IMAGES
of America

MURPHY

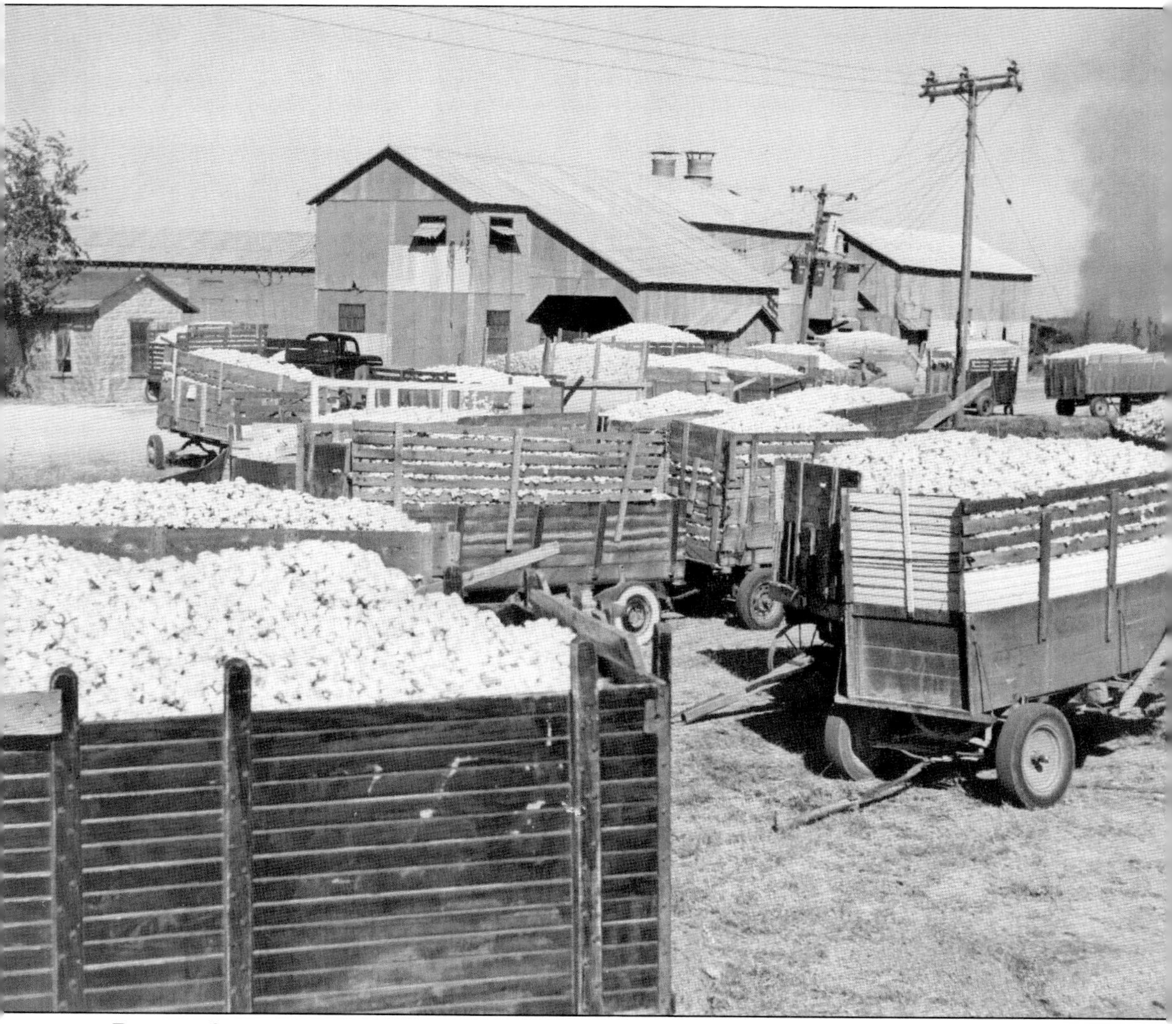

Bumper Crop, 1953. Many cotton wagons are waiting in 1953 to be weighed and processed at the Daniel Brothers Implement Company in Murphy. In the early farming days, cotton was stripped by hand and collected in six-foot bags. The introduction of modern machinery called "cotton strippers" eliminated the need for picking cotton by hand. (Inez Daniel.)

On the Cover: Studebaker Corporation. Lee Turney worked for Studebaker; here he is photographed with the regional sales managers, fifth from right in the top row. The Studebaker Corporation, producers of wagons for farmers, the military, and miners, was founded in 1852. By 1904, it produced gasoline-powered automobiles. The last Studebaker automobile was assembled in 1966. (Dessie Haker.)

IMAGES
of America

MURPHY

Donna Brumit Jenkins

ARCADIA
PUBLISHING

ISBN 978-0-7385-8538-3

Published by Arcadia Publishing
Charleston, South Carolina

Printed in the United States of America

Library of Congress Control Number: 2011937410

For all general information, please contact Arcadia Publishing:
Telephone 843-853-2070
Fax 843-853-0044
E-mail sales@arcadiapublishing.com
For customer service and orders:
Toll-Free 1-888-313-2665

Visit us on the Internet at www.arcadiapublishing.com

This book is dedicated to the past, present, and future citizens of Murphy, Texas.

Contents

Acknowledgments

Roses is red Violets is blew When this you see Think of me.
—Henry Dixon Maxwell on March 10, 1870.

The intent of this book is to preserve the history of Murphy through images and captions and to share the history of Murphy. What history? After all, the historic buildings in Murphy, except the First Baptist Church of Murphy and the old Murphy School, have long since disappeared. What history lies hidden in their walls? The vestiges of four cemeteries harboring the graves of the pioneering families have stories waiting to be told. Where are the old family trunks holding letters, diaries, and photographs?

In elementary school, I recall a student living southeast of Plano was considered a "Murphy kid" because the school bus route was called the Murphy route. What is special about being a Murphy kid? The memories of people, farms, fields, barns, farm animals, and the Murphy store are all that remain. The names of the families, the events of their lives, and memories of a bygone era must be preserved.

This book on Murphy includes images and memories collected about the pioneer Murphy families from their children, grandchildren, and great-grandchildren. Citizens provided photographs from the decades between 1900 and 2001. Thank you to the contributors, too numerous to name, who shared your family histories and photographs. You have made an important impact on preserving the history of Murphy and Collin County. This book would not be possible without Aimee Neimer's help with city history. Mary Maxwell shared the Maxwell family history and a copy of the *Day Books of Henry Maxwell from 1850–1860.*

Living in Murphy Revisited, by Bev Zavitz, was a valuable resource about Murphy's history. Dessie Haker and Margaret Smith provided books, photographs, and primary-source documents from the Turney, King, and Murphy families. Thank you for your help with the book and other Murphy projects.

Also, I want to thank my magnificent family and friends for their encouragement and understanding when I was researching, interviewing, scanning, and writing. My gratitude and love I give to Robert, my husband, for his supportive attitude to yet another project.

INTRODUCTION

Murphy, located in the southeastern corner of Collin County, was once part of the Peters Colony empresario grant issued by the Republic of Texas in 1841. The grant was issued to 20 investors led by William Peters who viewed the colony simply as a business venture. Murphy, or Maxwell as it was first called, was settled in the area known as the Decatur Road District. The boundary of Murphy was always fluid but once ran about eight miles north of Rowlett Creek and FM 544 to Parker Road, about eight miles east to Maxwell Creek and beyond to McCreary Road, and south to the Dallas County line.

Today, the political boundary is about four square miles; however, the census disclosed Murphy was the fastest growing Collin County city in 2010. The population in 2000 was approximately 4,000, but the growth steadily increased, and the population today stands at 17,708. In spite of its population growth, Murphy continues to protect the country-living atmosphere and community involvement demonstrated in the 1840s, when the first families arrived.

Collin County, carved out of the Blackland Prairie Region, was once covered with tall native grasses such as bluestem, buffalo, and mesquite that grew in the fertile black clay soil. The abundant rainfall and moderate temperatures provided an excellent combination for farming. This, together with the beckoning of cheap land, drew the first settlers to the area.

Other inducements for settling in the area were the more or less friendly tribes of Native Americans. The Caddo Indians living in North Texas were one the friendliest tribes in the Republic of Texas. They discovered the fertile soil and grew crops of potatoes, beans, squash, and corn. Nomadic tribes such as the Comanche and Apache usually roamed farther to the west hunting buffalo and seldom ventured into Collin County, but there were some raids and one massacre documented near Plano.

There were numerous small streams with water and abundant timber for use in building cabins. Native trees included pecan, elm, bois d'arc, ash, walnut, willow, hackberry, persimmon, and oak. Pioneers found the bois d'arc wood extremely valuable for fence posts and cabins. Game such as deer, bear, and rabbit inhabited the woods, and fish were plentiful, as were wild pig and turkey. Fruit, nuts, and honey were available to sustain the pioneers until they could cultivate land for the first crops. Some pioneers brought cattle and sheep to begin ranching.

Settlers in the Peters Colony received up to 640 acres of land per family or 320 acres per single man. The empresarios provided surveys, titles, and in some cases powder, shot, seed, or a crude cabin. In return the empresarios could retain up to one-half of the grant as payment for services. Often this led to disagreements over ownership, such as the Hedgecoxe War, in which the agent declared he was the final authority in determining land rights. Pioneers raided his office and found the land grants missing, and he was run out of the county. George Pegues represented Murphy in meetings concerning the grants, and settlers eventually received their grants. It was through such grants that the founding fathers of Murphy came to colonize and settle on the prairie of North Texas. The liberal land policy was an important factor in drawing settlers who were looking for cheap land and a better way of life.

Collin McKinney, one of the 56 signers of the Texas Declaration of Independence and for whom the county, Collin, and county seat, McKinney, are named, authored a state law creating the counties in the northern part of the state. Collin County was created out of an act of the legislature on April 3, 1846, and was originally part of Fannin County. Settlers to Murphy originated from Arkansas, Missouri, Virginia, North and South Carolina, Alabama, Indiana, Illinois, Ohio, and Kentucky.

Pioneers who came to Murphy were rugged individualists, hard-working, and sturdy stock. They braved bad weather, drought, and diseases for a new life promising a better future in Texas. The earliest individuals were Scotch-Irish, Presbyterians, and Democrats, and many were illiterate. Some could only sign an X for their name on land titles, but they retained an indomitable spirit. They were joined later by doctors, lawyers, shopkeepers, teachers, and preachers.

These innovators settled on Maxwell Creek, a branch of the East Fork of the Trinity River sometimes called Muddy Branch. They named the community Maxwell after James William Maxwell, who came to the area with his wife, Hannah, and family in the 1840s. Maxwell; his sons, Henry, James W., Andrew; and other kin gained head rights that became the core of the Murphy community. Unfortunately, in 1865, Henry Maxwell, enticed by the success of Oliver Loving and the lure of ranch land, moved west to engage in cattle ranching in Parker County. He and his son-in-law, A.J. Joyce, encountered Indians while on the range rounding up stock. Maxwell was shot with an arrow in the back and scalped. He is buried in Parker County.

Soon other families settled near the Maxwell head rights. Comfort Allen McMillan and his wife, Lydia, and their relatives settled along Maxwell Creek. William and Dorothy Murphy also settled on Maxwell Creek. About a dozen grants would be established adjacent to Maxwell Creek and Rowlett Creek. These grantees included the Sachse, Herring, Hogge, Marshall, Pegues, McCreary, and Mitchell relations.

In the 1870s, residents of the Maxwell community tried to develop a town site along present day Murphy Road and Maxwell Creek. When they applied for a post office, they found there was already a post office named Maxwell, so they renamed the community Decatur. Decatur had several streets and stores frequented by settlers from the surrounding communities of Dublin, Sachse, Parker, and Nickleville, a settlement later renamed Wylie. Citizens created schools in their homes to teach students the fundamentals of reading, writing, and arithmetic. They hoped for the railroad to pass through and make the town successful but had to wait until the late 1880s for this event. When James William Maxwell died, more of the Maxwell families began to scatter west in search of better ranch land.

Decatur began to decline until the railroad came to the area in the 1888. James Murphy, son of William and Dorothy Murphy, donated a right-of-way to the railroad for a depot. In exchange, he asked the railroad to reroute through his land, and the depot was named Murphy. Later, the community was renamed Murphy.

From the 1880s until the late 1970s, Murphy remained a farming community, and the railroad depot became a vital shipping point for cotton, grain, and cattle. The agrarian lifestyle began to change drastically for small communities like Murphy when surrounding towns such as Plano, Richardson, and Garland began to grow. The Murphy School and the post office closed in 1950s. The 1960s were relatively uneventful for the sleepy little community. By 1970, the population had dwindled to only 136 citizens. Over the course of time, families began to work and shop in the larger cities. Farmers sold their land, and housing developments sprang up. Families moving to the area from the northern cities and west coast wanted homes with acreage. New residents were greatly influenced the idyllic notion of a country atmosphere where times were simple and neighbors formed a tight-knit community. Lot sizes ranged from one to five acres. Murphy became a bedroom community, and the agrarian landscape again began to change as land around Murphy was incorporated into the larger cities of Richardson, Plano, and Wylie. The population began to climb steadily in the 1980s and 1990s, and businesses began to return. Today, citizens continue to cherish and hold fast to the idea of living in a small town.

One

Founding Fathers

Maxwell, McMillen, Murphy, and Others

The following chapter contains documents and images of some of the first Murphy pioneers. Often, photographs of the founding fathers were not available or were very limited and of poor quality. No photographs of either James William or Henry Maxwell have been found. The only original photograph of William Murphy is now lost. Precious photographs were passed down through several generations only to be lost or destroyed by the next generation responsible for cleaning out the home place when parents and grandparents died. Their stories, however, are worth remembering.

Photographs of James and John Madison Salmons are also not available. The first Salmons colonists were French Huguenots who arrived in Virginia hoping to escape religious prosecution. John married Sarah Beck, who came from a prosperous Collin County family. The Becks and Salmons families lived on land near Dublin Road and FM 544 where they raised livestock and grew corn and wheat. John Salmons owned one of the first sawmills and was paid $26.28 by the county to build a plank bridge across Rowlett Creek, thus connecting the wagon trail from Plano to Murphy. This trail was to become FM 544. Salmons was elected a county commissioner and later also served as justice of the peace and constable. He died from an infected wound in his hand caused by a fish fin and is buried in the Decatur-Maxwell-Murphy Cemetery.

Another founding family, George and Elizabeth Pegues, settled near Rowlett Creek and Dublin Road with their seven children. George, a farmer, studied law in Collin County and attended to legal matters in the Murphy area. Elizabeth, who could neither read nor write, found life strenuous and sometimes frightening when she encountered Indians or a bear among the trees.

George Pegues and William Gage, a millwright, built a sawmill and a gristmill to serve local families. Abundant timber along Rowlett Creek made timberland valuable and work plentiful. The Pegues family members sold their land, sawmill, and gristmill and moved to McKinney when George was elected chief justice there. Now, it is time to revisit the images Murphy of long ago.

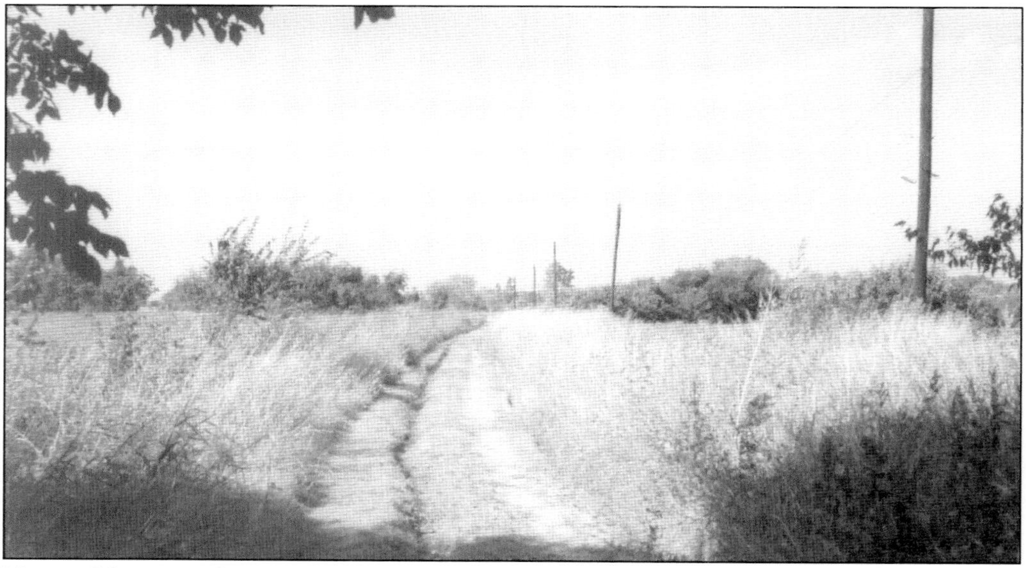

North Maxwell Creek and McMillen Road, 1989. To this area in the 1840s came the pioneering families of Murphy. These hearty Scotch-Irish settlers were a determined breed and never let hard work, threat of massacres, droughts, or floods scare them away from this Blackland Prairie. The tree-lined creek full of fish and game awaited the Maxwell, McMillen, and Murphy families. (Brad Lapsley.)

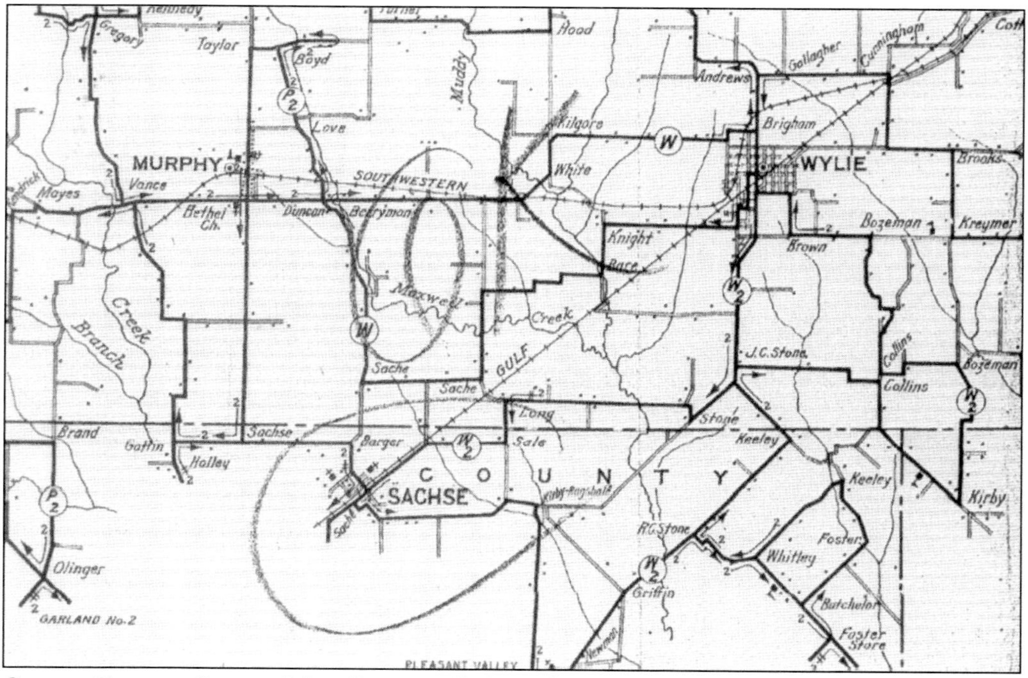

Collin County Survey Map. James and Hannah Maxwell settled on a branch of Maxwell Creek with three of their married children and four younger children in 1846. Henry Maxwell, their son, may have first settled in Red River County in 1938 before moving on to Maxwell Creek with his family. (Mary Maxwell.)

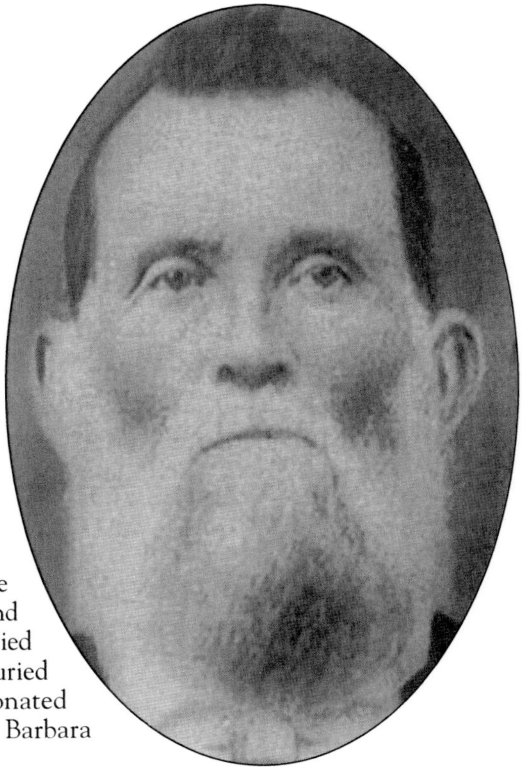

Comfort Allen McMillen and Lydia Maxwell McMillen. Comfort, born in 1818, and Lydia, born in 1821, came from Arkansas and settled in Murphy in 1846 along with their six children and Lydia's brothers James and Henry Maxwell. Also in the ox-driven wagon train were the William Willeford and Lewis Marshall families, accompanied by a herd of Comfort McMillen's sheep. The Maxwells dreamed of farming and ranching. Comfort and Lydia had six children, but only four grew to adulthood. One child drowned in a wash pot at the age of two, and another died at age 16. Comfort loved to have company over, and Lydia loved to cook for people. They were married for 66 years and lived in Murphy. Both are buried in the McMillen Cemetery on land they donated to the Corinth Presbyterian Church. (Both, Barbara Taylor Bennie.)

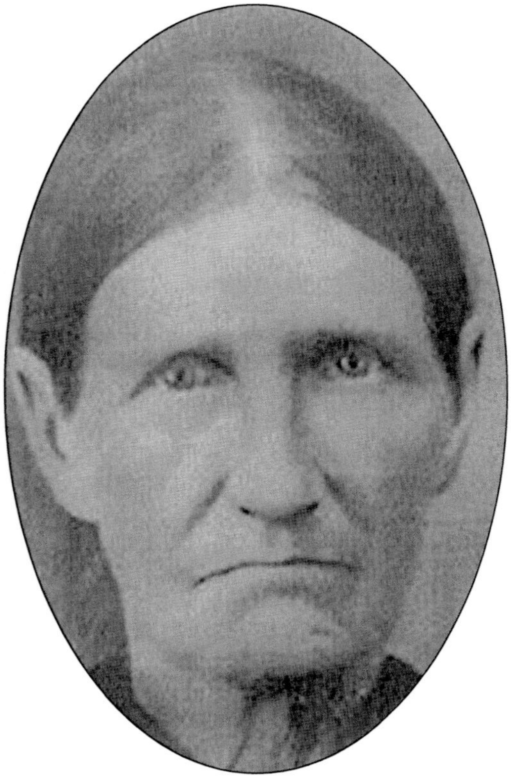

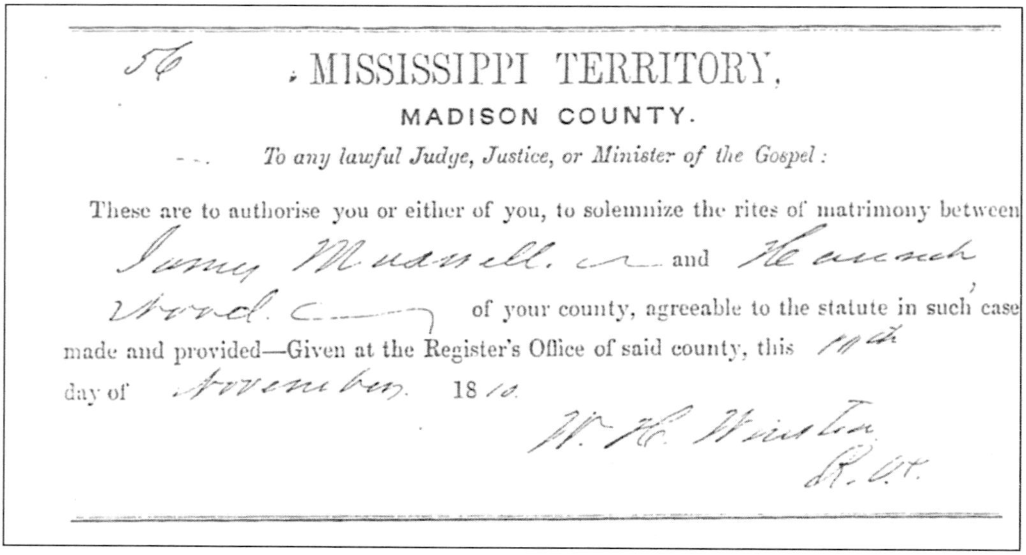

56 MISSISSIPPI TERRITORY,

MADISON COUNTY.

To any lawful Judge, Justice, or Minister of the Gospel:

These are to authorise you or either of you, to solemnize the rites of matrimony between Jamy Maxwell Sr and Hannah Wood of your county, agreeable to the statute in such case made and provided—Given at the Register's Office of said county, this 19th day of November 1810.

W. H. Winston R.O.

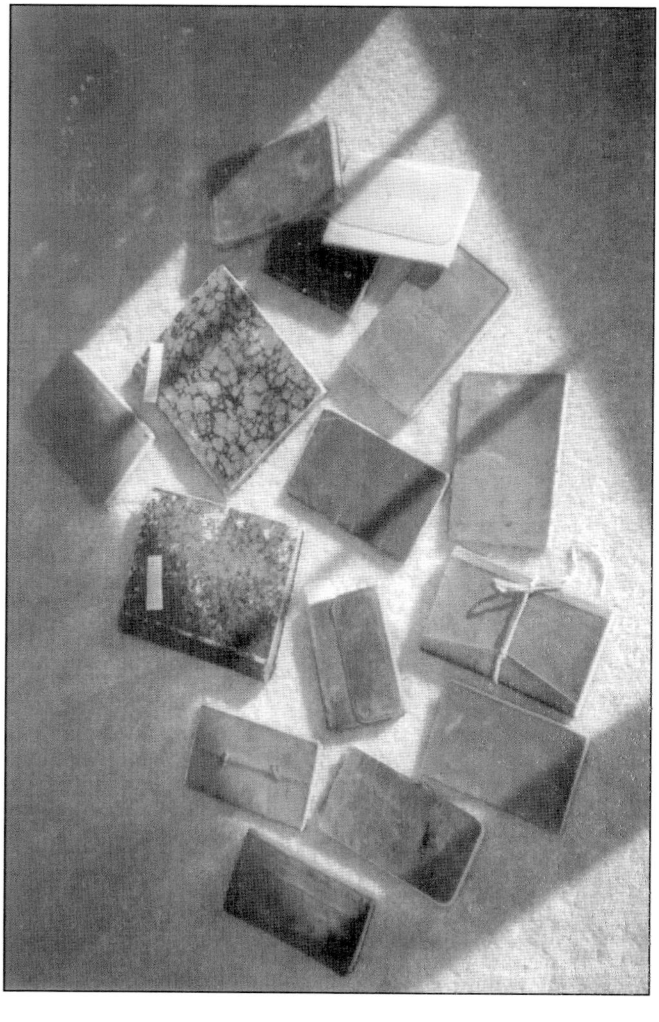

Marriage Certificate of James William Maxwell Sr. and Hannah Wood Maxwell, 1810. James Maxwell, born in South Carolina in 1773, came to Texas with his wife. James was 73, and Hannah 53 when they arrived in Collin County with heavily laden wagons on New Year's Day 1846. Maxwell's grant was first surveyed in 1836, but the land was not settled and no log cabin was built until 1845. (Mary Maxwell.)

The Maxwell Journals. Much of what is known about the Maxwell family was written in their daybooks or journals. Of the eight living Maxwell children, only Lydia remained in the Murphy area all her life. In 1850, James William Maxwell died and is thought to be buried on the land his son J.W. Maxwell donated to the Decatur-Maxwell-Murphy Cemetery. (Mary Maxwell.)

War of 1812 Battle Map. James William Maxwell Sr. served in the War of 1812. The photograph details the battles in which he participated. His son, Andrew, following his own patriotic calling, joined the "Sons of the South" during the Civil War. Little is known about James's war years except through Hannah Maxwell's applications for war pensions. (Mary Maxwell.)

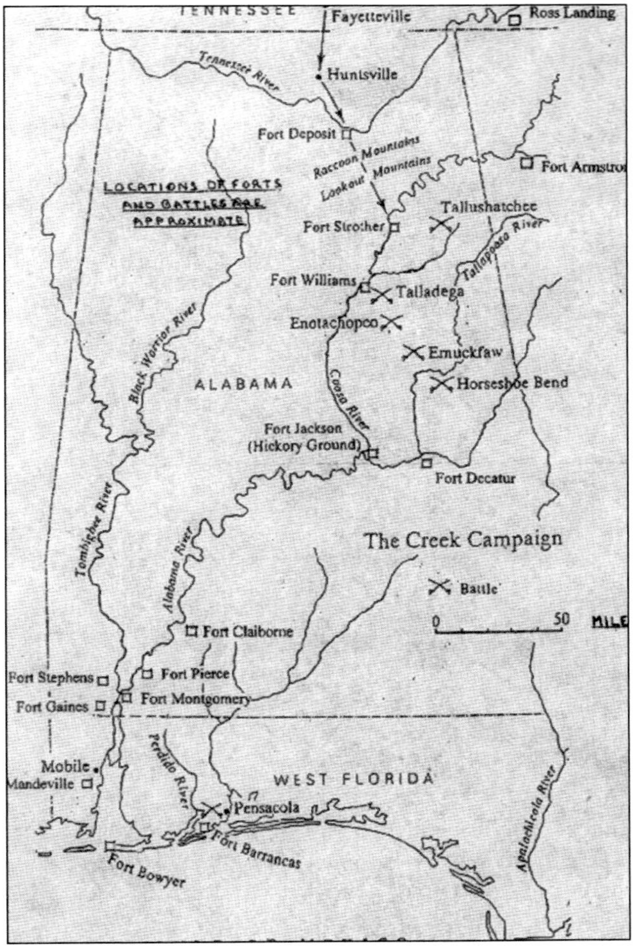

Decatur-Maxwell-Murphy Cemetery. James William Maxwell died in 1850, and both he and his wife are thought to be buried in the Decatur-Maxwell-Murphy Cemetery on land donated by his family. Their tombstones are missing. Not long after the death of James William, Henry and others in the Maxwell family began to go their separate ways, moving to Parker, Johnson, Hamilton, and Coryell Counties. (Inez Daniel.)

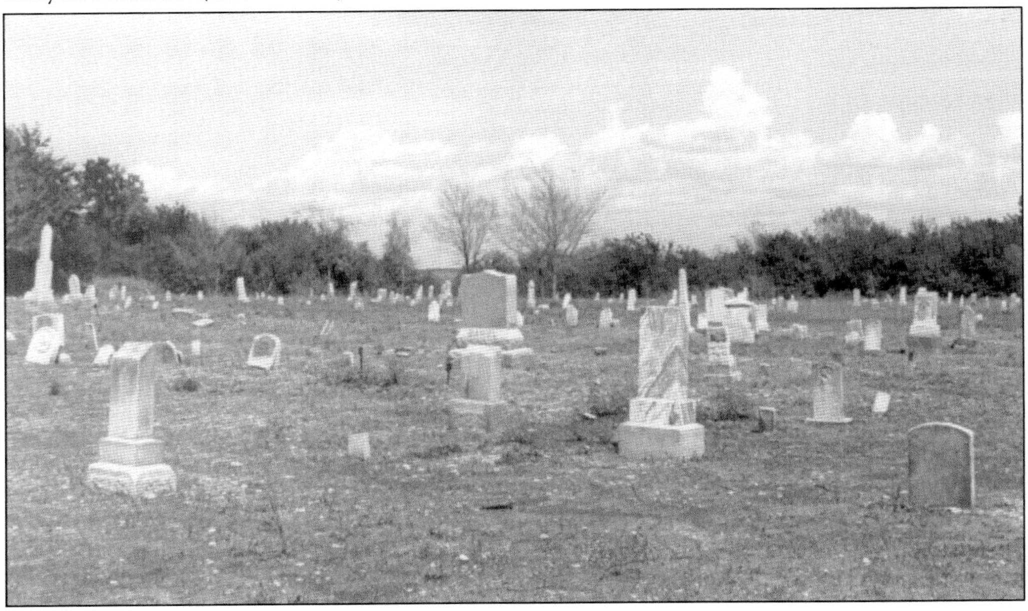

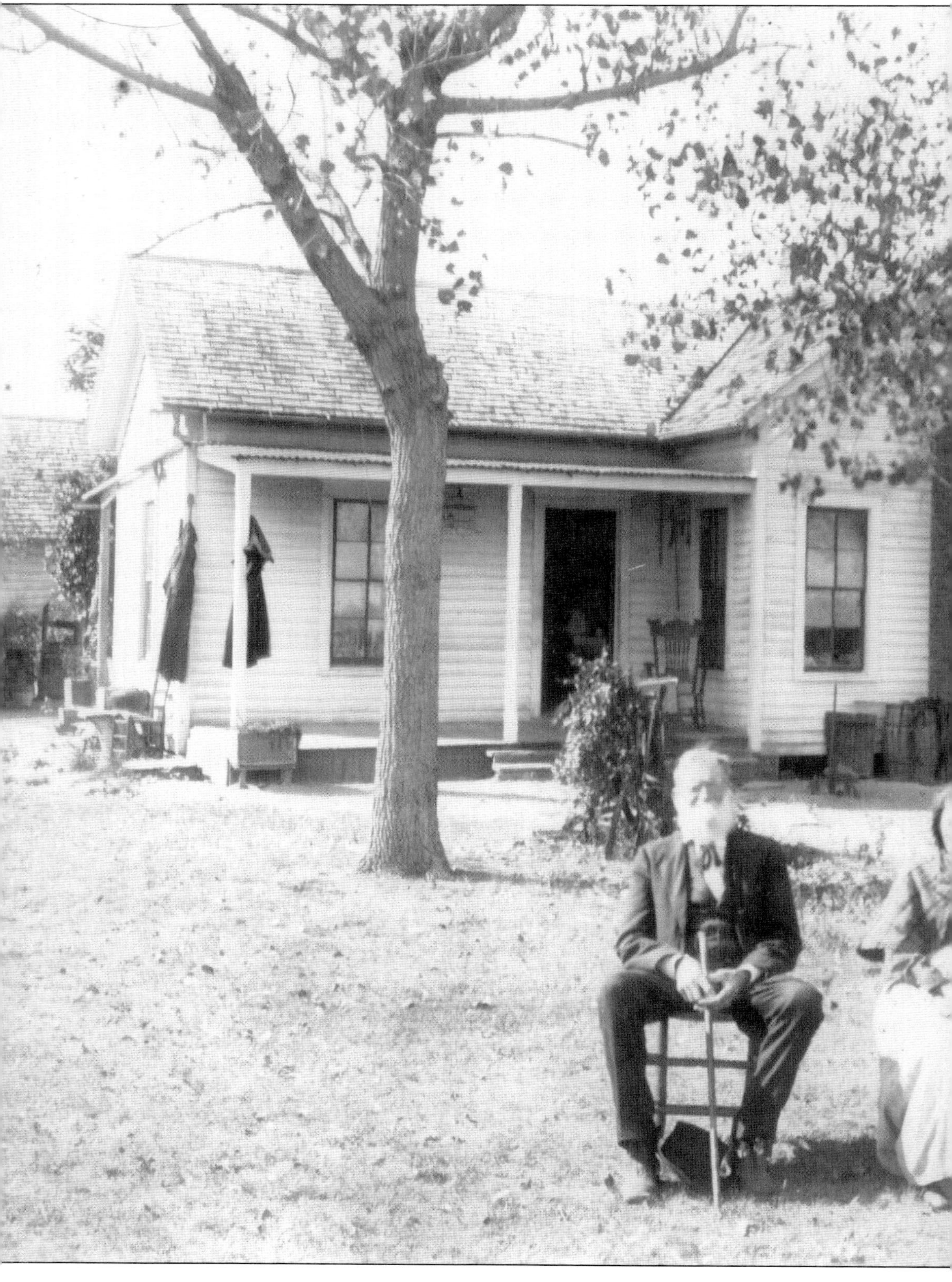

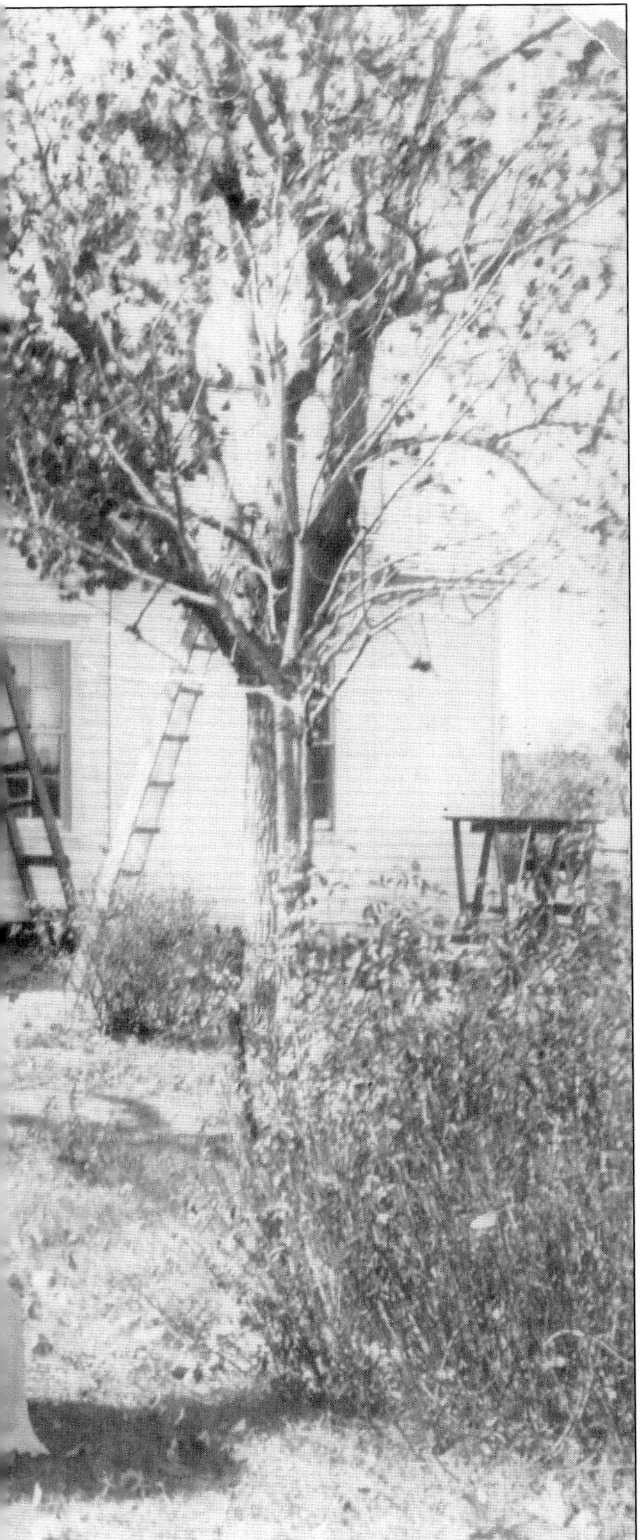

Comfort Allen McMillen and Lydia Maxwell McMillen at Home in Murphy. The McMillen homestead was located at Murphy Road and Betsy Lane near present-day Southfork Animal Hospital. For the first two years, they lived in a log cabin built on their head right along Maxwell Creek. There, they found ample water and fish, deer, bear, rabbit, and wild turkey. At this point, Comfort began one of the first businesses in the area. He sold sheep from the rams and ewes he brought with him from Arkansas. The McMillen relations were God-fearing Christians and strict Presbyterians. In August 1846, they organized the first church in the area, the Corinth Presbyterian Church, which first met in the Maxwell School House in Murphy. He was an accomplished Bible student devoted to memorizing entire sections of the Bible and singing religious hymns. (Barbara Bennie Taylor.)

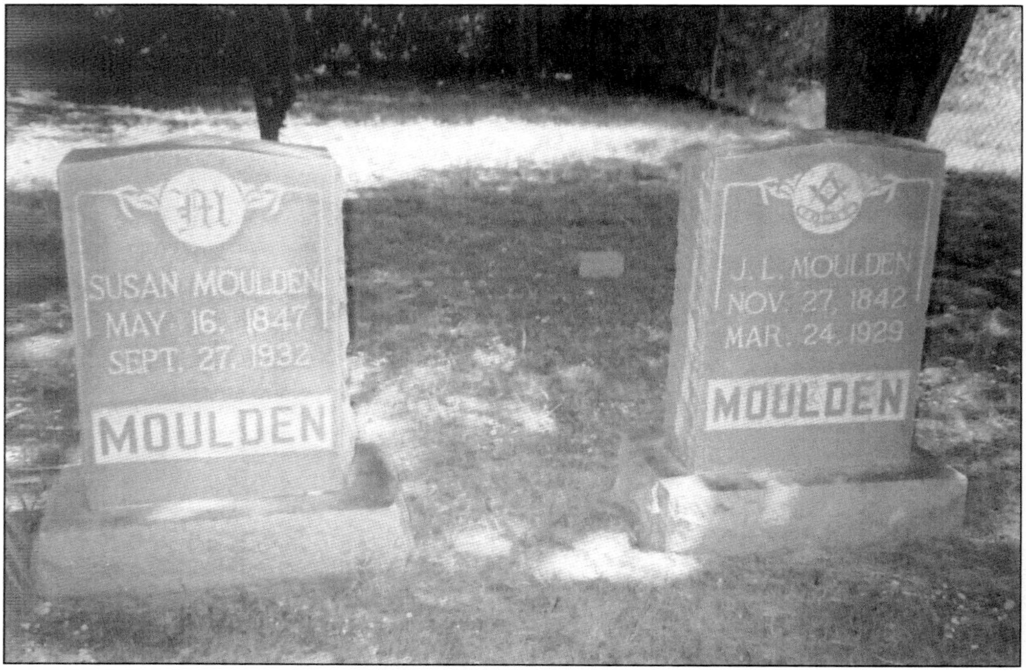

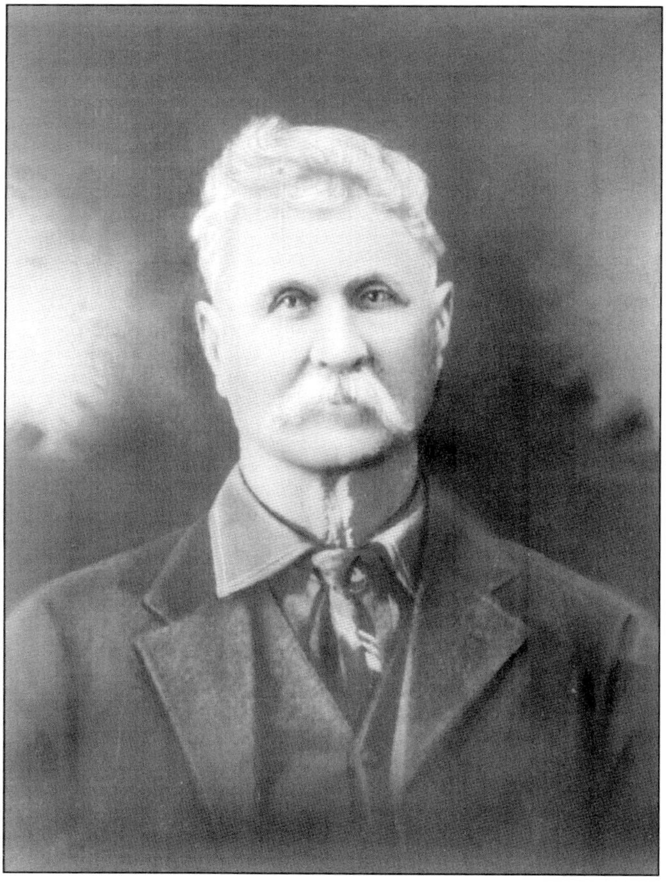

SUSAN AND J.L. MOULDEN HEADSTONES. Shown in the photograph above are the graves of Susan, daughter of William and Dorothy Murphy, and James Moulden, the nephew of Comfort McMillen, located in the Murphy Family Cemetery. James L. Murphy and J.L. Moulden were store owners in early Decatur. Moulden later became the first sheriff of Collin County. (Dessie Haker.)

FRANKLIN PIERCE MURPHY. Franklin was the sixth son born to William and Dorothy Murphy. He married Mary Louisa George on February 9, 1876, in the home of her mother, Susan George, who lived in the Murphy community. They moved to West Texas to farm and ranch. (Phyllis Stephens.)

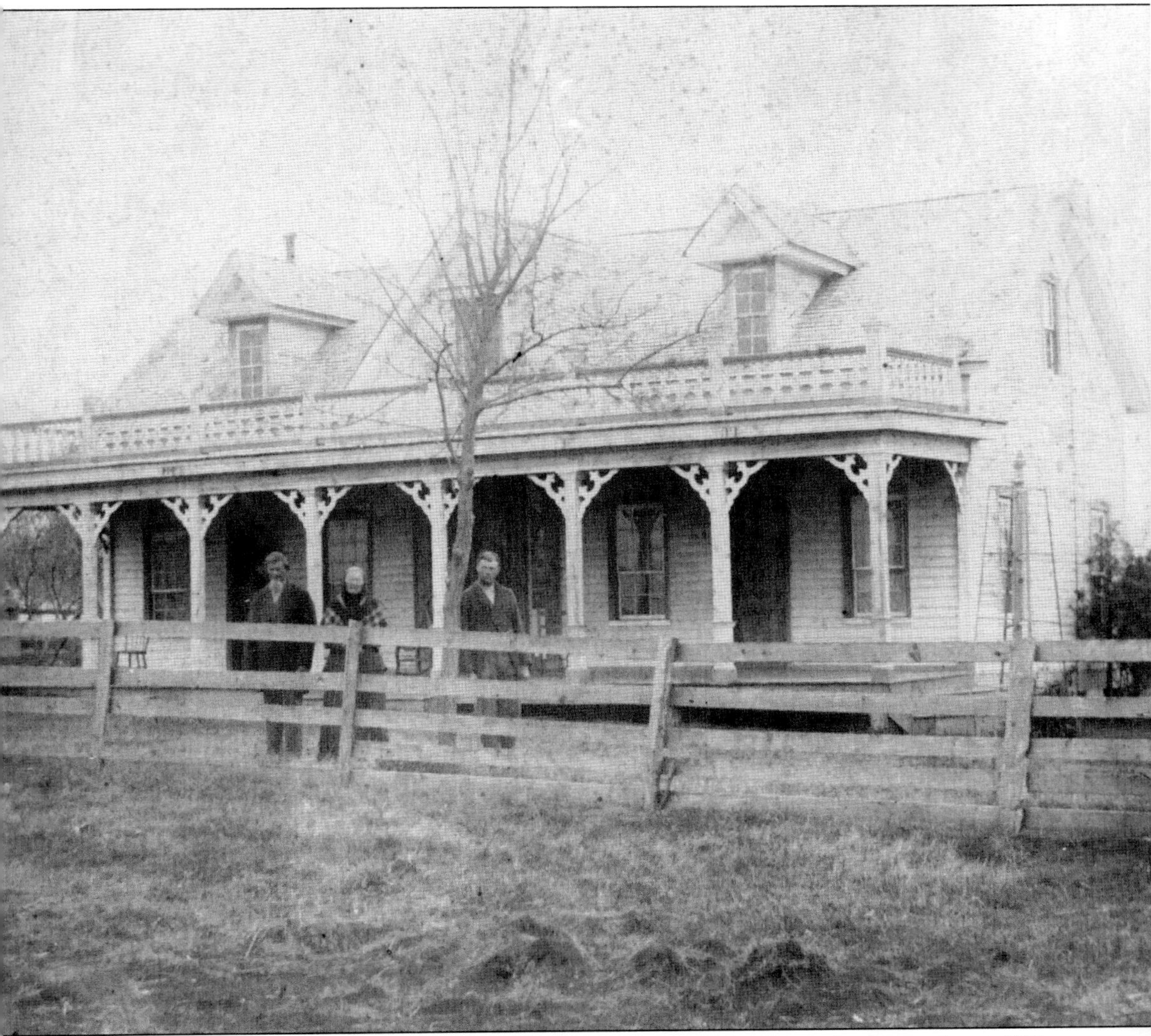

WILLIAM MURPHY HOUSE ON MAXWELL CREEK. William and Dorothy (Dorothea) Murphy and Eli Murphy, William's brother, came to Old Decatur in the 1850s. Standing in front of the Murphy house, built in 1874, are William and Dorothy and son John Murphy. In addition to John, William and Dorothy's children included Sarah, James, Susan, Nancy, William Jefferson, Franklin Pierce, Pleasant, Mary, Anne, and Dorothy. They farmed and raised cattle and horses, and William donated land for the Murphy Family Cemetery. The first Murphy families to come to the United States were from Ireland. William's father, James Murphey, settled first in North Carolina and spelled his name with an "ey," as did William's grandfather; however, his great-great-great-grandfather Daniel spelled his name Murphee with a double "e" on the end. (Dessie Haker.)

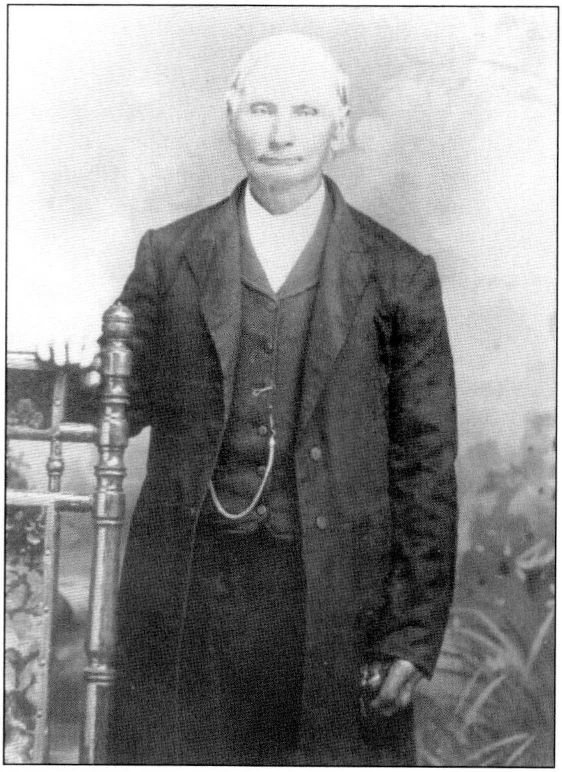

WILLIAM SACHSE. Born in Prussia, William Sachse owned land in both Collin and Dallas Counties and was a successful farmer, rancher, and trader. When the railroad passed through his land, he granted them the right-of-way, and citizens named the town Sachse. Although he was the namesake of Sachse, he amassed a large amount of land in and around the Murphy area. (Sachse Historical Society.)

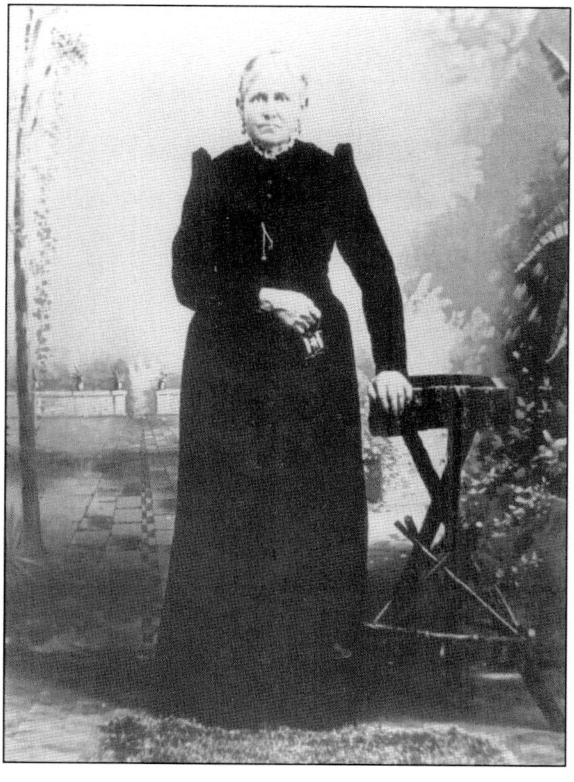

MARTHA ANN FROST SACHSE. "Marty" was the second wife of William Sachse and the daughter of Peters colonist Benjamin Frost. William had four children by his first wife, Elizabeth McCullouch. After the death of Elizabeth, he married Marty in 1852 and had 10 children. When each of the children married, he gave them a home and a large farm. (Sachse Historical Society.)

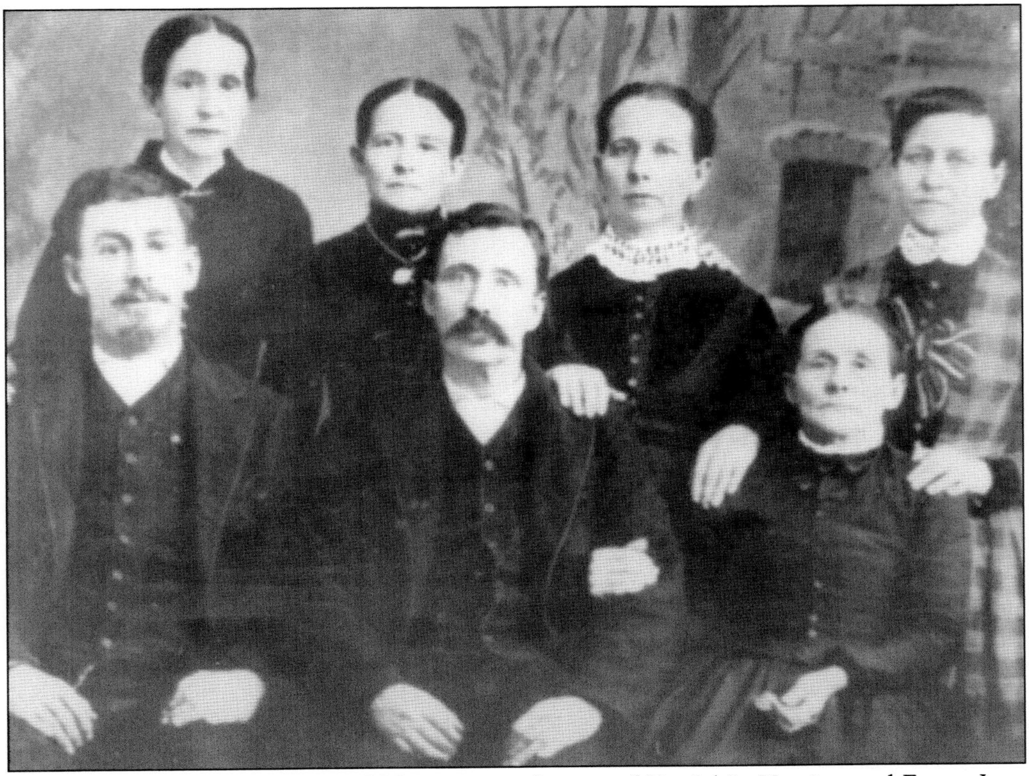

Daniel Herring Family. Daniel Herring was the son of Daniel L. Herring and Fanny Jane Creech from North Carolina. He moved to the Murphy area in 1848 with his brothers Issac and Sherwood and his widowed mother, Fanny Jane. The 1880s daguerreotype photograph above shows Daniel and Mary Deck Herring's children. Pictured are, from left to right, (first row) Joshua, John, and Anna (Loften); (second row) Sallie (Hogge), Mariah (Lee), Martha (McAmis), and Nancy (Parks). The Herrings constructed their home on the highest point of the farm, which was located on what is currently Sunset Drive in Skyline Acres. Mary died and was buried in the Decatur-Maxwell-Murphy Cemetery. Daniel married Elizabeth Newman and built a home in Sachse. Below is a photograph of the Herring-Hogge Cemetery, where Daniel and Elizabeth are buried. (Above, Sachse Historical Society; below, Brad Lapsley.)

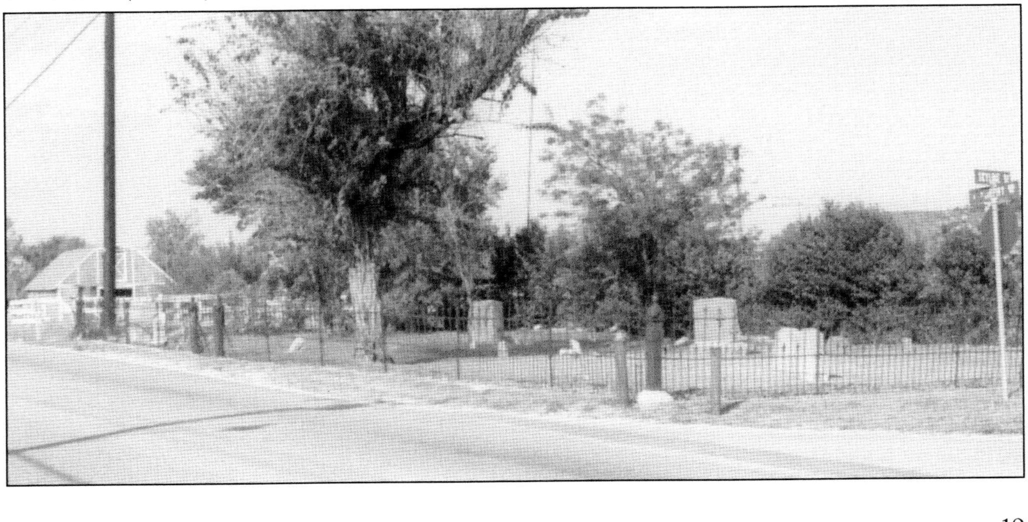

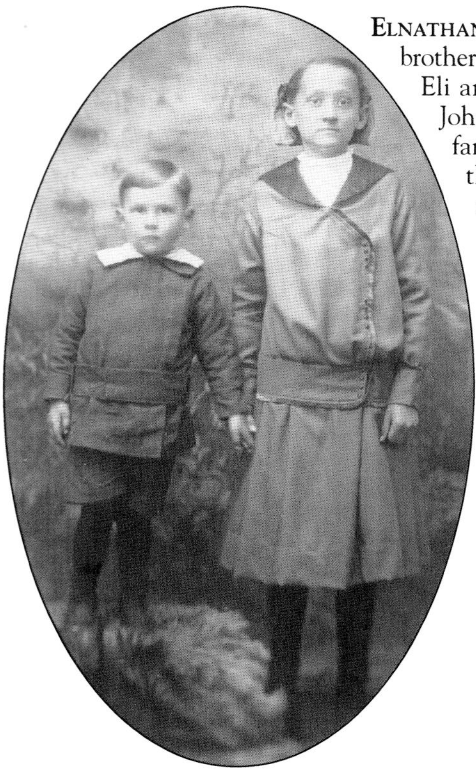

Elnathan and Anna Hogge. Elnathan and Anna, the older brother and sister of Eli Hogge, were born in South Carolina. Eli and Elnathan moved to Texas, and Anna married John T. Neely and moved to Illinois. The elder Hogg family spelled their last name Hogg. Once in Texas, the brothers changed the spelling to Hogge in order not to be confused with another Hogg family living in Collin County. (Mike Massey.)

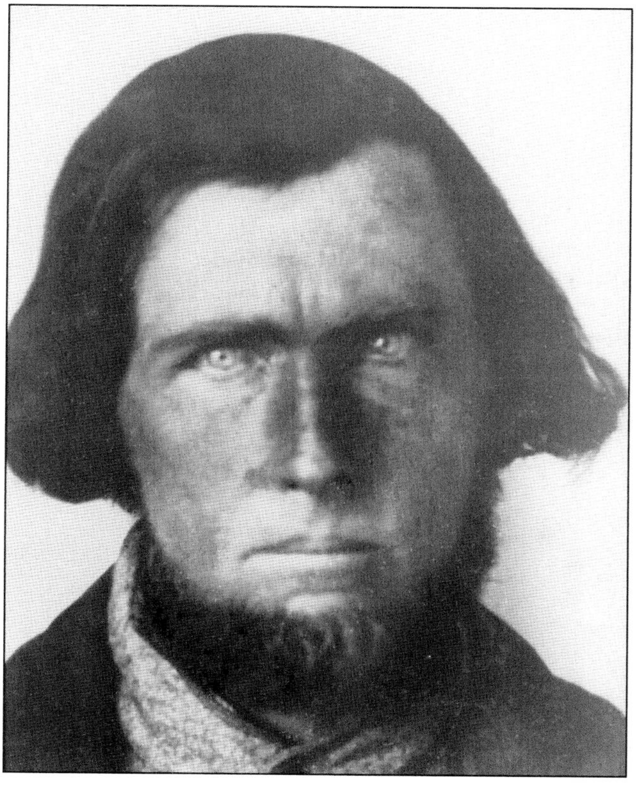

Eli Hogge Sr. In this photograph, Eli is 31 years old. He married Sarah Herring in 1856, and they had 11 children. The first-born twins were stillborn when Sarah was thrown from a horse. Other children included John William, James D., Eli Jr., Mary Ann, Sally, Thomas Elnathan, Charles, Frank, and Edna May. (Mike Massey.)

Older Eli Hogge Sr. Eli Hogge was born on September 7, 1828, in South Carolina and died in 1883 in Texas. He was the son of Thomas and Sarah Scott Hogg(e). Eli served in the Civil War under Gen. Joseph Johnson and was wounded in both legs at the Battle of Shiloh. (Mike Massey.)

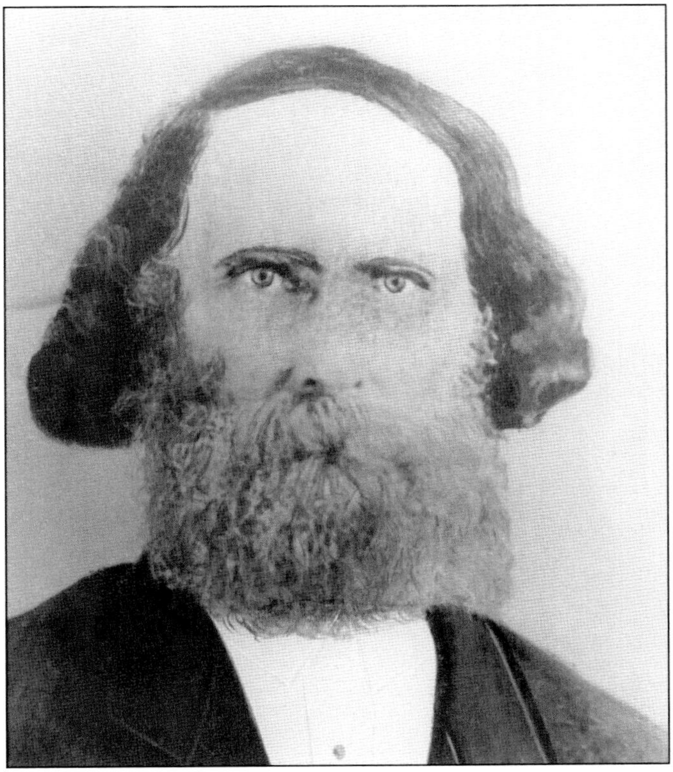

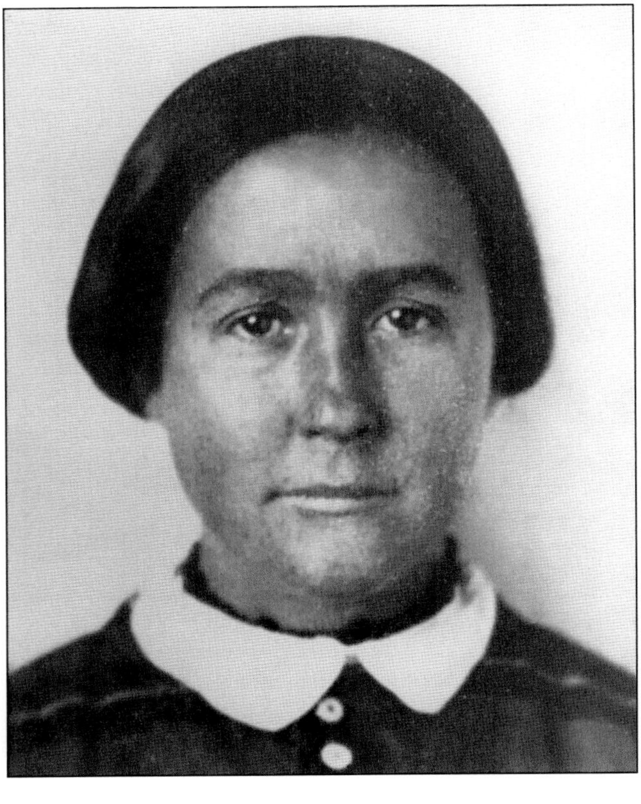

Sarah Herring. Known as "Sally," Sarah Jane Herring was born in 1838 in Illinois and came to Texas with her parents, Daniel and Mary Deck Herring, original settlers in the Murphy area. They arrived on Christmas Day, 1848. In the photograph, she is 21. She married Eli Hogge in Collin County. (Mike Massey.)

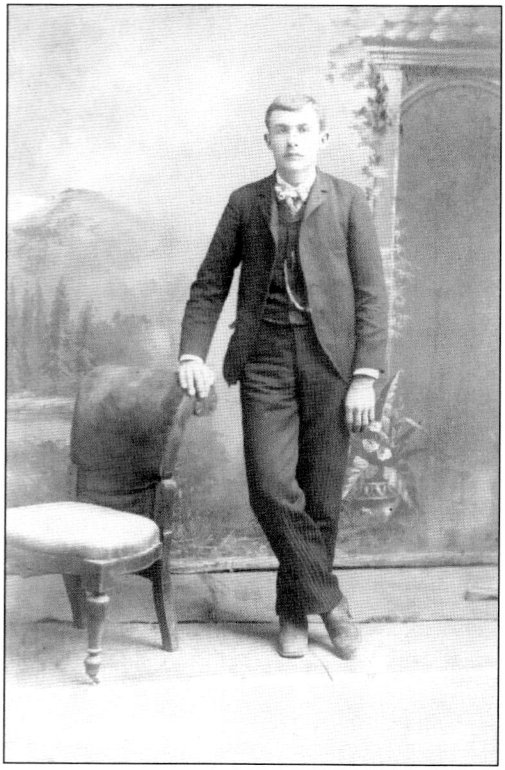

Elnathan Hogge. Elnathan, the son of Thomas and Sarah Hogge, was listed in the 1870 Mississippi census as a carpenter and saloon keeper. In 1880, he was listed in the Collin County census next to his brother Eli Hogge as a farmer. He first married Elvira L. Brian, and upon her death, he married Cornelia C. Wylie. Elnathan had nine children and farmed in the Murphy and Wylie area. (Mike Massey.)

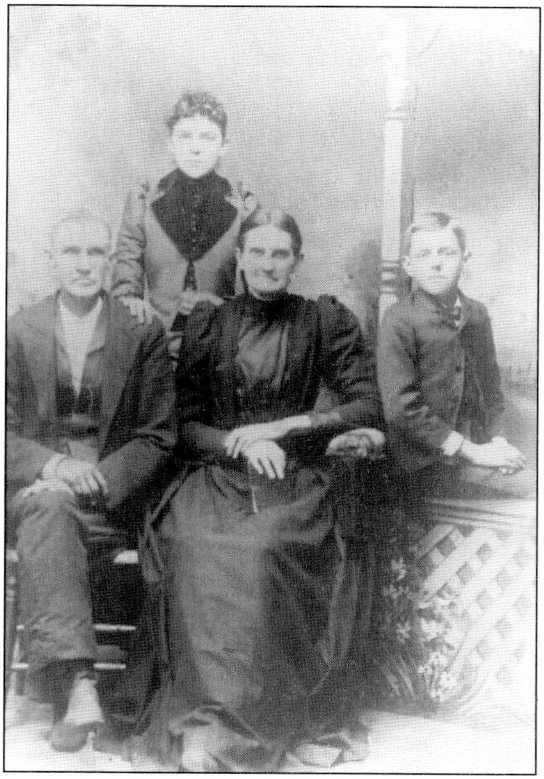

William J. and Mattie Echols Daniel. William and Mattie came to Texas in the 1860s from Alabama and settled in the Murphy farming community. They had six children, including Fannie, Josie, Minnie, Allie, Mattie, and William Oscar (known as "Kid" or "Willie"). Shown in the picture are William and Mattie, daughter Mattie, and son Willie. (Inez Daniel.)

Mary Jane Cheatham. In the photograph, Mary Jane Cheatham sits in a cotton field in Murphy. In order to keep the sun from burning her skin, she wore a bonnet and a long-sleeved dress to work in the field. Farm women did not want tanned skin as is the custom today. The cotton sack on her shoulder could hold over 100 pounds of cotton. (Ema Jean Christian.)

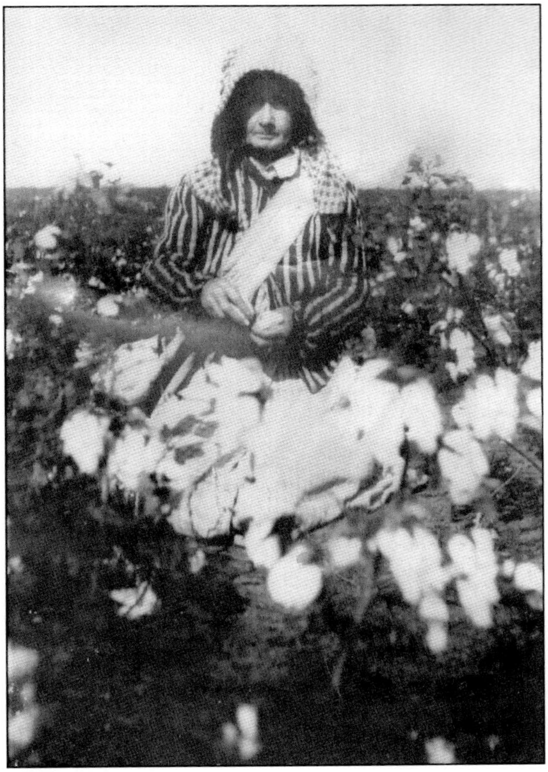

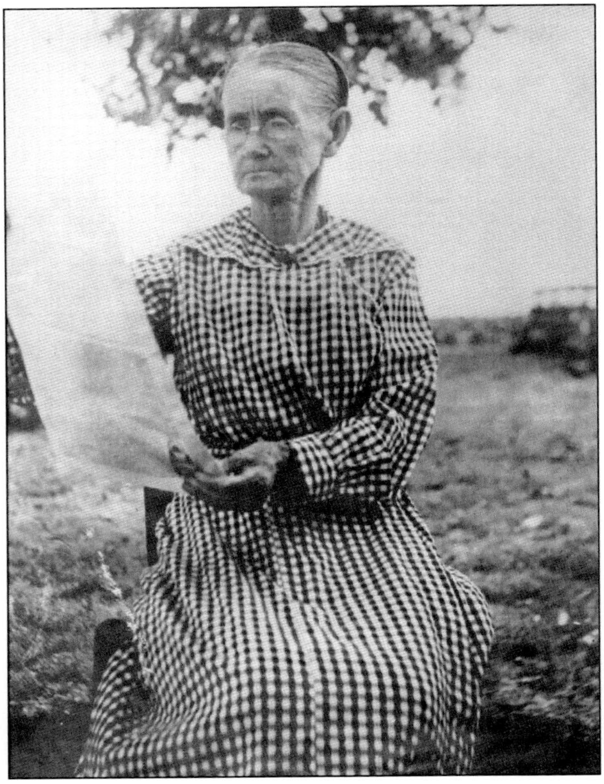

Mary Reading the Newspaper. The daughter of Thomas M. and Martha Gordon Marsalis, Mary Jane was born in Mississippi in 1844. When her husband died, she and her five children moved with her parents to Louisiana. In 1875, she and her parents moved to Collin County. Life was difficult for a widowed woman, five children, and aging parents. (Ema Jean Christian.)

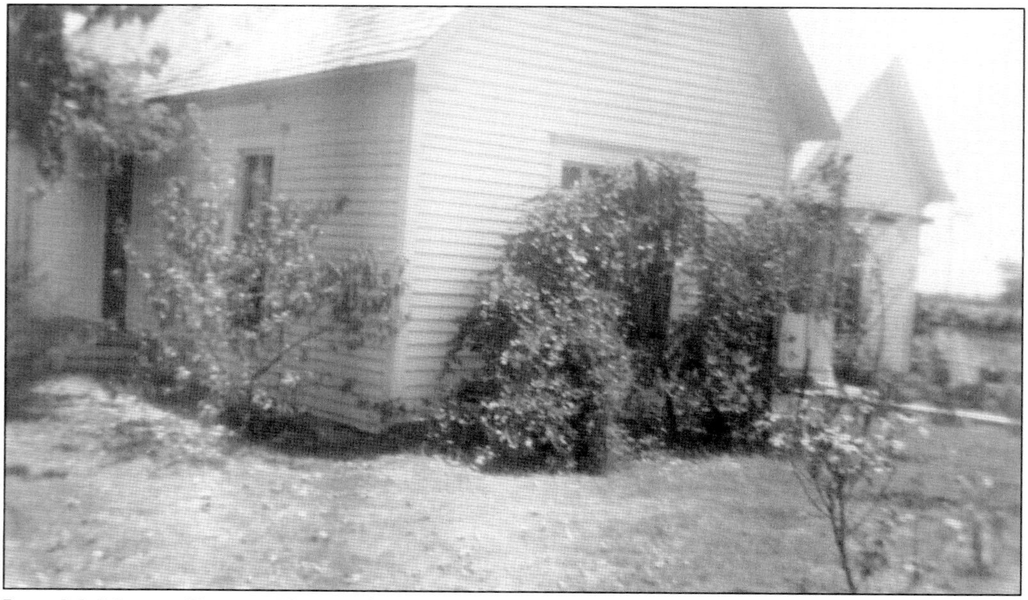

Jane McMillen Taylor Home. Shown in the photograph above is the home first owned by the McMillen family. It was located on North Murphy Road. Jane lived in this home her entire life with her children. H.T. McMillen and T.C. McMillen were sons by her first husband, William Allen McMillen. With Arthur Upshur Taylor, her children were Albert C. Taylor, Julia Inez Taylor, and Mary Taylor. (Barbara Taylor Bennie.)

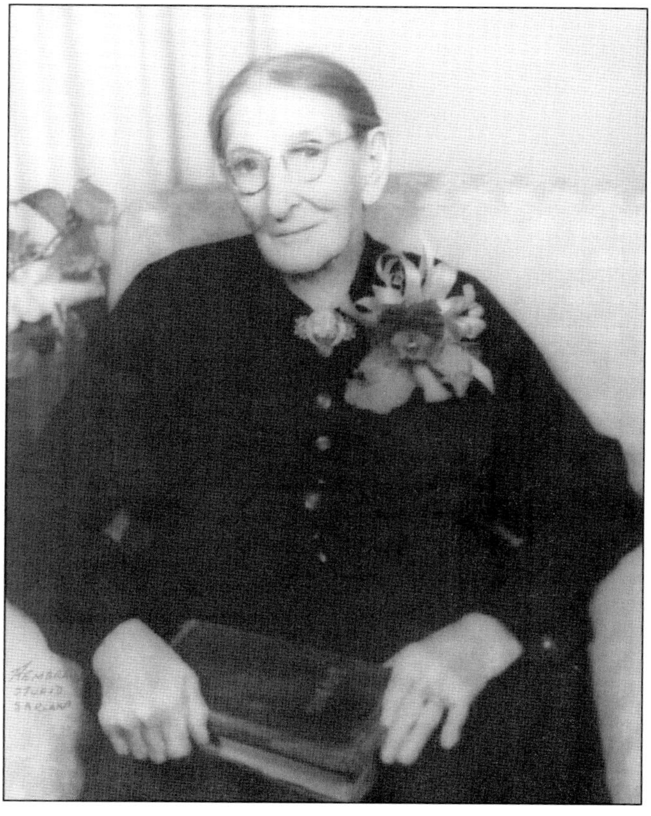

"Martha" Jane McMillen. Jane, daughter of Comfort and Lydia McMillen, was born on the family farm. This picture was taken in honor of her 93rd birthday. Her first marriage was to William Allen McMillen, a cousin, whose parents were Almeda and Lewis McMillen. Upon William's death, she married Arthur Upshur Taylor. She again was widowed when a passenger train struck Arthur Taylor. (Barbra Taylor Bennie.)

Two

Agrarian Roots
Early Farming and Livestock

Most immigrants came to Murphy with the idea of farming. Before the land could be farmed, trees must be felled, land cleared, and shelter erected. The pioneers often camped on a creek or stream until a cabin could be raised. Early houses were often one- or two-room log cabins, such as the one built by Daniel Herring. In 1862, he built a two-story frame house that stood on what is now Sunset Drive in Skyline Acres. Settler William Sachse first lived in a partial dugout with windows before he built his rock house in the 1850s. Building took much time and effort, and logs of elm and oak were used. Boards were sawed and worked by hand with neighbors offering help. Because there were no sawmills nearby, sawn lumber was hauled from Jefferson, Texas, by wagon and was expensive. The first homes were small, with a room for sleeping and sitting. Kitchens were detached because of the threat of fires.

Few settlers near Murphy had livestock, but the Maxwell and Murphy families drove their breeding stock beside the wagon train. Cattle, sheep, and pigs roamed freely on the open range. Animals were rounded up, marked, or branded in the spring after they gave birth to offspring. Oxen, mules, and horses were essential to cultivation, planting, and harvesting crops. Horses and mules were also vital as transportation. Dr. Henry Dye of Plano rode many miles on the back of a mule to visit a sick patient. By 1866, Collin County was the leading mule-producing market west of the Mississippi. Early animals were crossbred; however, by 1910, some farmers, such as Clairborne Christopher Gregory, raised purebred horses and ran a racetrack near Parker.

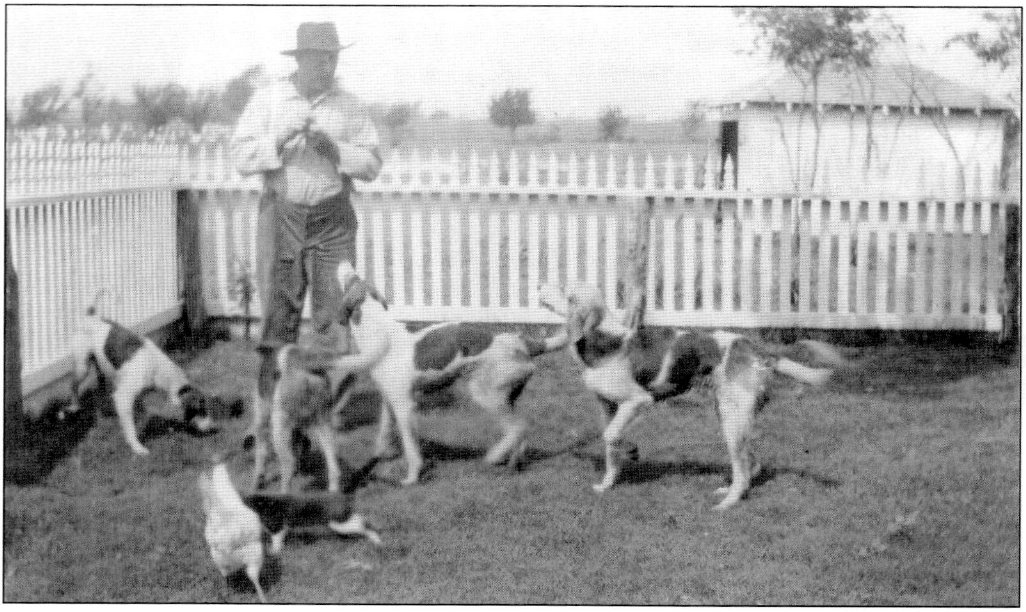

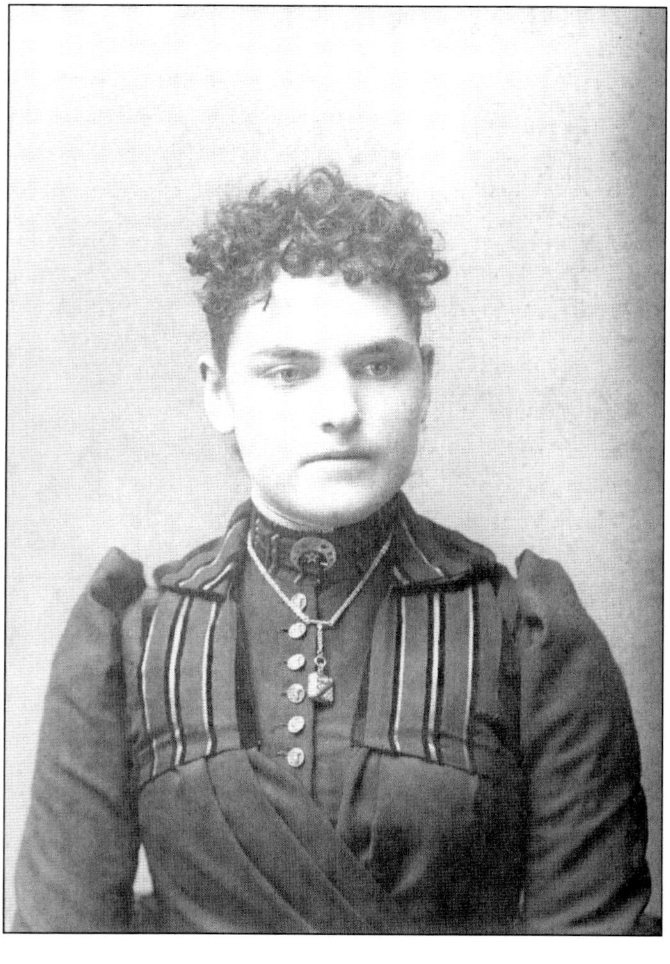

Ran Strange in His Front Yard. John Randolph "Ran" Strange was born in 1874 in Tupelo, Mississippi. His parents, Robert and Emma Strange, moved to Texas when he was nine years old. They had four sons and three daughters. Ran married Allie Daniels in 1898 and moved to Murphy. He is pictured in the front yard of his Murphy home with his hunting dogs, chickens, and cats. (Betty Strange Prince.)

Allie Daniel Strange. Allie, daughter of William J. Daniel and Martha A. Echols, was the first of the Daniel children born in Texas. Her siblings were James M., Fannie Catherine, Josephine Lovella, Minnie Lillian, Mattie Bell, and William Oscar. She was married to Ran Strange. All the siblings married into prominent Murphy families. (Betty Strange Prince.)

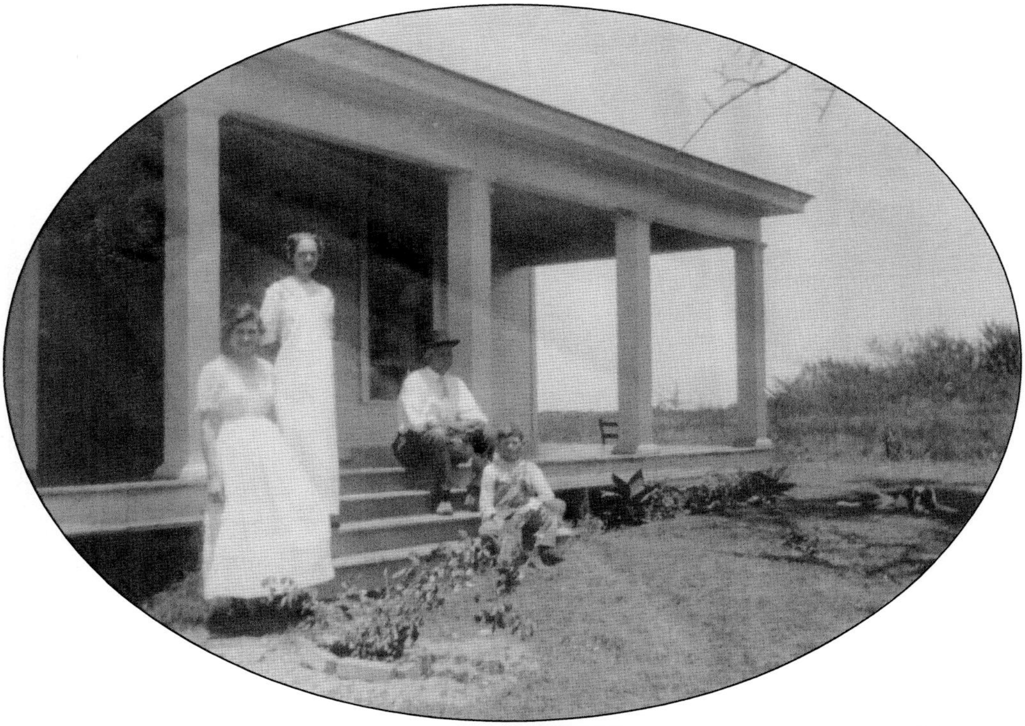

Ran Strange Family. On the front porch of their Murphy home, Allie and Ran appear with their children Faye and Rex. Faye, their first child and only daughter, was born in 1900. Rex Strange was born in 1902. Not pictured is Reginald, who was born in 1904 and died in 1906. He is buried at the Decatur-Maxwell-Murphy Cemetery beside his grandmother Martha Daniel. (Betty Strange Prince.)

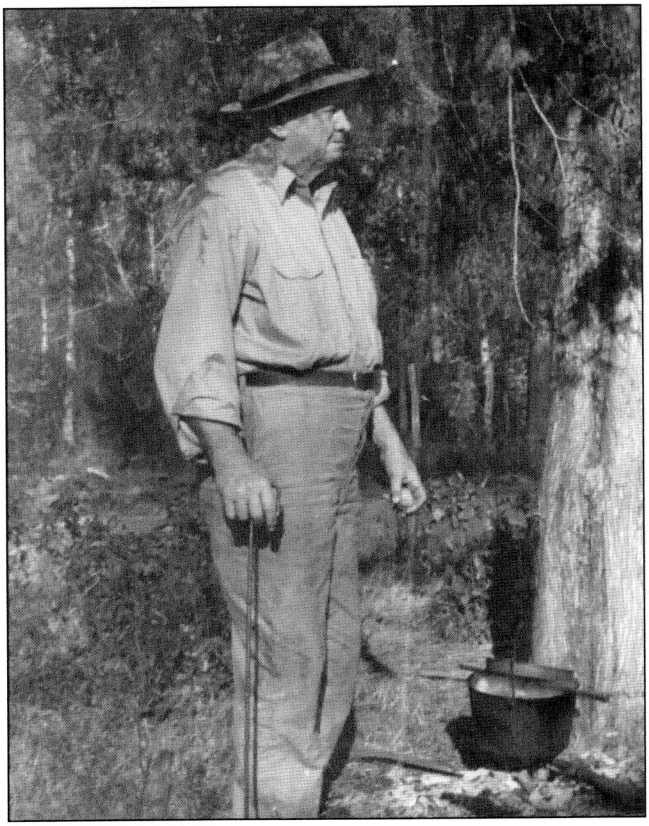

Hunting Camp. Ran Strange was known as an ardent fox hunter who raised hunting dogs and enjoyed the days he spent at the hunting camp. Foxes were abundant in the Collin County woods. He was a member of the Woodsmen of the World, a fraternal benefit society whose objective was to volunteer and help those in need. Fishing was another of his favorite sports. (Betty Strange Prince.)

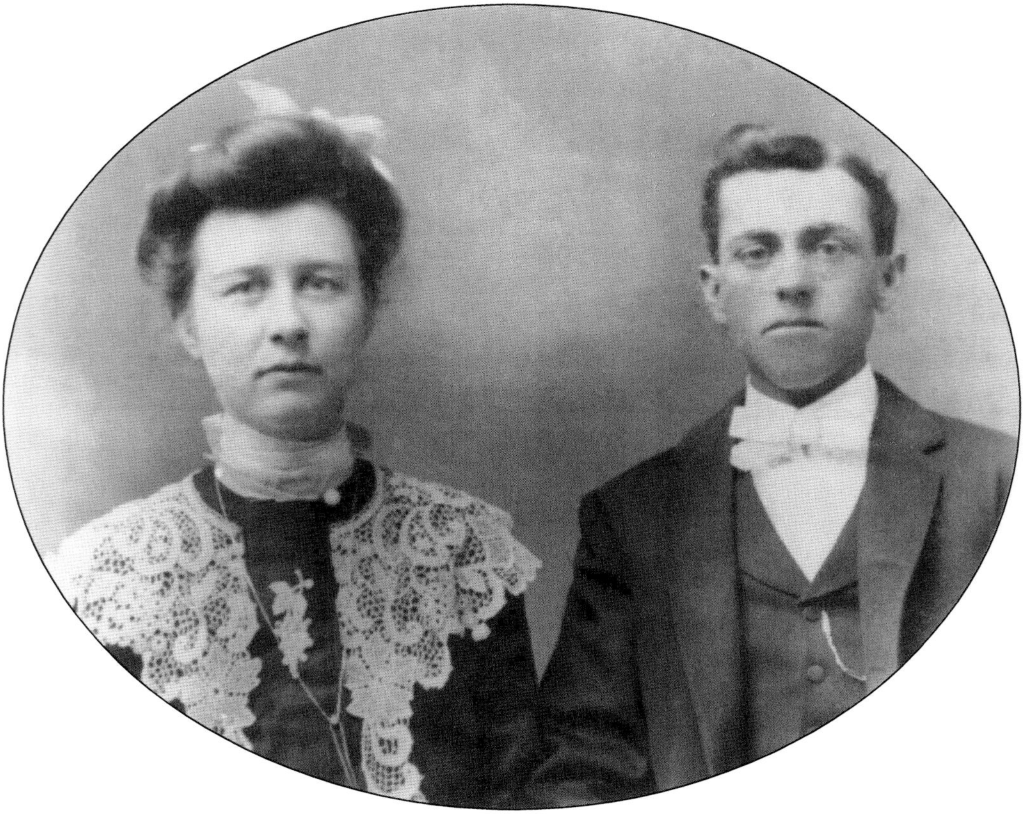

William Oscar "Willie" and Jimmie Harrison Daniel. "W.O.," as he was known in his adult life, was born in Collin County in 1876. He and Jimmie Harrison, a Murphy schoolteacher, were married in 1903. A respected farmer, he founded Daniel Implement Company in 1948 and became one of the early mayors. W.O. and Jimmie had five children, including Max, Madge, Robert, Janice, and William O. Jr., called "Dub." (Inez Daniel.)

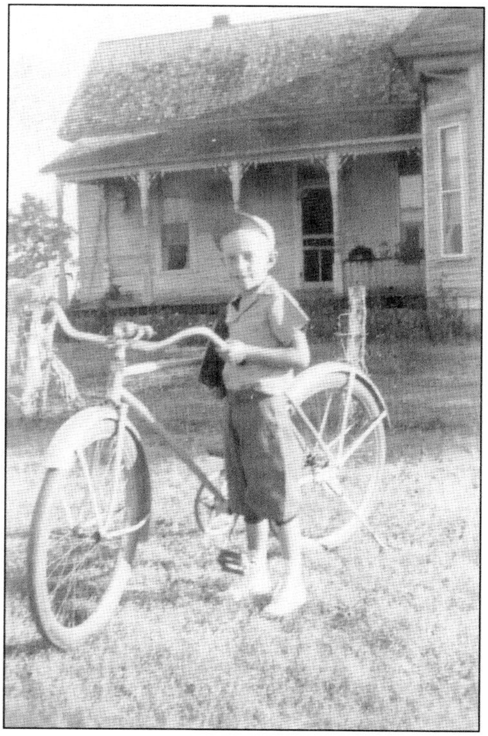

Early Daniel Home. In this photograph, Jimmy Daniel, W.O. and Jimmie's grandson, stands in front of the Daniel home with his bicycle. The home was located at the intersection of Murphy Road and McMillen Road. W.O. was a distinguished resident of Murphy and a stalwart member of the Murphy Baptist Church. (Jim Daniel.)

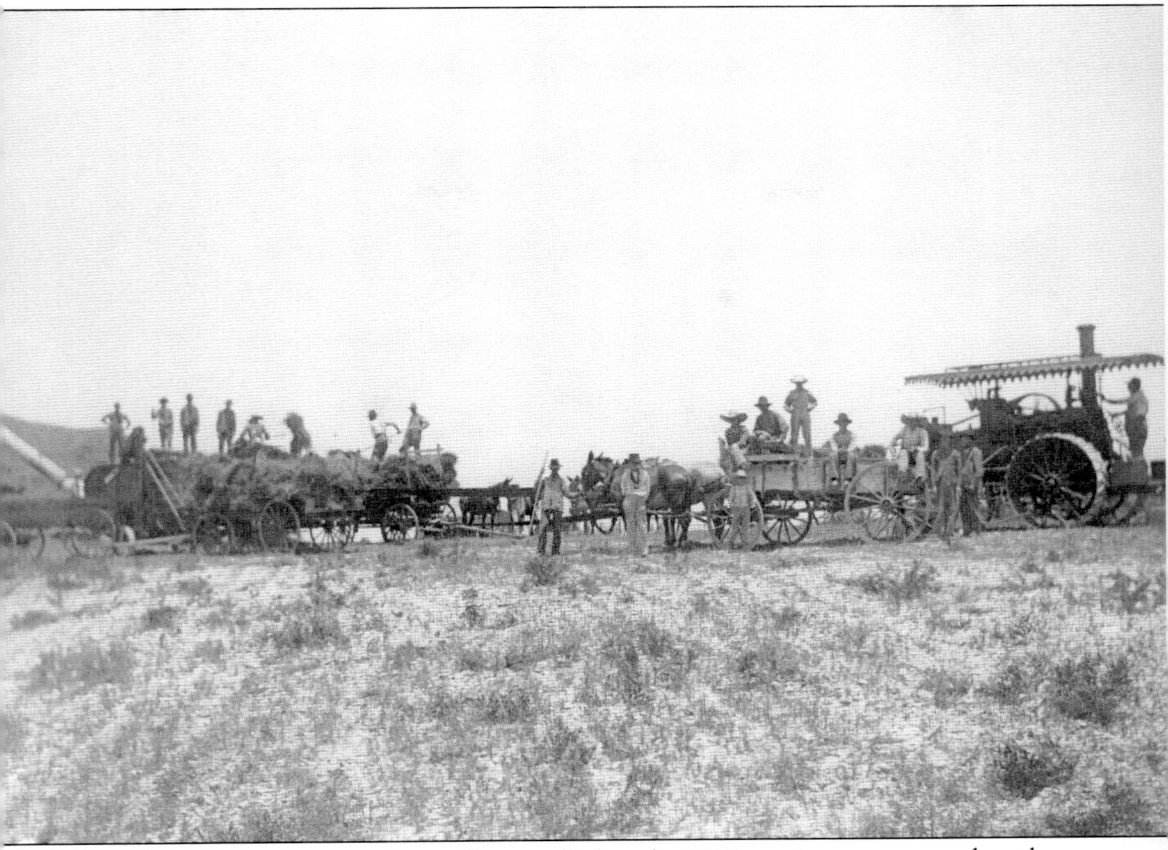

C.C. GREGORY THRESHER AND STEAM ENGINE. Before the 1880s, grain was sown and cut by hand. A farmer using a cradle could cut two acres of grain per day. Wheat was threshed with a stick called a flail. With the invention of the steam thresher, farmers could work more efficiently. Threshers were expensive, and farmers like C.C. Gregory hired out threshers to other farmers after cutting their own crops. Turner, Herring, and Salmons also owned threshers and cut grain for miles around. Pictured is the steam-powered thresher on the Gregory farm near Murphy. Farmers employed a crew of up to 25 men, according to Roy Hall. There was an engineer who operated the steam engine, men with teams of horses and wagons to collect the grain and straw, one wood wagon and one water wagon to feed the engine, and a cook to feed the men. Often, it was the farmer's wife who fed the crew. (Ema Jean Christian.)

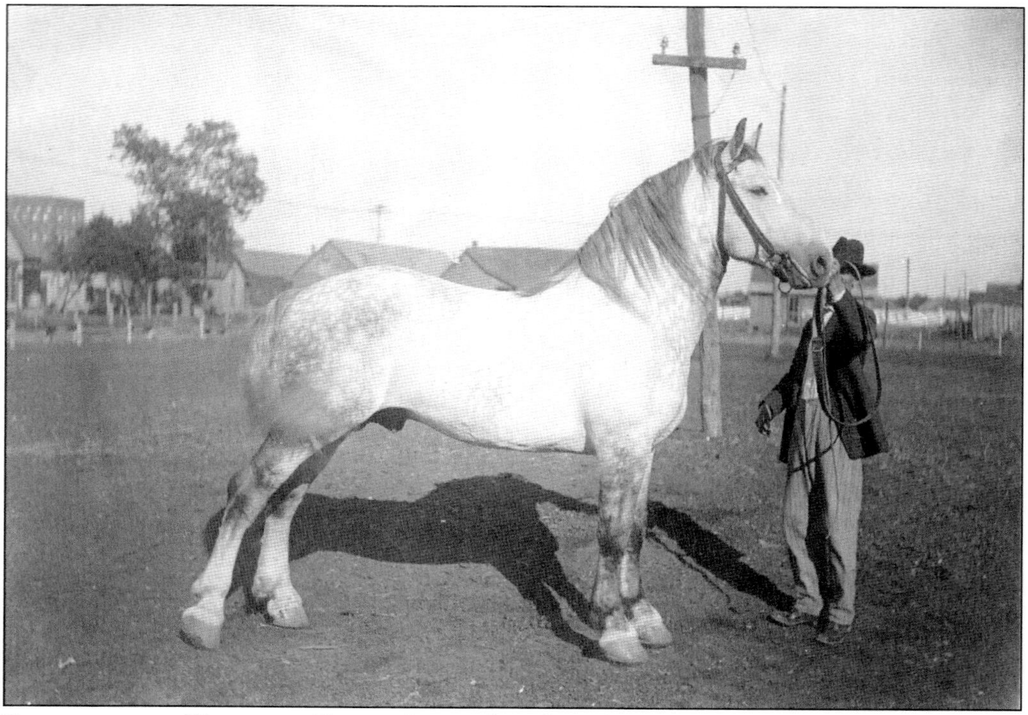

RACEHORSE AND HORSE AND BUGGY. Pictured on the right above is C.C. Gregory with his prize stallion. He bred and raced horses and even had his own racetrack near Parker. When pioneers first came to the area, they often had oxen to provide the heavy work. Later, horses and mules were used for both work and transportation. By the early 1900s, men were purchasing livestock for breeding purebred animals, including horses. Henry Maxwell owned at least 48 horses before he left Murphy for West Texas. Once, he traded 320 acres for a fine horse. In the 1960s, horses were valued from $75 to $200. In the picture below, C.C. Gregory is to the left with his horse and buggy. Races were held with a horse and a lightweight carriage and on horseback. (Both, Ema Jean Christian.)

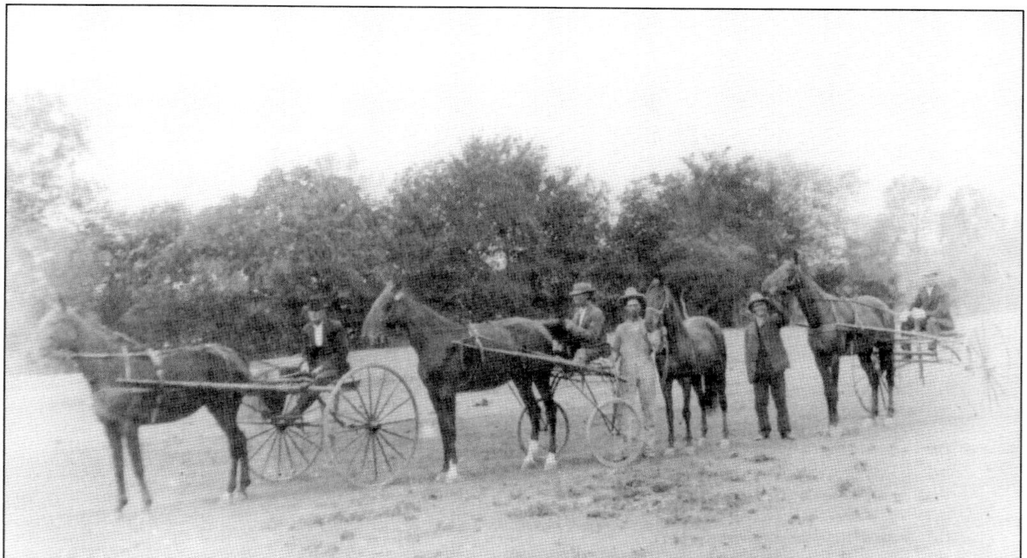

Three

Agribusiness
Farmers, Stockmen, and Businessmen

The first farmers sometimes supplemented their income by engaging in other occupations. Preachers such as S.M. Wilkins and R.R. Dunlap supplemented their income by teaching at a school located in a church. Other families built stores, gristmills, and much later cotton gins. The Salmons, Gage, and Pegues families were engaged in farming as well as the sawmill and gristmill business. General stores were constructed carrying a variety of staple goods, such as coffee, calico, sugar, salt, tobacco, and whiskey, which were considered necessary items on the farm. Stores became the voice of the community when men met to make purchases and discuss farming and ranching. The farmer's wife met other wives while making purchases. They discussed their gardens, children, churches, and illnesses. Notices were tacked to the walls of the stores to announce births, deaths, and community activities.

As early as 1855, Henry Maxwell sold lots along the future FM 544 between Murphy Road and Maxwell Creek in anticipation of the coming railroad. Men who purchased lots were craftsmen and tradesmen and men who would support the Maxwell ranching needs. Streets were named after trees like Locus, Mulberry, and Chestnut. Others were named Houston, Galveston, and Texas. Members of the Sidwell family farmed and owned a blacksmith shop, making horseshoes and wagon wheels. Their dream of the coming of the railroad in 1857 died, and it was not until 1888, when the railroad tracks were laid, that agribusiness began to thrive.

Agribusiness, or businesses making and selling products used in large-scale farming and ranching, began to grow around the beginning of the 20th century. Businesses were located on the corner of Murphy's crossroads of FM 544 and Murphy Road or near the train depot. James Murphy became the first postmaster. Early businessmen included the Allison brothers, Daniel brothers, Chaddicks, Harveys, McCrearys, Taylors, and Swindalls. A drugstore, doctor's office, bank, and feed store were built near the depot facing Murphy Road. Photographs in this chapter showcase the farmers, stockmen, and businessmen who contributed to the growth of Murphy.

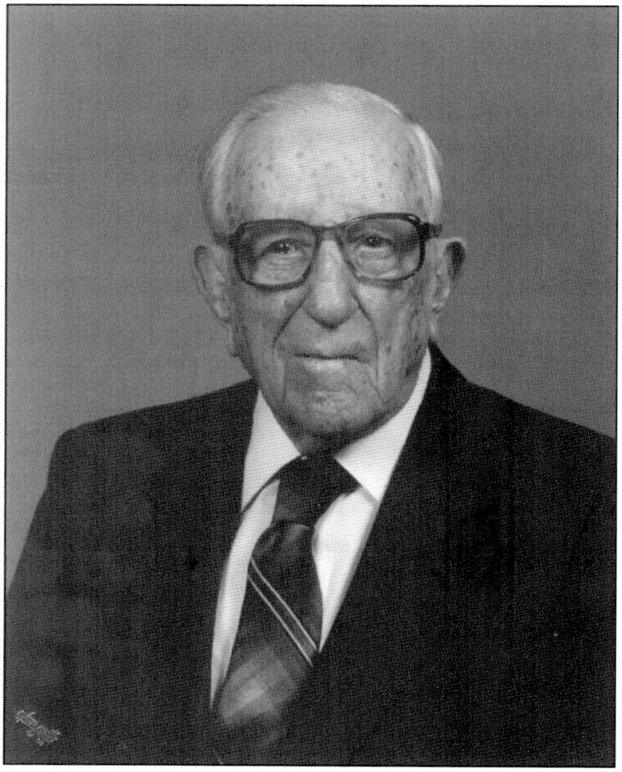

ALBERT C. TAYLOR. Albert, son of Arthur and Jane McMillen Taylor and grandson of Comfort Allen and Lydia Nobel Maxwell McMillen, was born in Murphy and attended one of the two wooden school buildings that occupied the site of the old Murphy School built by the Works Progress Administration (WPA). Albert's father, Arthur, was a farmer and ginner who managed the Trinity Oil Company Gin in Murphy. (Barbara Taylor Bennie.)

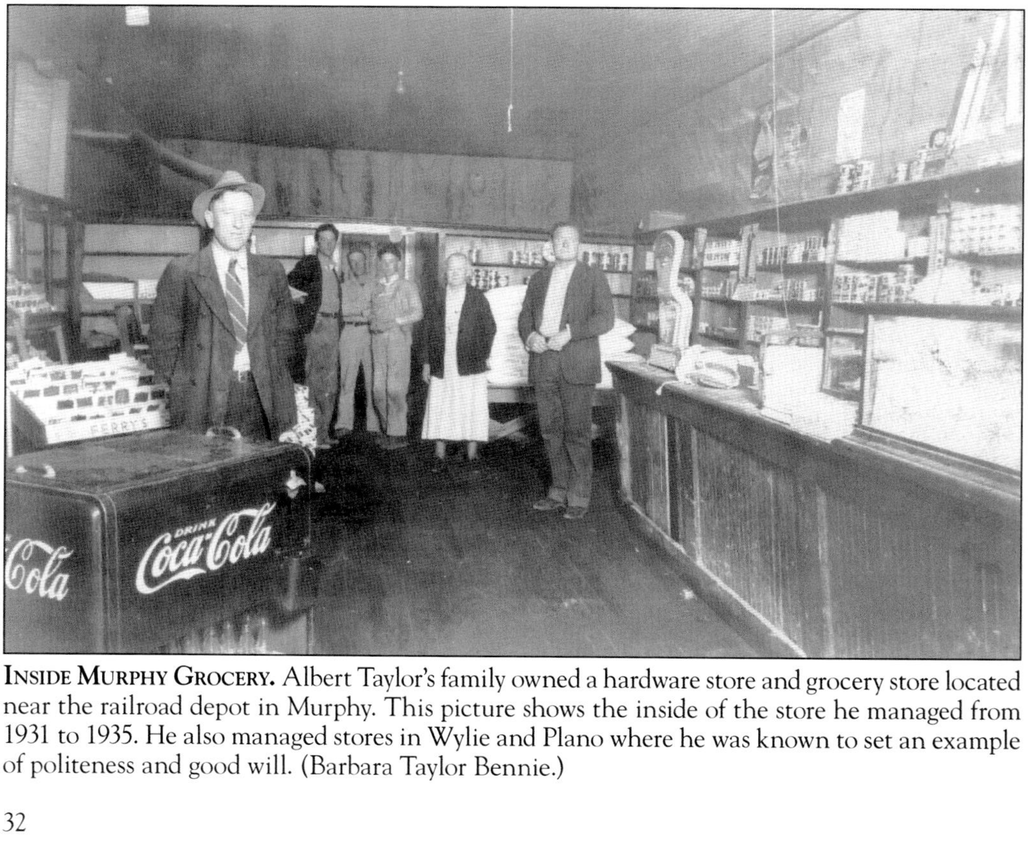

INSIDE MURPHY GROCERY. Albert Taylor's family owned a hardware store and grocery store located near the railroad depot in Murphy. This picture shows the inside of the store he managed from 1931 to 1935. He also managed stores in Wylie and Plano where he was known to set an example of politeness and good will. (Barbara Taylor Bennie.)

ARTHUR CARLYLE TAYLOR. Known as Carlyle and born in Murphy, Arthur was the son of Albert Carlyle Taylor and Willie Lee McCleary Taylor. He attended school in Murphy most of his school years and graduated from Plano High School in 1935. Few students had cars, and there were no school buses. Arthur caught a ride to and from school with classmates. (Barbara Taylor Bennie.)

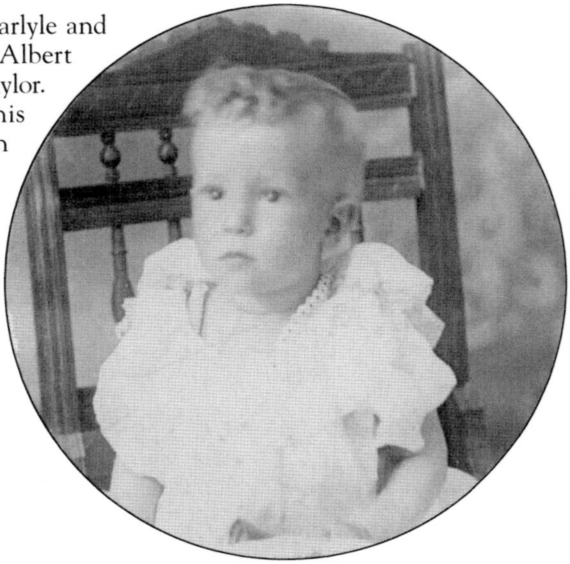

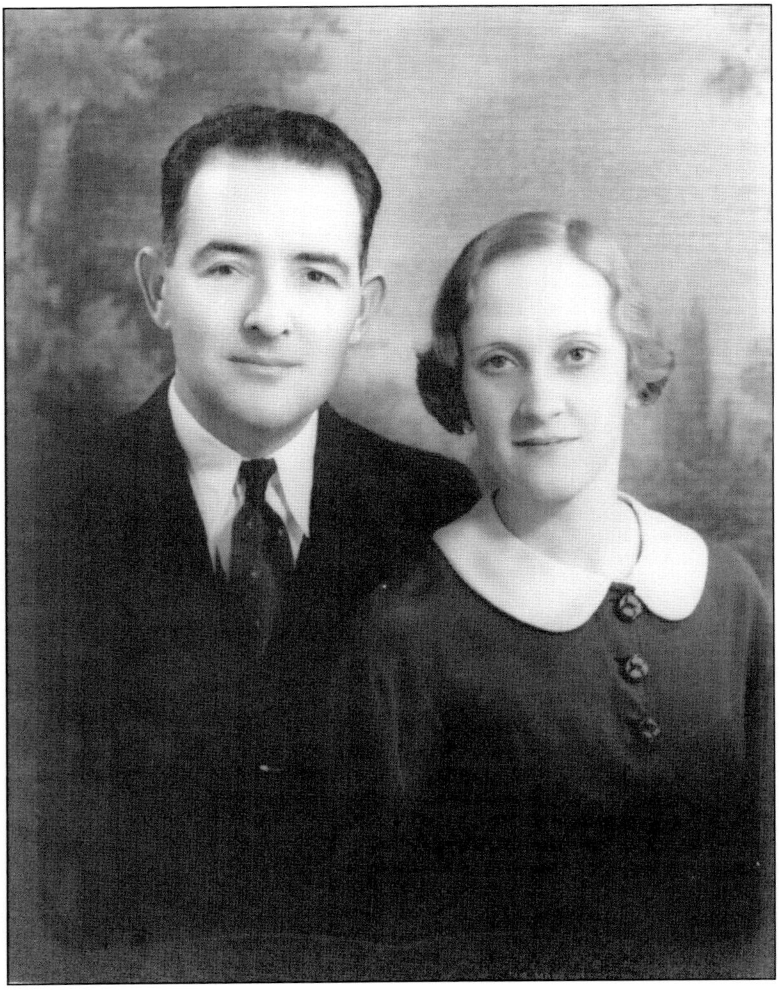

JOHN HENRY AND JANICE BAILEY. John Henry Bailey and Cleara Janice Daniel, the daughter of W.O. and Jimmie Daniel, were married in 1930. The Daniel girls all married into prominent Murphy farming families. Fannie married William Brigham. Josie married Thomas Poindexter. Minnie married Bruce Bedell, and Allie married Ran Strange. Mattie married Charlie Love. (Inez Daniel.)

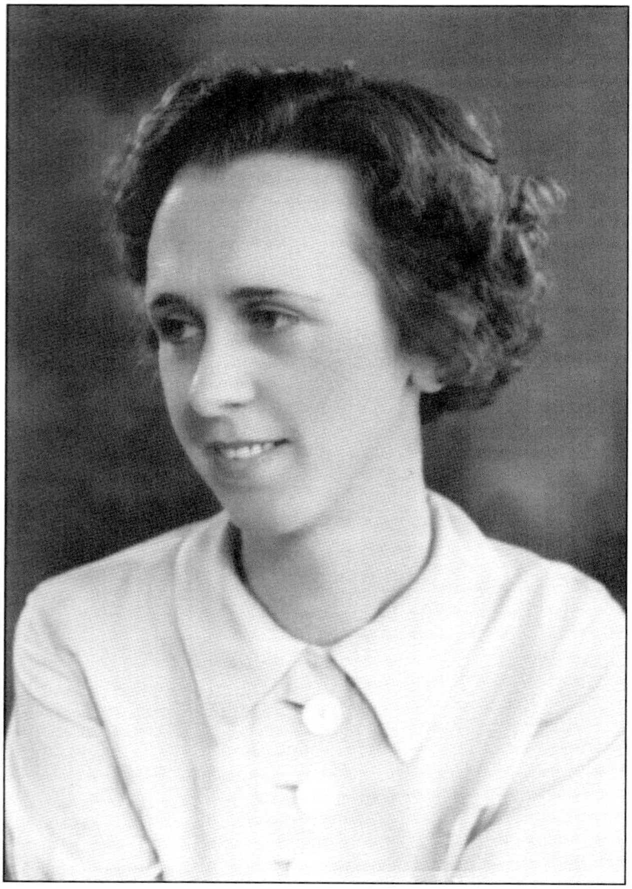

"MARY" MADGE DANIEL. Madge was a well-known citizen of Murphy and lived on the old family farmhouse on Murphy Road until her death. She taught school in Wylie in the 1940s and sometimes caught the train home for only a dime. Later, she taught English at Garland High School. After retirement, she remained active, serving as the city secretary and playing the organ at the Murphy Baptist Church. (Inez Daniel.)

MAX AND INEZ DANIEL. Max Daniel, born in 1910, married Inez Sarver in 1933. Surprising their family and friends, they eloped to Durant, Oklahoma. Returning to Murphy, they began their married life together on the family farm. This picture was taken at their home on their 25th wedding anniversary. They had one daughter, Kathy. (Inez Daniel.)

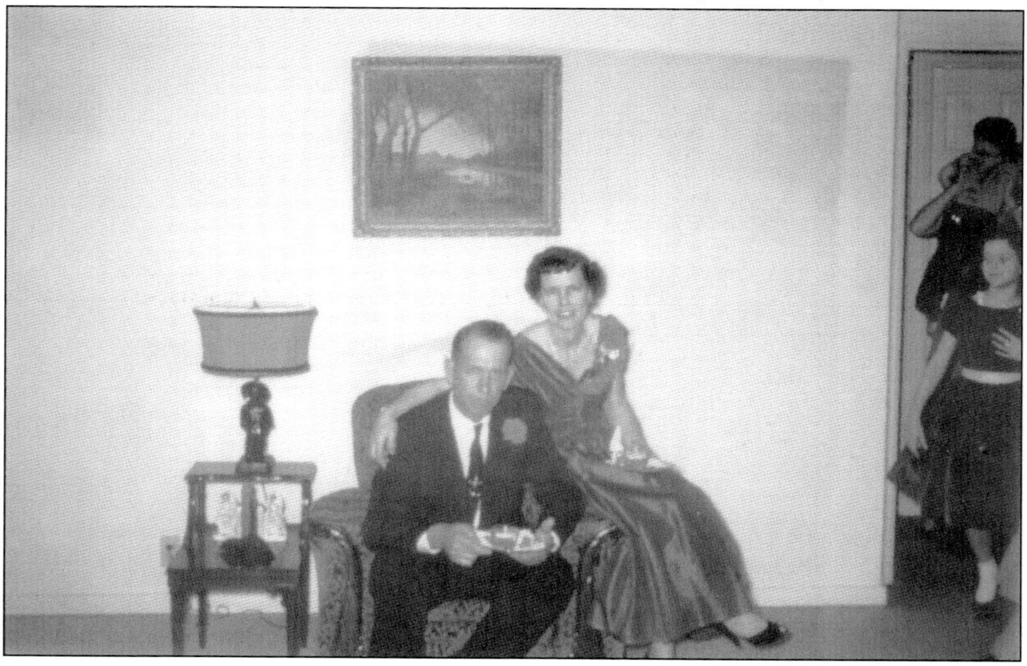

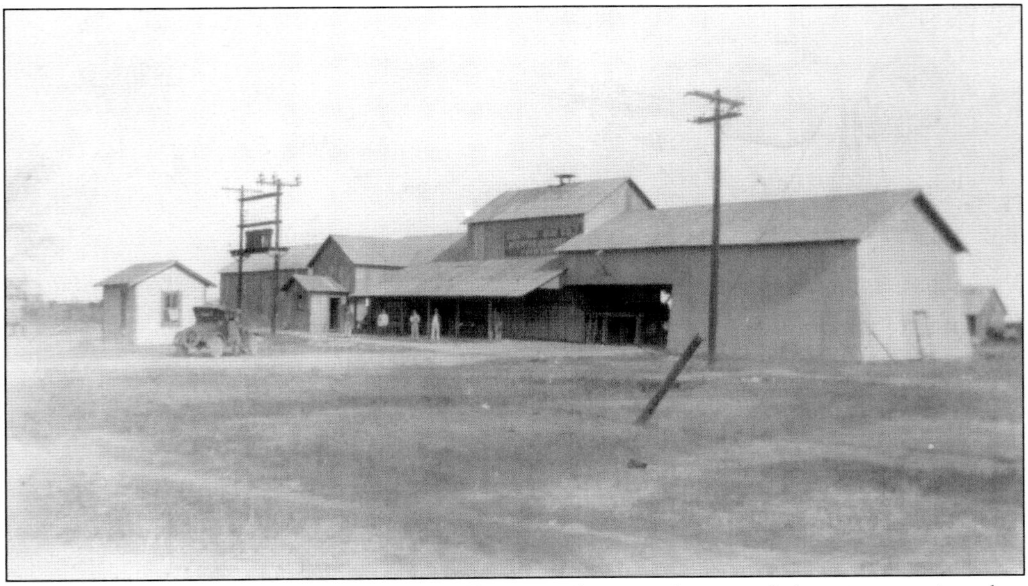

W.O. DANIEL AND O.H. MCENTEE GIN. Farmers often supplemented their income in other businesses, such as ginning. Daniel and McEntee formed a partnership in the early 1930s. The gin was located southeast of Murphy Road along the railroad tracks; however, as was the history of many gins, it was destroyed by fire. (Inez Daniel.)

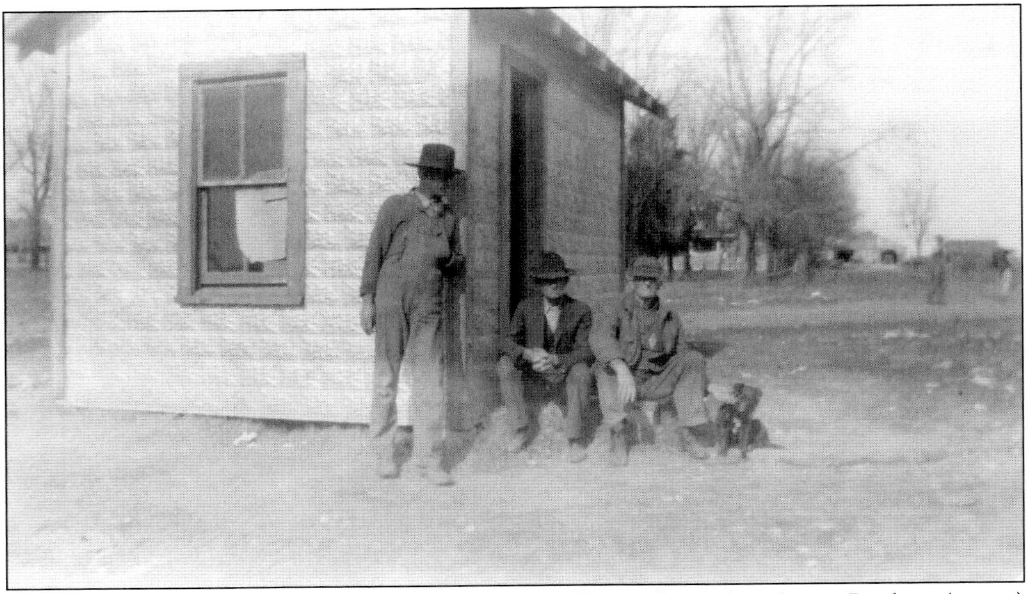

GIN OFFICE. Standing beside the gin office is farmer Hillen, and seated are farmer Brigham (center) and farmer Greer. Farmers brought their crop to the gin, had it weighed, and waited outside the office to have the information recorded. Flora Daniel kept books for the gin and would record the information and write a check for the transaction. (Inez Daniel.)

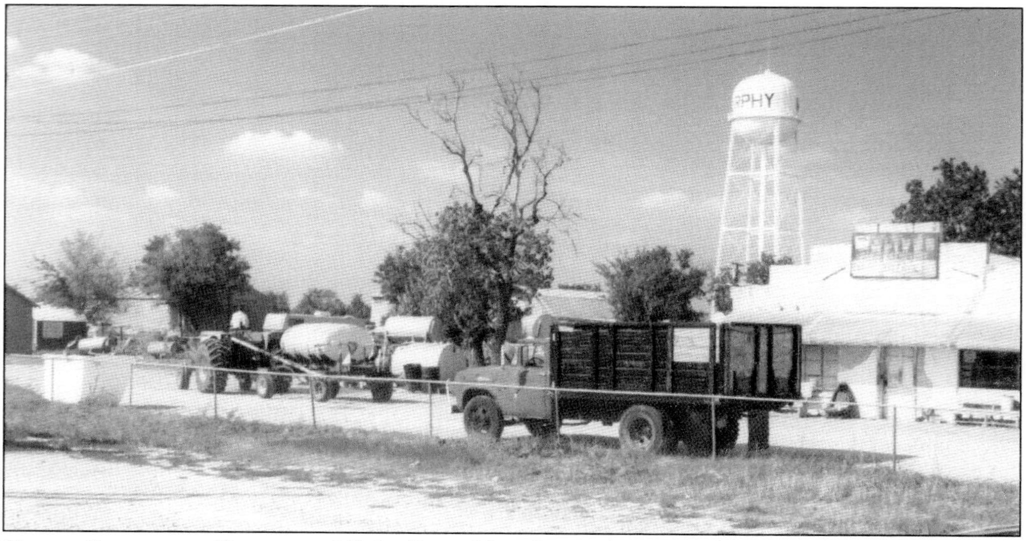

Daniel Implement Company. All the Daniel family members were farmers who also prospered in business. In 1949, W.O. Daniel Jr. built an implement company on the north side of the railroad tracks. He operated the business in Murphy and expanded operations into Frisco, Forney, and Grandview. His wife, Flora, helped manage the Murphy and Forney stores. (Inez Daniel.)

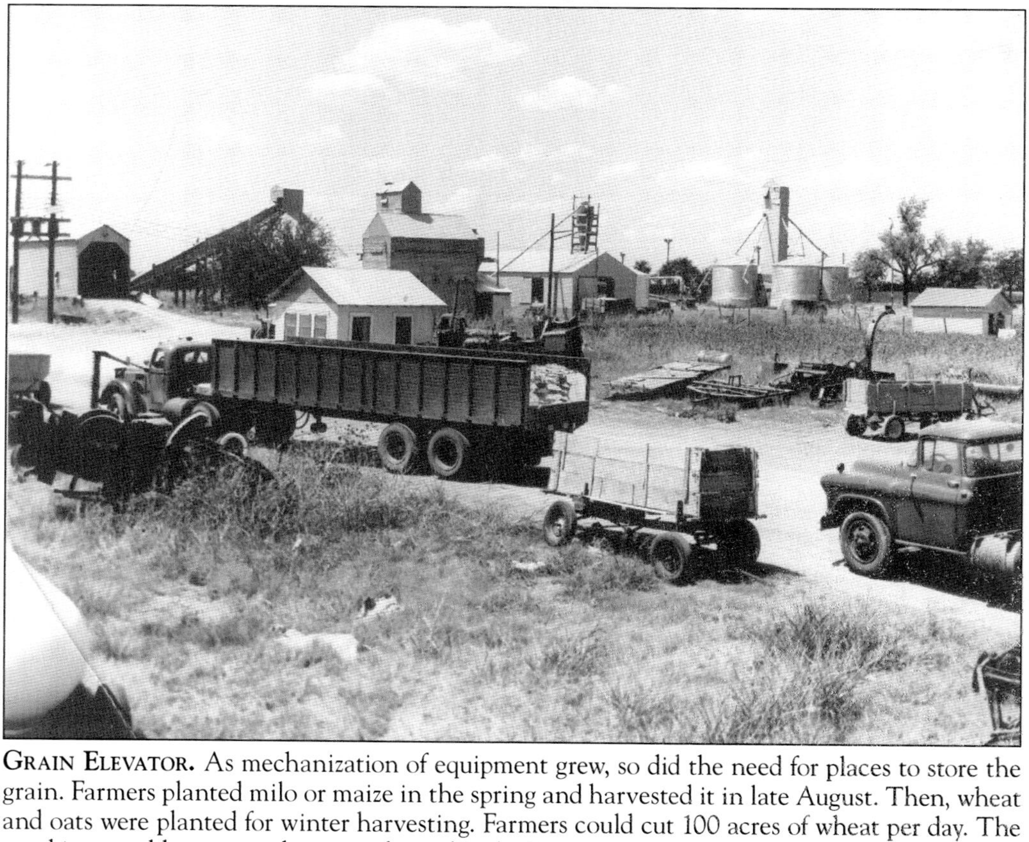

Grain Elevator. As mechanization of equipment grew, so did the need for places to store the grain. Farmers planted milo or maize in the spring and harvested it in late August. Then, wheat and oats were planted for winter harvesting. Farmers could cut 100 acres of wheat per day. The combine would separate the grain from the chaff. Then, the grain was transported to storage tanks. (Inez Daniel.)

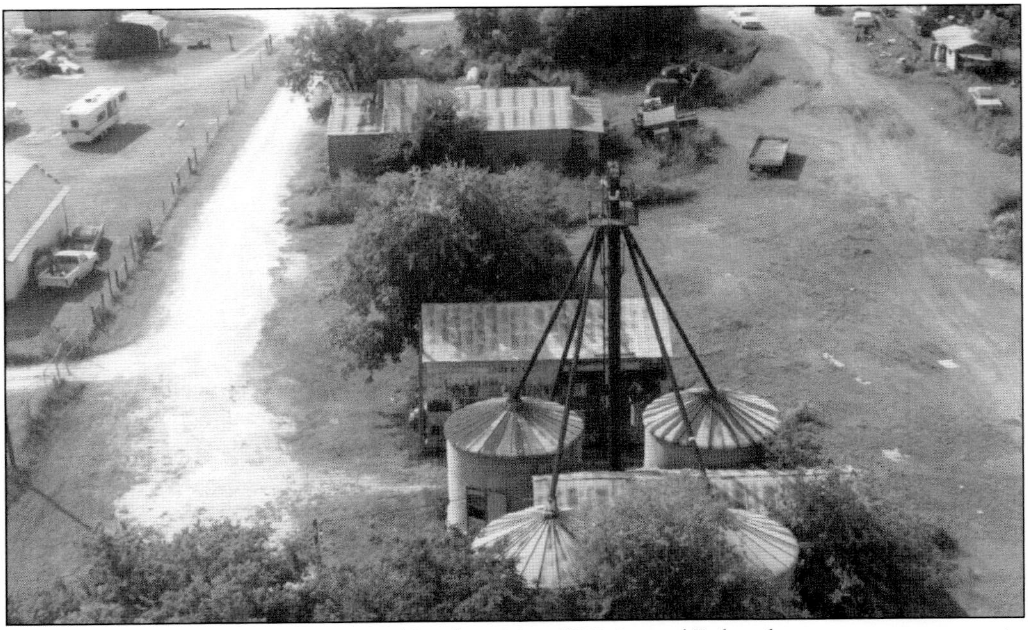

GRAIN ELEVATOR AND GIN. The Daniel brothers Max, W.O. Jr., and Robert began to grow more grain and cotton and formed a gin and grain elevator company. They did not have livestock or pastureland but grew milo and cotton on their farmland. This picture shows the surrounding fields and the gin and grain elevator as seen from the top of the old Murphy water tower. (Brad Lapsley.)

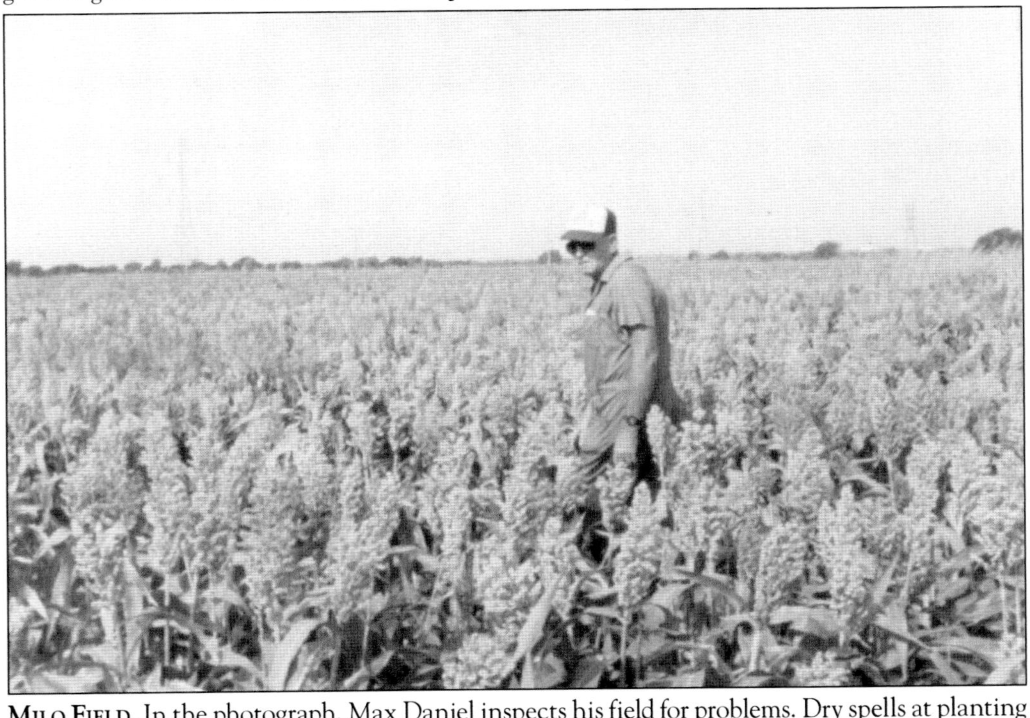

MILO FIELD. In the photograph, Max Daniel inspects his field for problems. Dry spells at planting time or rainy spells at harvest were always a concern for farmers. Insects and diseases could wipe out a crop, as could a hailstorm. After milo was combined and stored in tanks, it was taken to market. After harvesting, fields were plowed for the next crop. (Inez Daniel.)

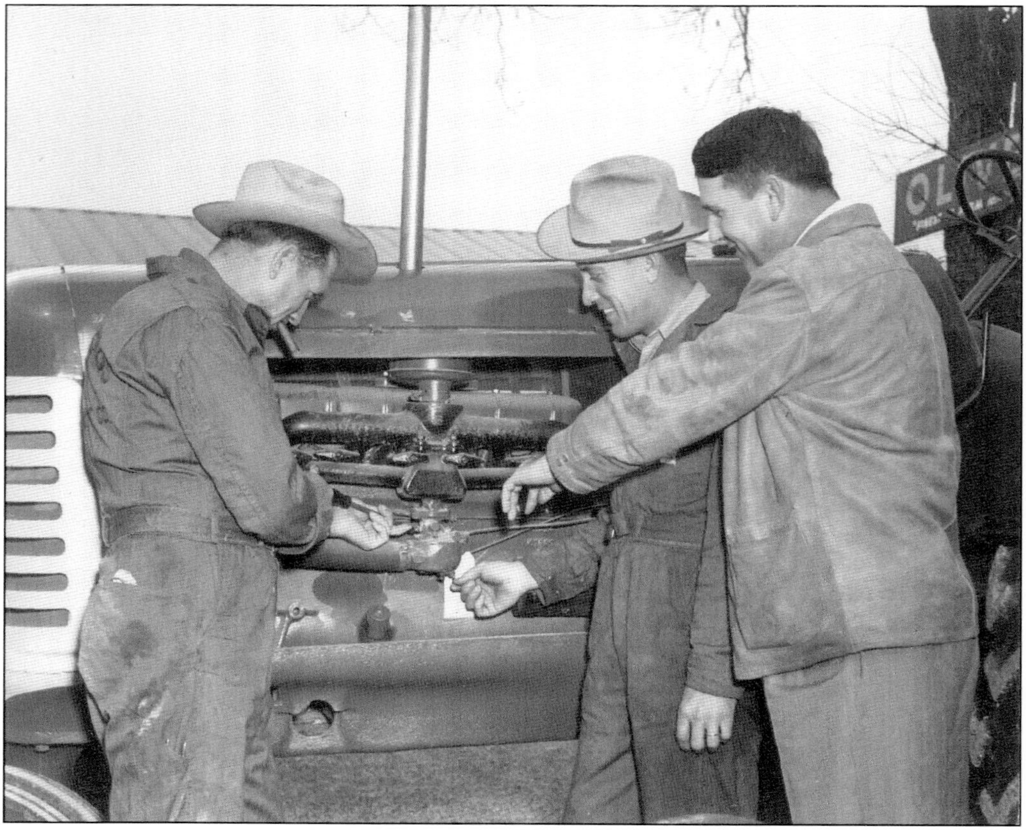

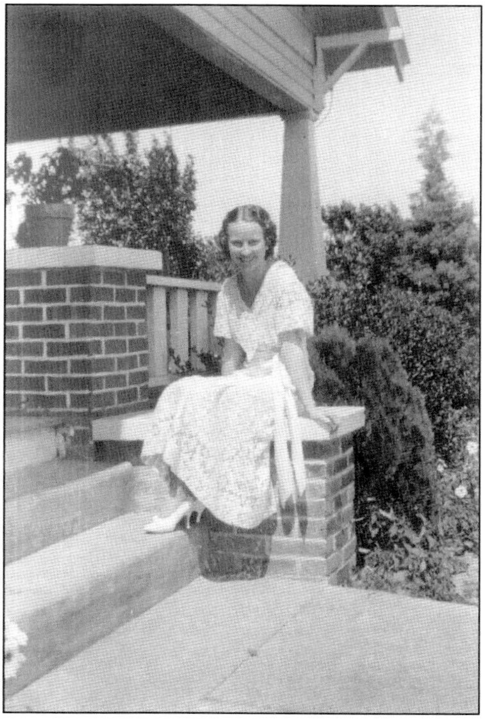

Oliver Equipment Company. In this photograph, from left to right, Max and W.O. Daniel Jr. and W.W. Keeran inspect an Oliver tractor. The Daniel brothers began to sell Oliver equipment in the 1950s. Large tractors, big combines, and heavy plows and planters were needed to run the 2,000–4,000 acres of farmland in and around Murphy. They sold tractors, trailers, and a variety of other equipment to area farmers. (Inez Daniel.)

Flora Grace James. Flora, daughter of Pearl and Frank James, posed for this picture in her wedding dress. Her parents owned a farm between present-day Jupiter Road and Spring Creek, and her family donated the land for Big Springs Baptist Church. Frank was a deacon at the church. (Flora Daniel.)

FRANK JAMES. Frank James plowed his fields on the Spring Creek farm with a plow and mules. He and his wife, Pearl, were outstanding members of the Spring Creek community and productive members of the Big Springs Baptist Church. He was a church leader and deacon. (Flora Daniel.)

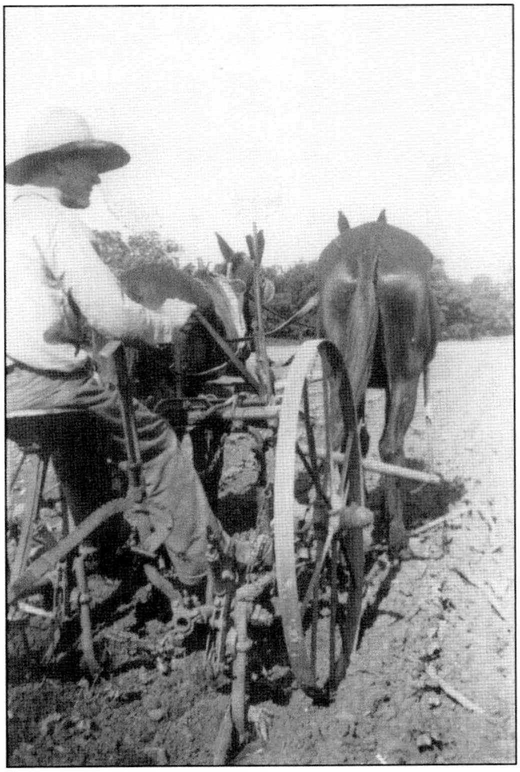

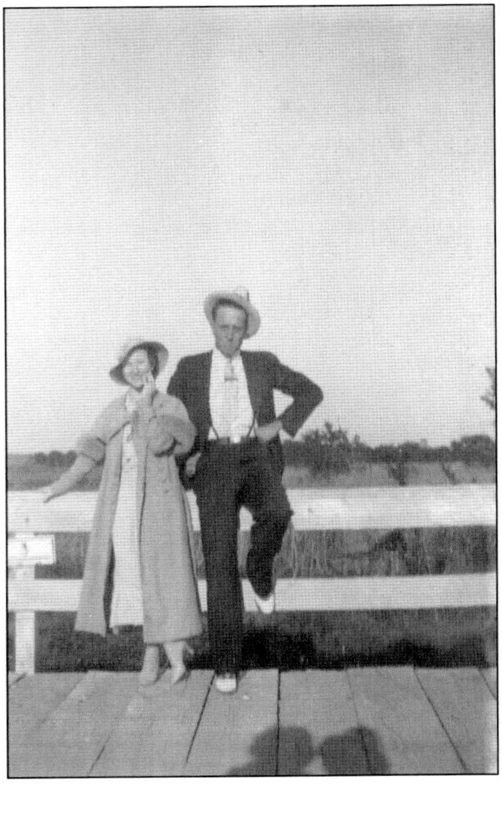

FLORA AND WILLIAM OLIVER DANIEL. Flora and W.O. Daniel Jr. of Murphy were wed on April 5, 1935, in McKinney at the home of the Baptist minister, Brother Jenkins. Flora and W.O. were members of the Murphy Baptist Church, where Flora taught Sunday school and W.O. was a deacon. (Flora Daniel.)

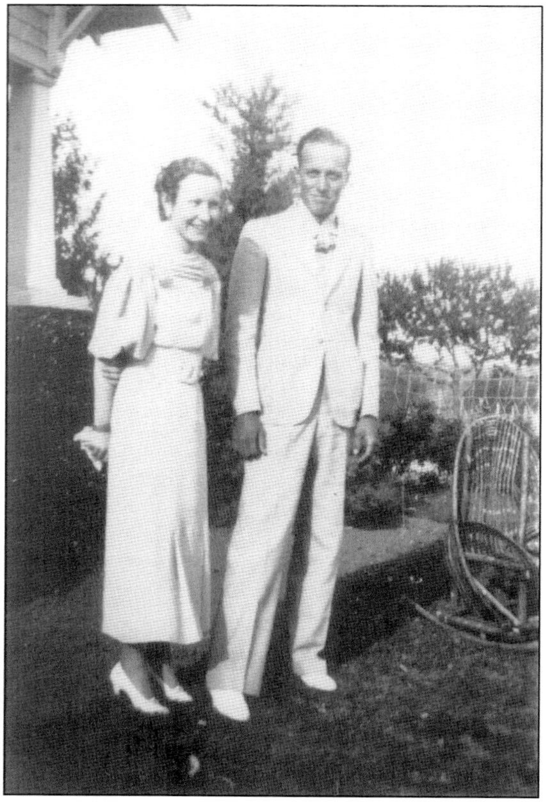

Flora and W.O. Daniel. Flora and W.O. are dressed for church as they stand in front of their Murphy home. The Daniel family was all farmers working the land and planting grain and cotton. The Daniel brothers joined their father and expanded the implement company in Murphy catering to local farmers and small stockmen in the surrounding areas. Flora worked in the office and kept books. (Flora Daniel.)

Robert and Norma Daniel Wedding. Shown in the photograph are Robert, the youngest son of W.O. Sr. and Jimmie Daniel, and Norma Jean Lenore on their wedding day on November 24, 1946. They moved from Murphy, making their home in Wylie, where they owned a laundromat. Their children were Robert Lee, Mary Cynthia, and Lisa Jeanene. (Inez Daniel.)

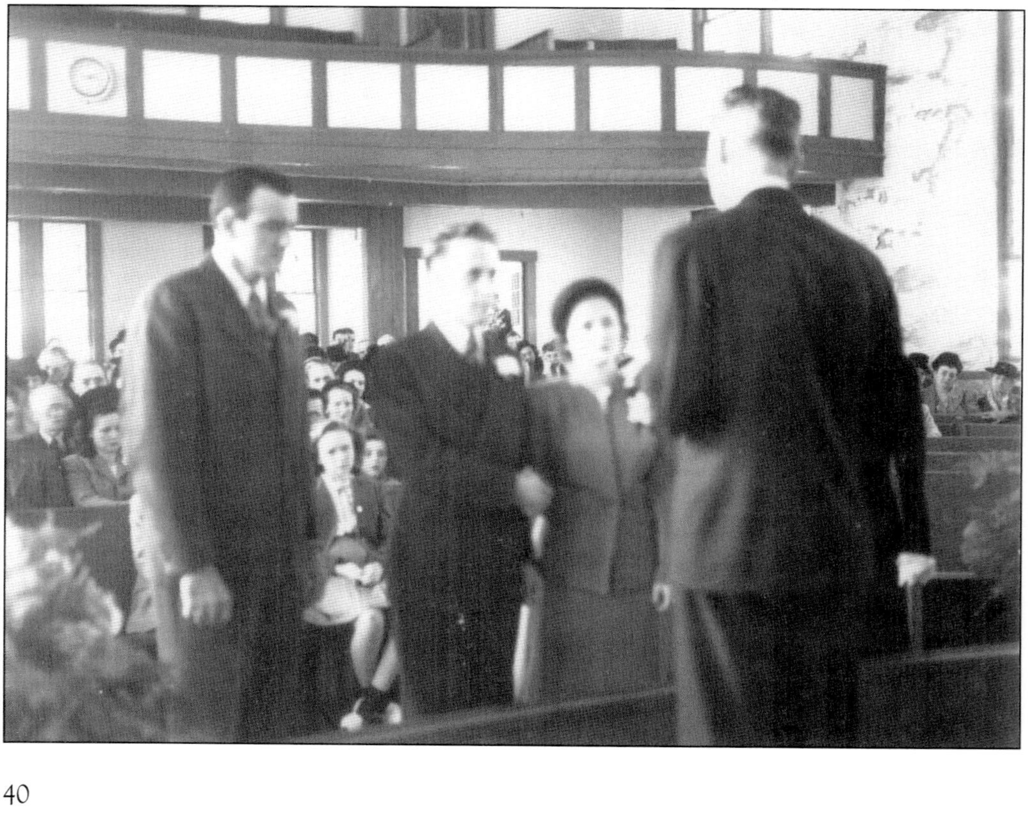

CELIA AND JIM DANIEL. Jimmy Frank Daniel, born in 1936, and Celia Faye Daniel, born in 1940, were the children of Flora and W.O. Daniel Jr. As children living in Murphy, they played together and with their neighbors. Whether it was freckled-faced Jim singing tunes for his grandfather or playing cowboys or Celia having a backyard tea with her dolls, they were a close-knit pair of siblings. Jim attended the Murphy school, which was located down the street from his house on Murphy Road, until the school closed in the 1950s. Both Jim and Celia graduated from Plano High School. Jim went to college at Baylor University and married the 1958 Baylor Homecoming Queen, Dotty Brocksmith. Celia married Donald Teague. Pictured are Celia and Jim in the early 1940s and again in the 1950s. (Both, Jim Daniel.)

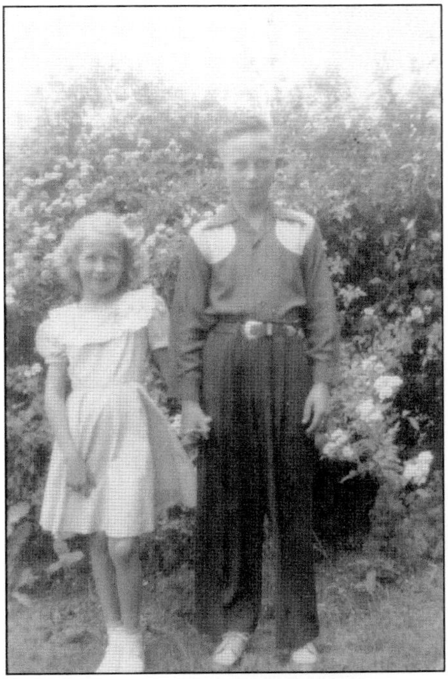

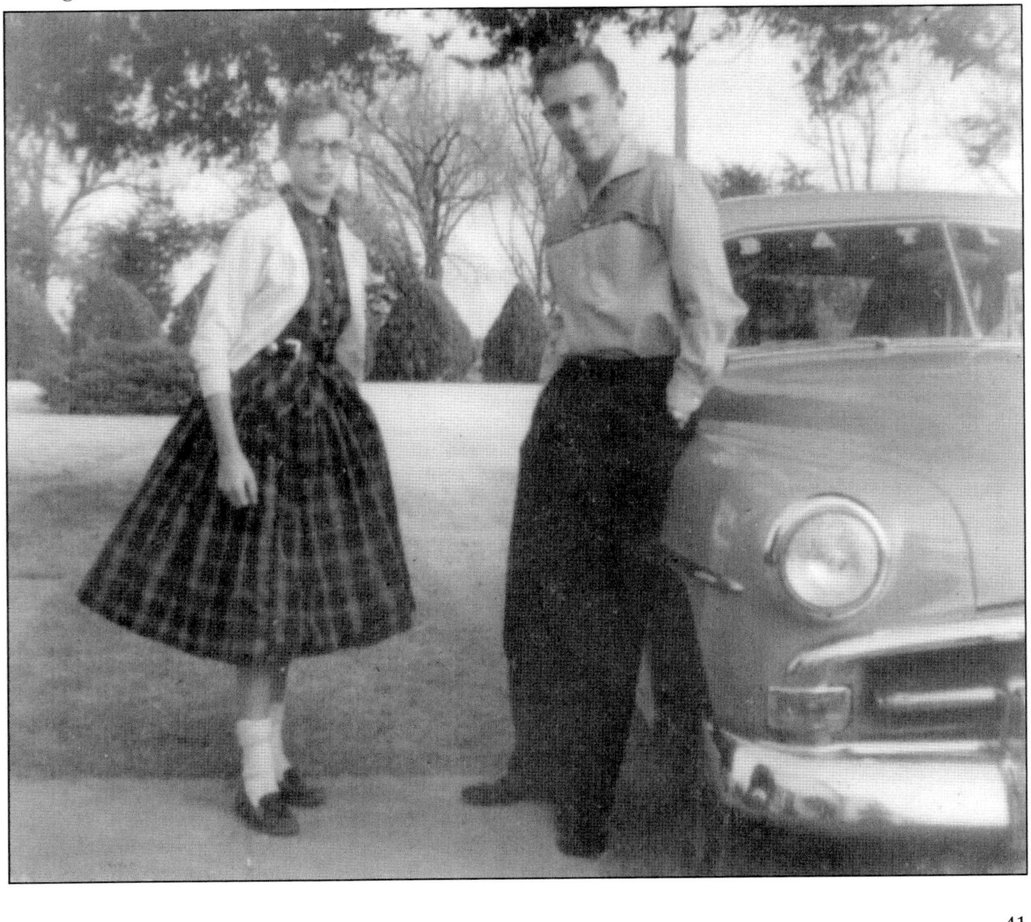

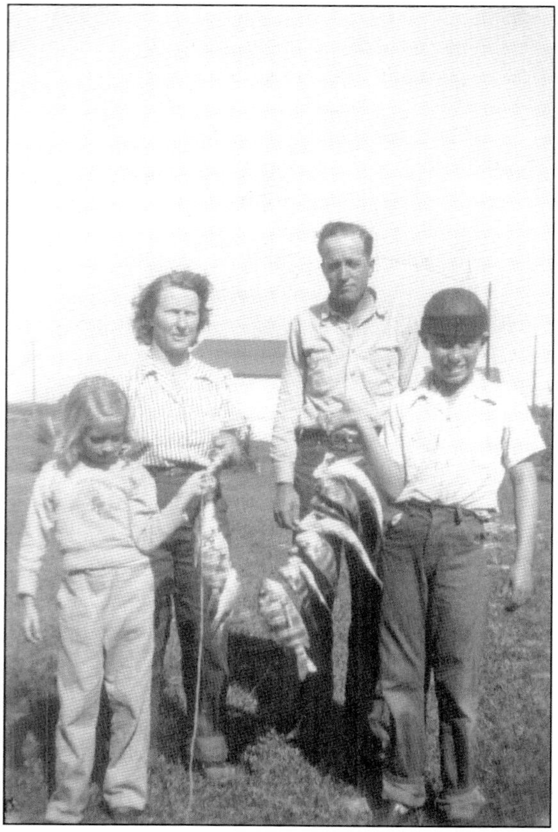

FISHING. Jim Daniel proudly displays a string of fish he caught. Fishing was a fun activity for many of the families in Murphy. Both boys and girls fished along creek banks and in Rowlett Creek. Family fishing trips were sometimes followed by a fish fry with slaw, fried potatoes, and beans. Pictured are, from left to right, W.O., Flora, Celia, and Jim. (Jim Daniel.)

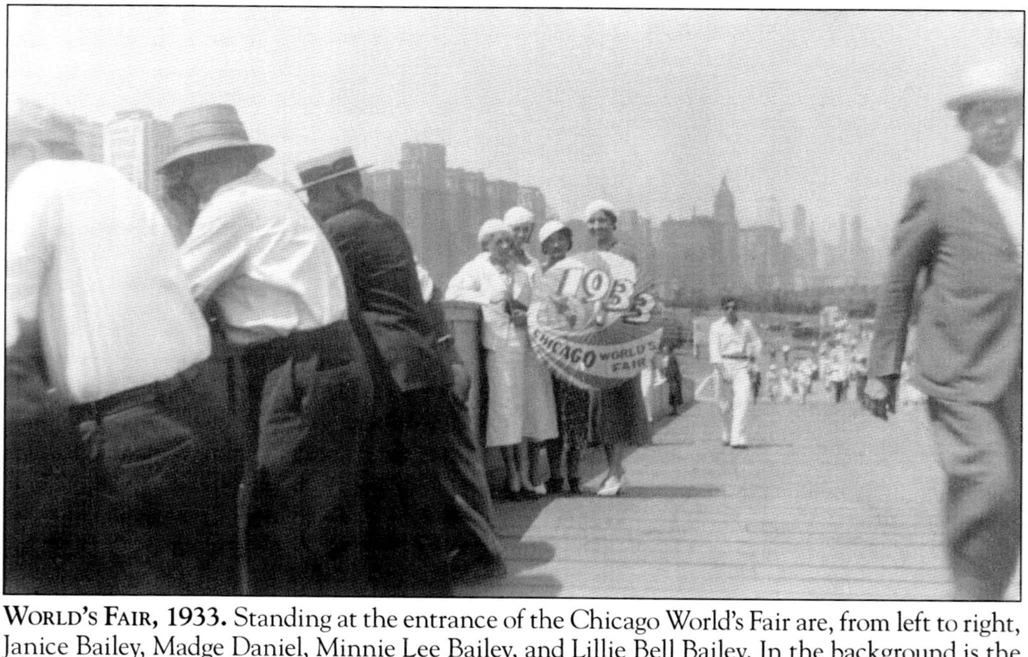

WORLD'S FAIR, 1933. Standing at the entrance of the Chicago World's Fair are, from left to right, Janice Bailey, Madge Daniel, Minnie Lee Bailey, and Lillie Bell Bailey. In the background is the Chicago skyline. The Murphy women enjoyed visiting the fair, whose theme was "A Century of Progress." (Inez Daniel.)

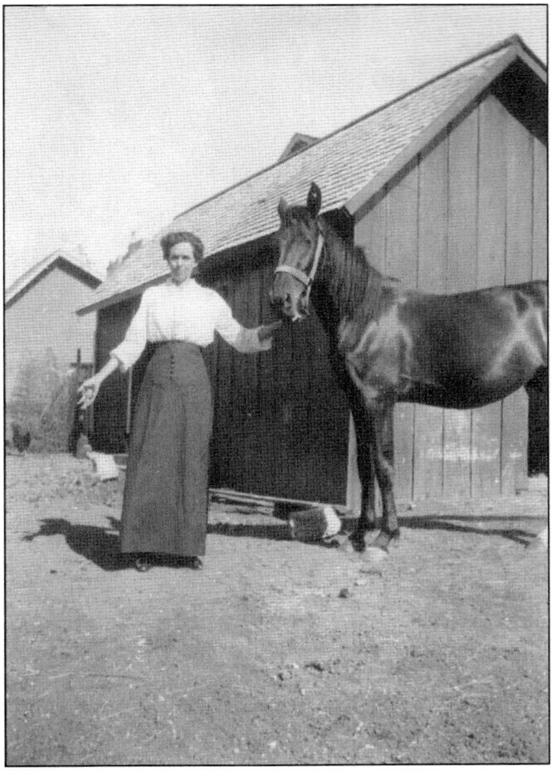

Mattie Daniel Love. Mattie Daniel was the daughter of William J. and Mattie Echols Daniel. She was married to Charlie Love, and they lived in Murphy with their son, Herbert Love. The photograph shows her as a young lady standing with her horse in front of the barn on the Daniel home place. (Inez Daniel.)

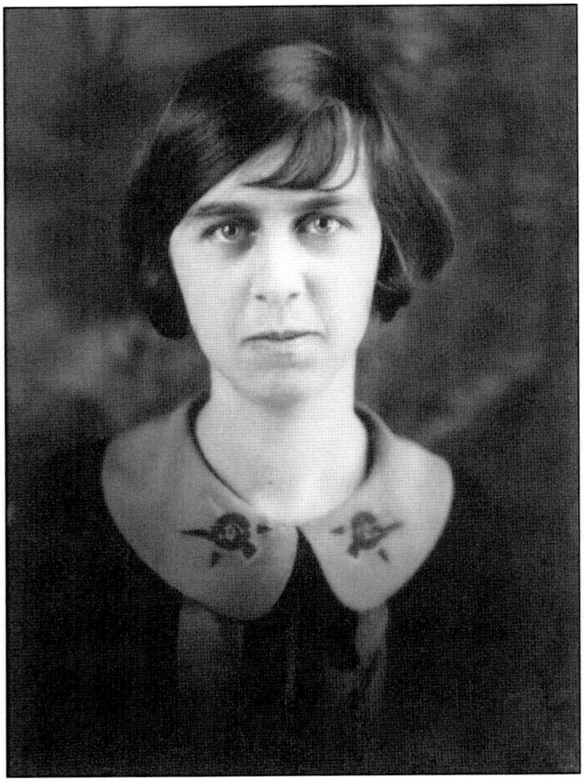

Madge at North Texas Teacher's College. Madge was born to W.O. and Jimmie Daniel. She never married and lived and died on the same farm where she was born. Madge was a teacher and a well-known citizen of Murphy. She served as an election judge and was involved in the first Murphy government, formed in the 1950s. Madge appears as a college senior in this photograph. (Inez Daniel.)

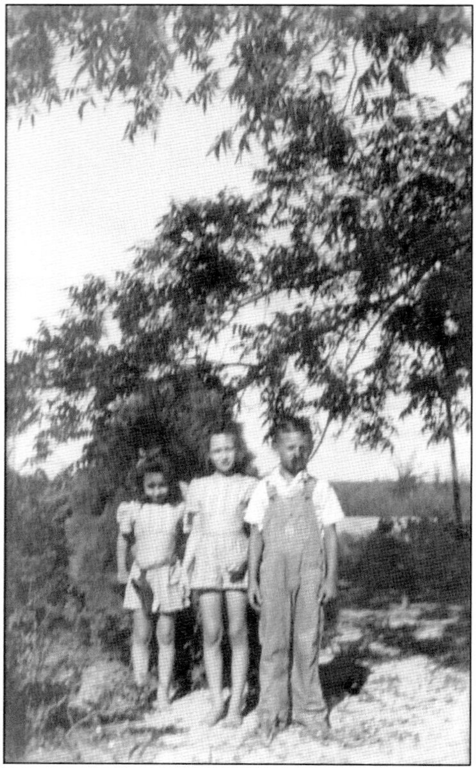

Barnes Farm on Brand Road. Pete Barnes (right) is shown in this photograph with Eddie Carpenter (left) and Dorothy Barnes (center). He and his seven brothers and sisters lived on the family farm on Brand Road and walked to Murphy School by following the railroad track into Murphy. His parents were J.K.P. (John Knox Polk) and Olive Barnes, who purchased the Brand Road farm in 1928. (Brenda Barnes Coleman.)

Grandma Barnes and Ollie Mae. Olive Barnes (left) is shown in the picture with Ollie Mae Herbert. Ollie Mae and her husband, Leon, lived on the Ingram farm on Brand Road. Leon farmed while Ollie Mae cooked and cared for members of the Barnes family. Ollie Mae was sitter for numerous Murphy children during the 1970s and was remembered for her habit of chewing tobacco. (Brenda Barnes Coleman.)

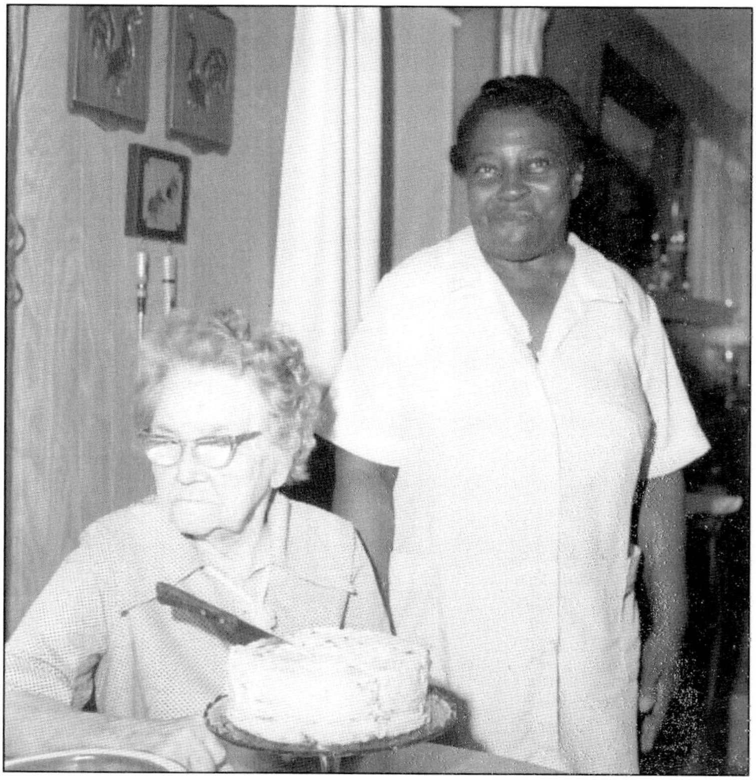

LULA SUE AND CHARLES TRAVIS. Charles Christopher Travis and Lula Sue Pitts were married and moved to the Travis farm in Murphy about 1934. Charles was the youngest son of John Roland and Nancy "Nan" Williams Travis from East Texas. Lula Sue was the daughter of John Wesley and Permeilia Andrews Milan. Charles and Lula Sue had three daughters, Merle Strange, Lillian Harvey, and Anna Ruth Merritt. (Betty Strange Prince.)

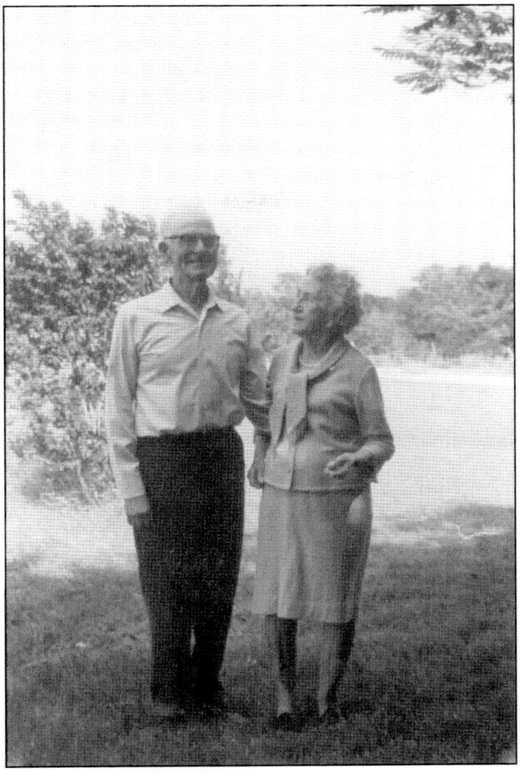

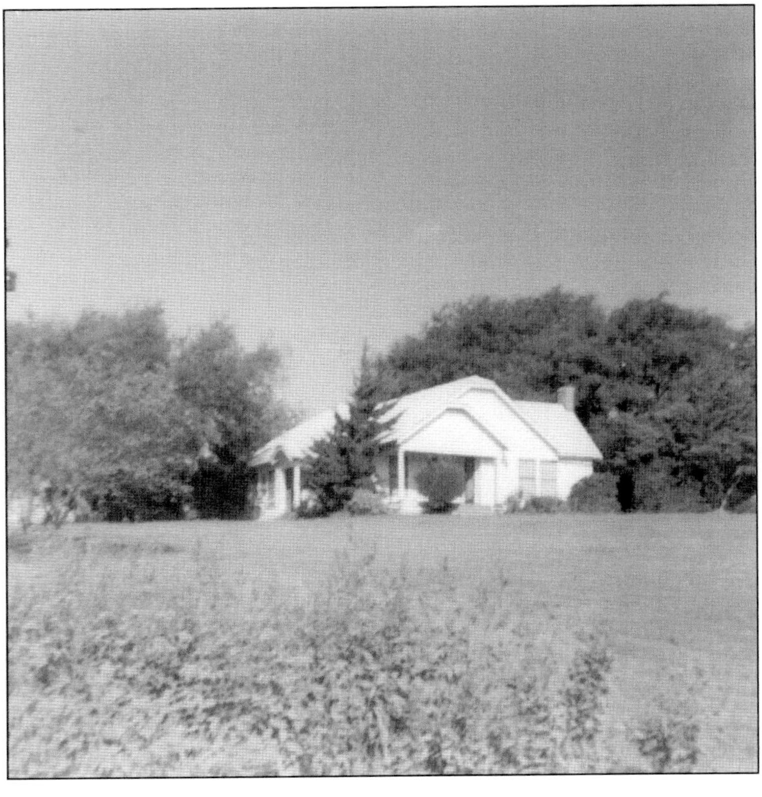

TRAVIS HOME, 1930S. The grandchildren remembered visiting often. During the daylight hours, they would make use of the outhouse, and they would use a chamber pot, or "slop jar," placed beside the bed at night. Cold running water was used for baths. Water was heated on the stove for warm baths of only two to three inches of water. Years later, indoor plumbing and hot water were added. (Betty Strange Prince.)

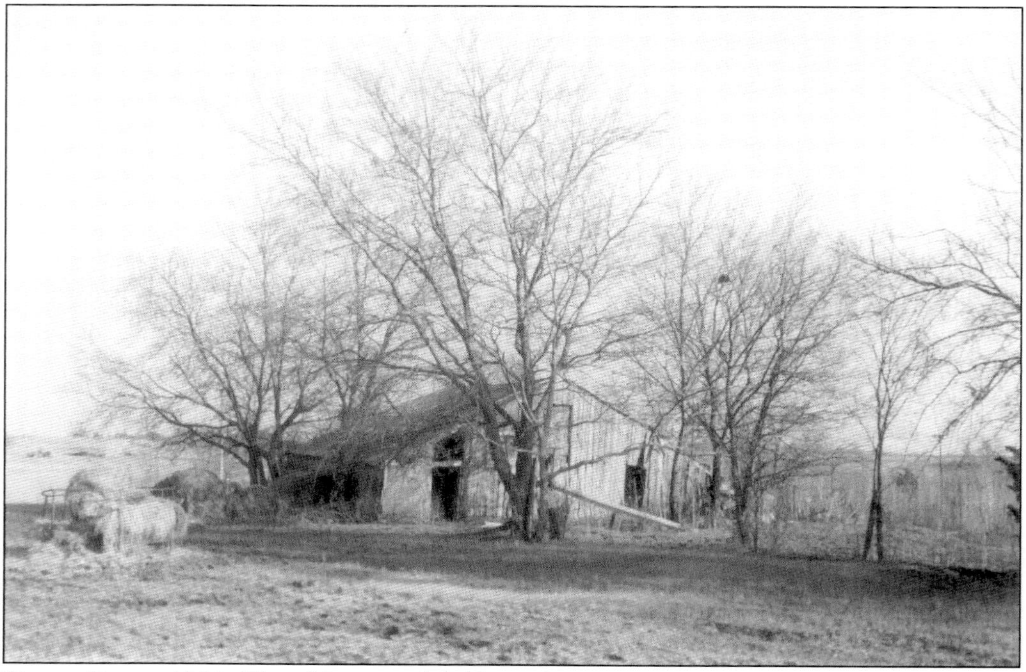

TRAVIS BARN, 1998. The oldest grandchildren, Gary, Ronnie, Martha, and Betty, loved the barn that was torn down shortly after this picture was taken. They played in the hayloft and corncrib and watched the windmill fill the water tank. Watching "Paw Paw" milk the cows and plow the fields was exciting. There was always milk, buttermilk, butter, vegetables, and fruit from the farm. (Teresa Ganis.)

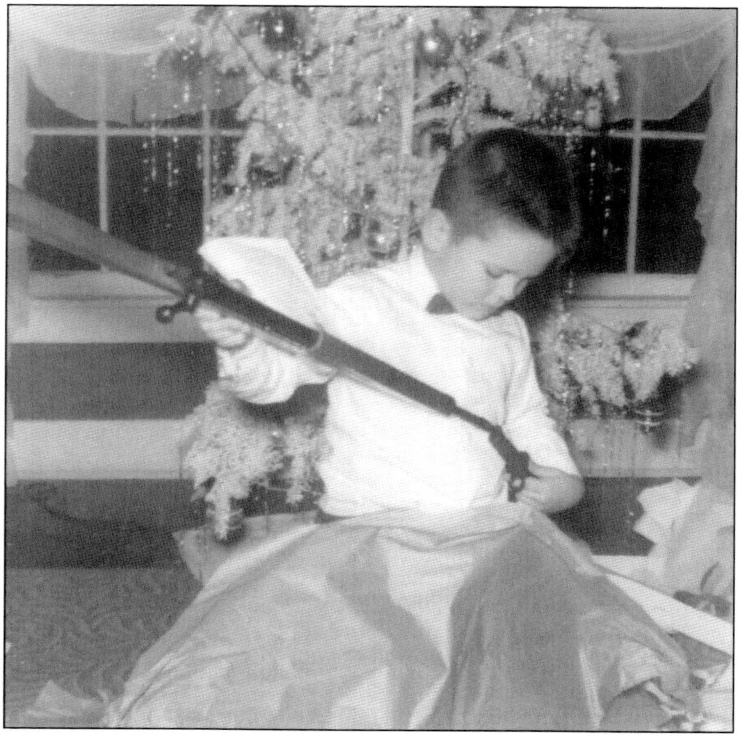

CHRISTMAS, 1959. Shown in the picture is Mike Merritt, the Travises' grandson. Christmas was a time for family, and being frugal, the family used the same farm cedar tree year after year. The tree was painted white and stored hanging in the garage and taken down to be redecorated each year. Wrapping paper was saved, and grandchildren ironed the paper every Christmas Eve before everyone began to wrap gifts. (Betty Strange Prince.)

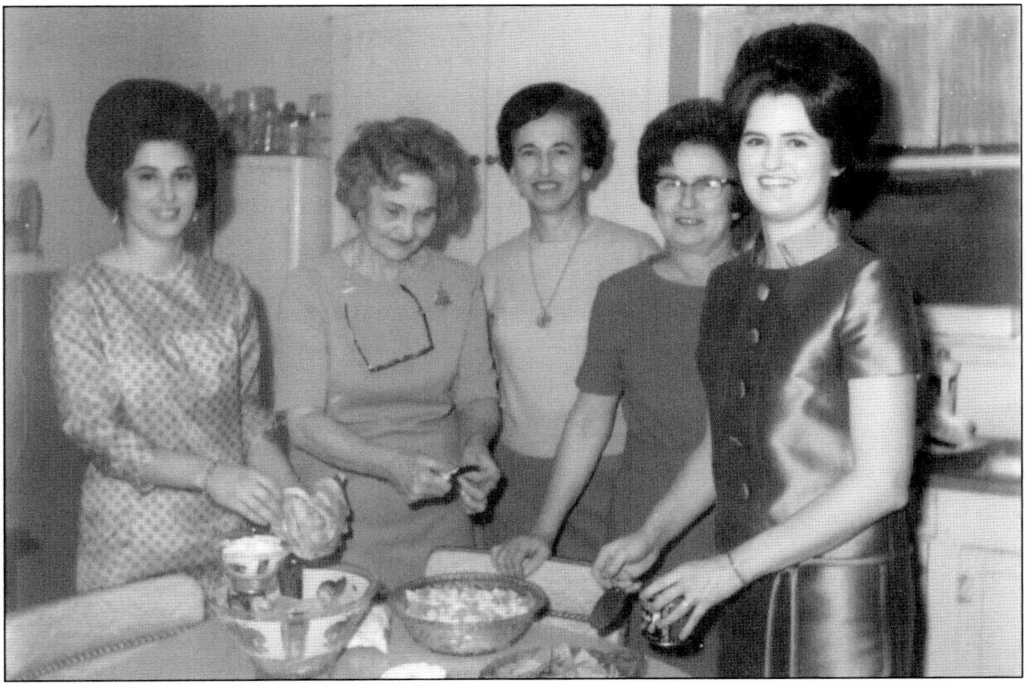

CHRISTMAS, 1968. Pictured are, from left to right, Faye Strange, Lillian Harvey, Merle Strange, Lula Sue Travis, and Betty Prince. The family gathered on Christmas Eve for "The Christmas Tree." They assembled at 6:00 p.m. for ham, potato salad, and homemade cucumber and beet pickles. Later, they sang hymns, read the Christmas story, and opened gifts. Then, dessert and a traditional punch with pink sherbet and ginger ale was served. (Betty Strange Prince.)

EASTER SUNDAY, 1974. Easter was a time to dress up and attend church. The Travis family members were ardent contributors of the Murphy Baptist Church. Charles was a deacon, and Lula Sue taught Sunday school and vacation Bible school, a summer program for children and young teenagers. The pastor and his family were often visitors at Sunday dinner in the Travis home. (Betty Strange Prince.)

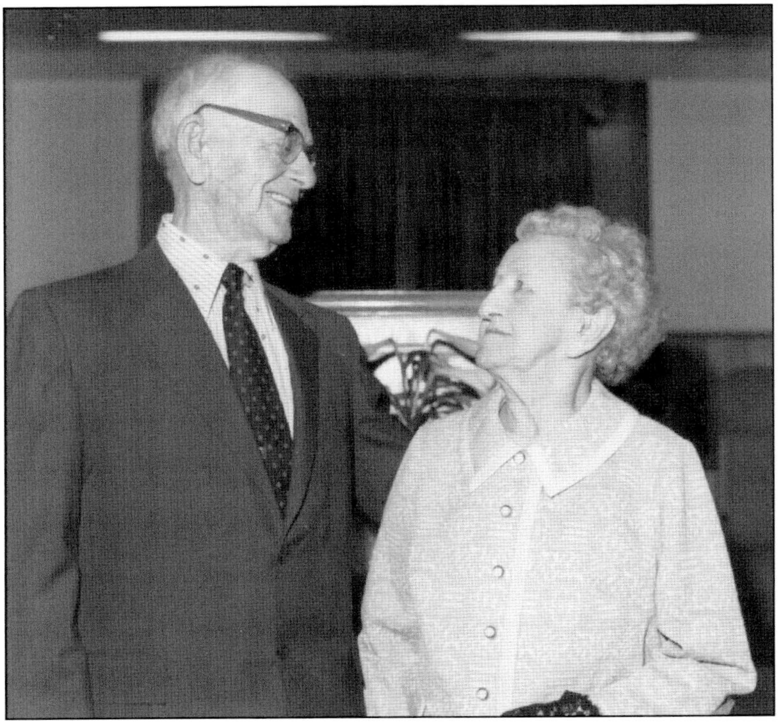

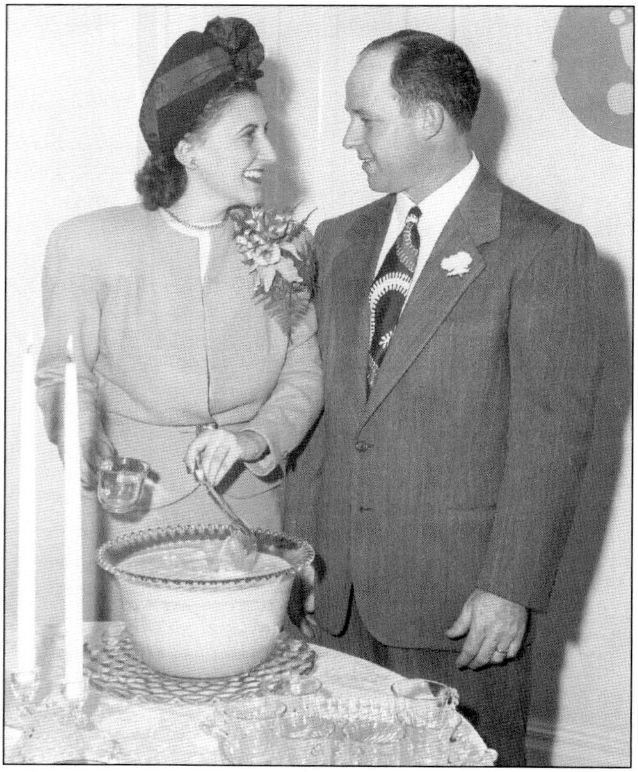

TAYLOR WEDDING. Albert Carlyle Taylor, son of Arthur and Jane Taylor, graduated from the US Naval Midshipman School in 1942 and served in World War II. He married Mary Alice Painter from Wylie in 1946, and later moved to Plano where he owned an automotive parts business. The Taylors had two daughters, Barbara Taylor Bennie and Ginny Taylor Logan. (Barbara Taylor Bennie.)

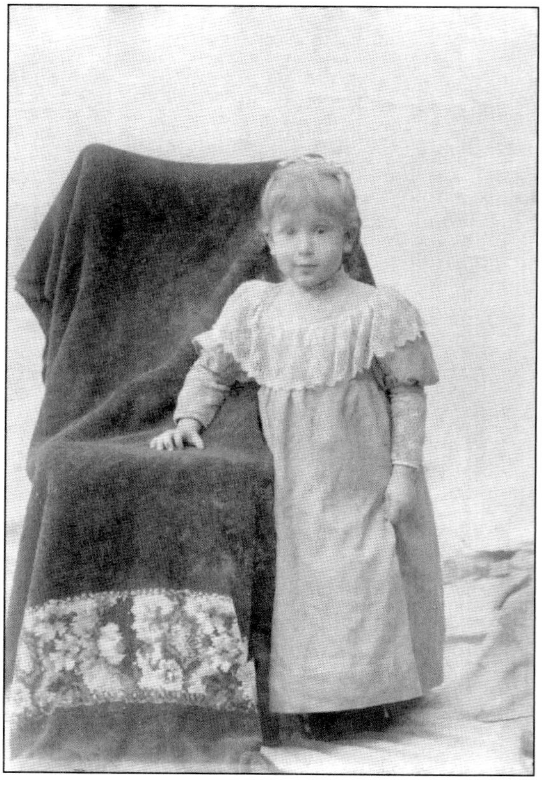

MARY "VIRGINIA" TAYLOR. Mary was the daughter of Arthur Upshur and Jane McMillen Taylor. She came from strong Murphy roots, as she was the granddaughter of Comfort and Lydia McMillen and the great-granddaughter of James and Hannah Maxwell. Living on the family farm, she never married and devoted her life to the care of her invalid sister, Julia. (Barbara Taylor Bennie.)

Julia Ines Taylor. Julia Taylor, a lifelong resident of Murphy, was the last daughter of Arthur and Jane McMillen Taylor. She was born with disabilities and needed constant care. After the passing of Julia's parents, her older sister Mary Taylor had the responsibility of caring for her. (Barbara Taylor Bennie.)

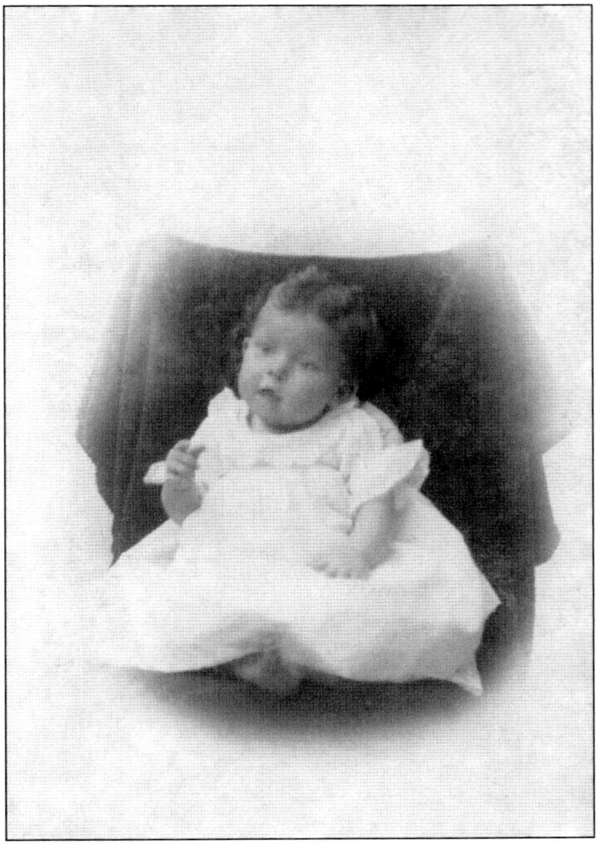

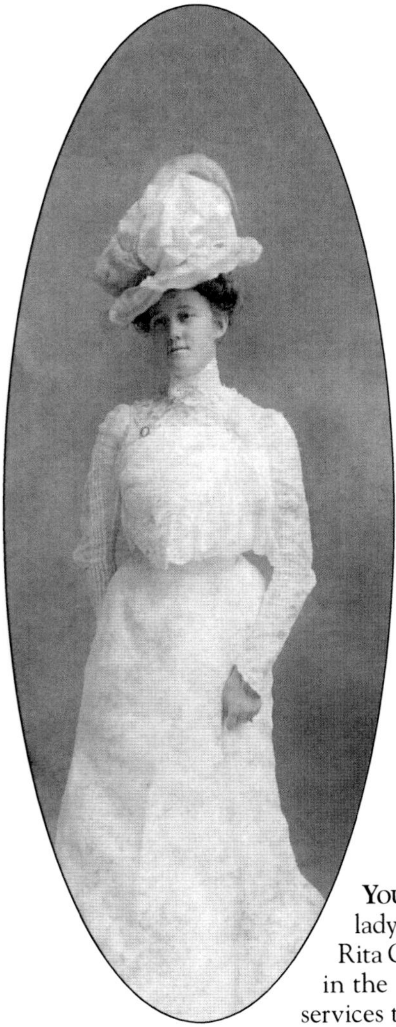

Young Lady. Mary Taylor was a beautiful and fashionable young lady who graduated from Murphy School in 1909. According to Rita Gallagher Smith, she was an excellent seamstress, and people in the Murphy community and surrounding areas sought out her services to sew stylish garments. (Barbara Taylor Bennie.)

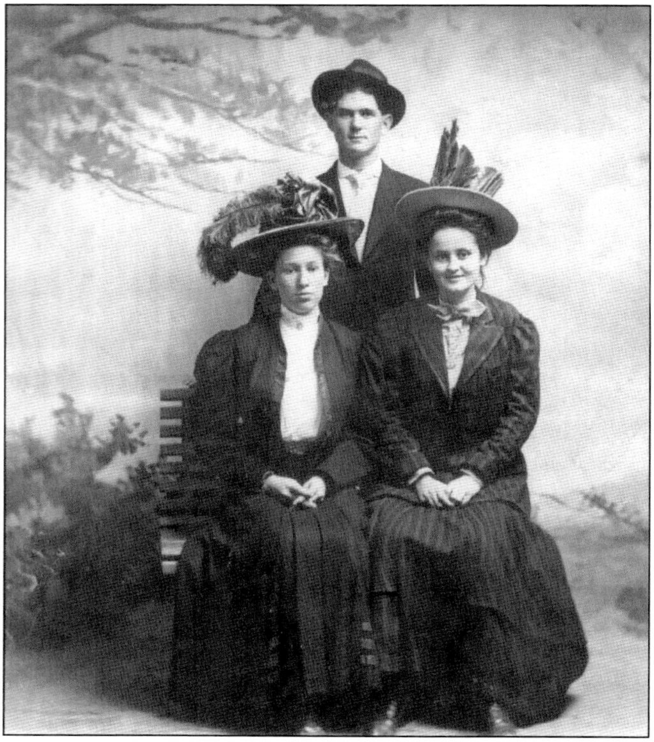

Friends. Always popular and out-going, Mary Taylor (left) was friends with people all over the Murphy community. She poses in this photograph with Fred Forman, who lived in Plano, and Birdie Gregory (right), who lived in Parker. Later, as postmistress and train agent, she was one of the mainstays of the community. (Barbara Taylor Bennie.)

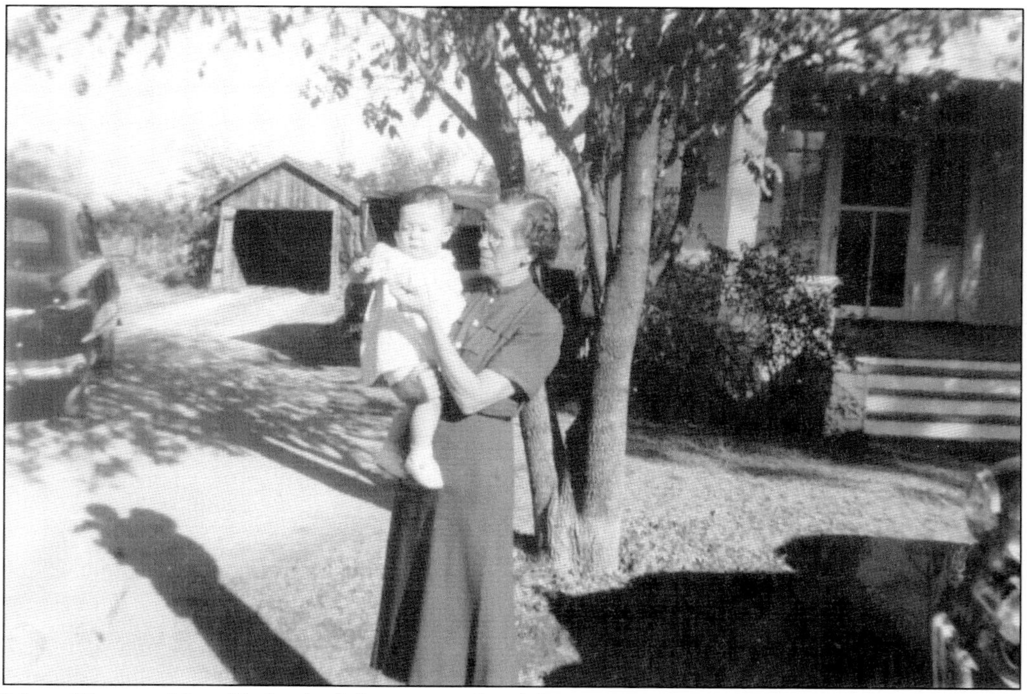

Mary Taylor. Mary Taylor (right) is pictured with her great-niece Barbara Taylor. Children loved to go the post office and train station to visit. Mail was sent by placing the mailbag on a hook outside the depot, which was then collected by the conductor with a long hook as the train passed. Mail was delivered in a leather bag thrown onto the train platform. (Barbara Taylor Bennie.)

Charlie on Tractor. Charlie King's parents were Ernest and Lillian Belle McCracken King, who owned a farm at the intersection of Blackburn and Murphy Roads. Ernest King was originally from Tennessee and was part Algonquin Indian. Belle King used her inheritance from her family sawmill to purchase land for $19 per acre. Cotton, corn, and maize were grown, and the Herring farm bordered the King farm. (Martha Williams.)

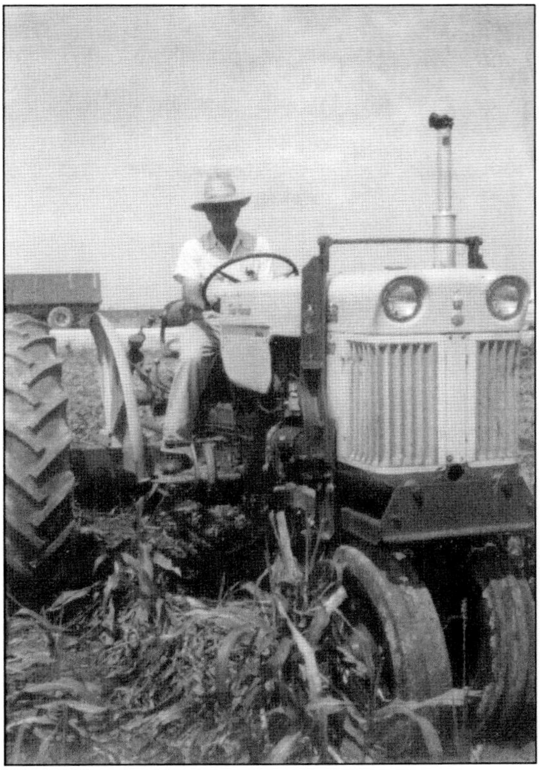

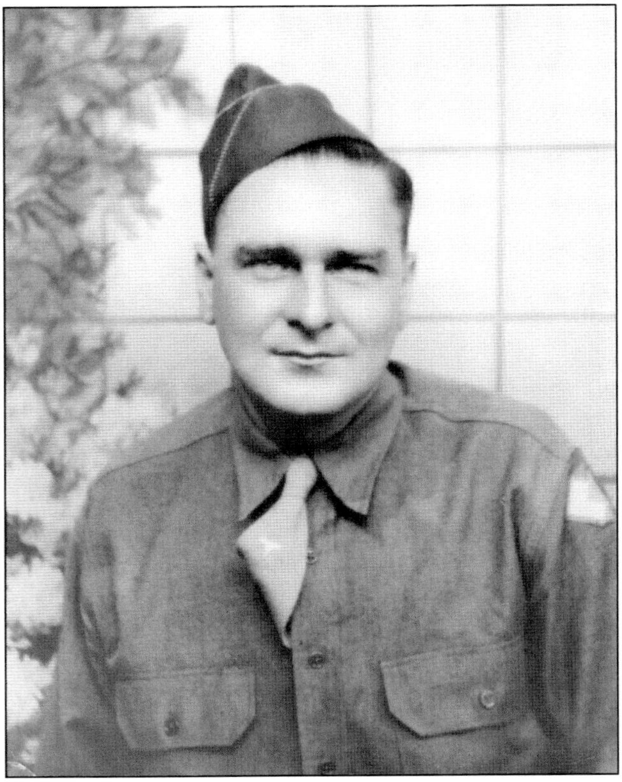

John King. When Ernest King died, the eldest son, John, and Belle undertook the running of the farm. Soon, World War II broke out, and John was called as a medic. While helping a fallen soldier, he was shot in the back and died. Bell never recovered from the shock of the deaths of her husband and son. (Martha King Williams.)

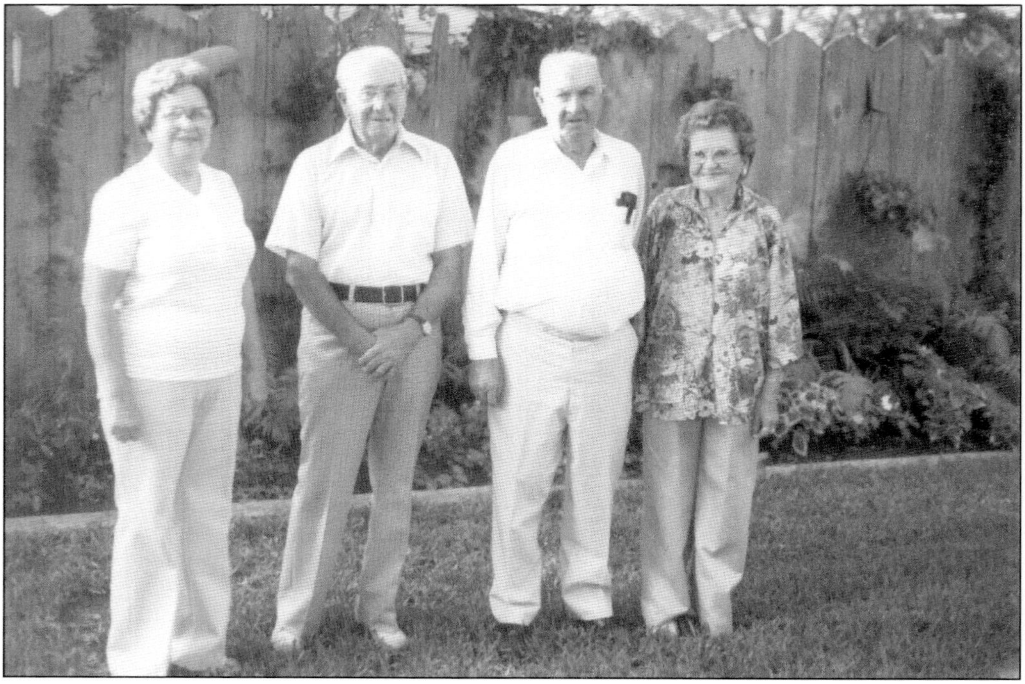

KING FAMILY. After his brother John died, Charlie and Mildred King took over the Blackburn Road farm. Charlie was one of seven siblings. In the photograph are, from left to right, Margaret King Bailey, Charlie King, Raymond King, and Nona King Greer. Not pictured are Boonie King Boyd, Gladys King Bickle, and John, who died in World War II. (Martha King Williams.)

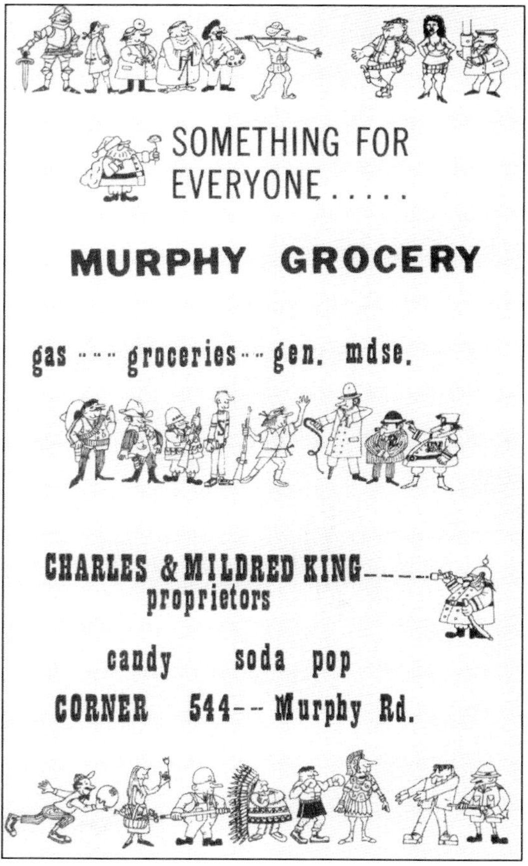

MURPHY GROCERY ADVERTISEMENT. Charlie and Mildred King purchased the Murphy Grocery in the early 1960s. The advertisements for the establishment offered "something for everyone." They sold gas, groceries, candy, soda pop, fishing supplies, thread, and other general merchandise. Murphy children remember the free bubble gum provided by Charlie and Mildred as well as the penny candy jar, 5¢ Coca-Cola and Nehi sodas, and peanut patties. (Brad Lapsley.)

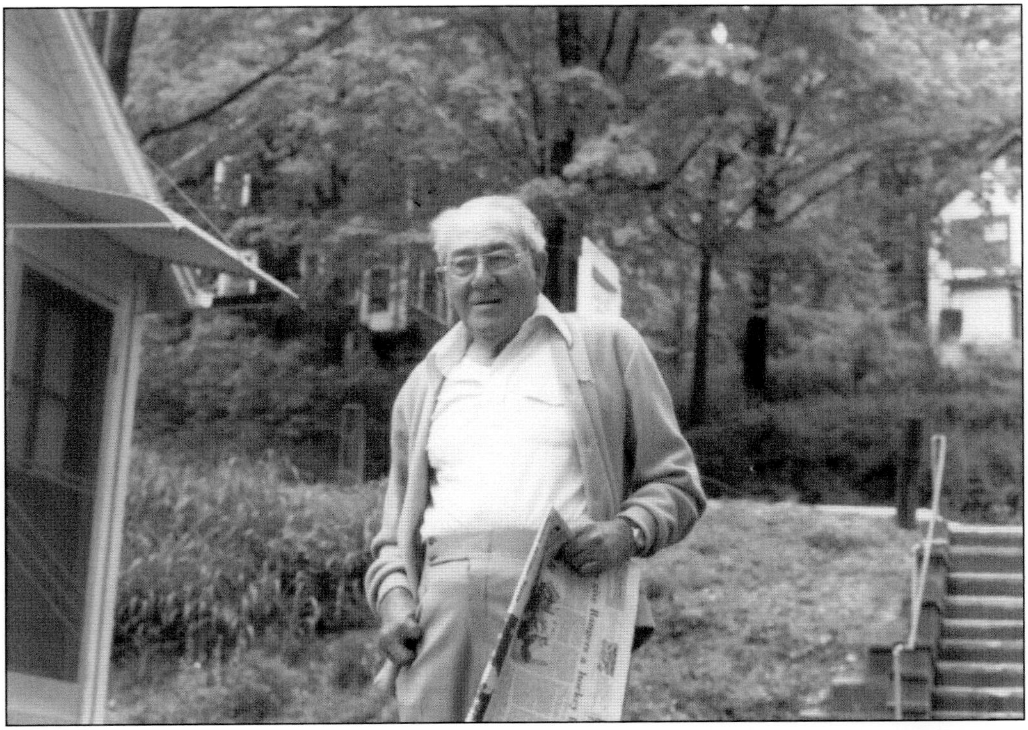

CHARLIE AND MILDRED KING. The Kings were married during the Depression and had three children, Martha, Donna, and Mike, while living on the Blackburn Road farm. Tilling the soil was satisfying but hard work during the early years of their marriage. They retired from farming and then spent the next 15 years tending the Murphy Grocery. Charlie and Mildred were Murphy icons. The grocery provided more than supplies; it was a place to find information on Murphy or play a game of dominoes. Mildred was known for her fried chicken and German chocolate cake made from scratch. The Kings attended the Sachse Christian Church and participated in many area activities. Charlie served on the city council, and Mildred was always busy with the Murphy Fair or a church event. Pictured above is Charlie, and at right is Mildred. (Both, Martha King Williams.)

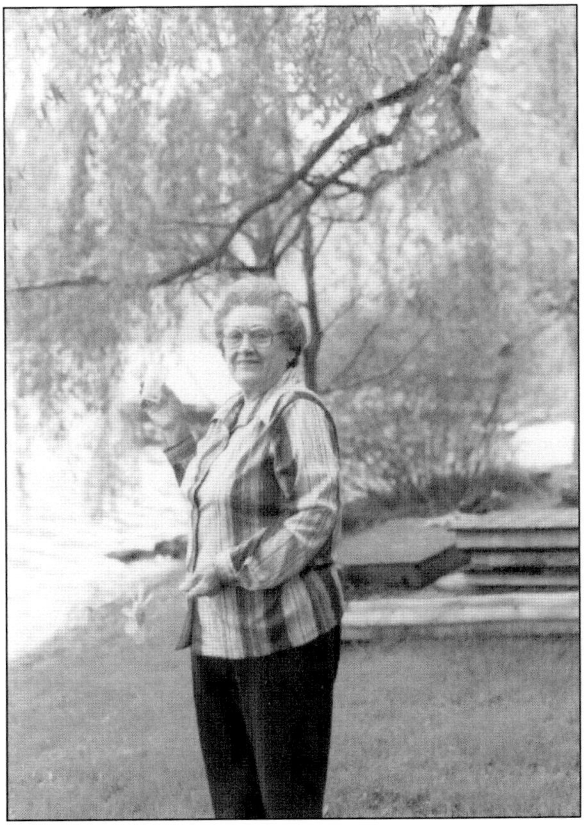

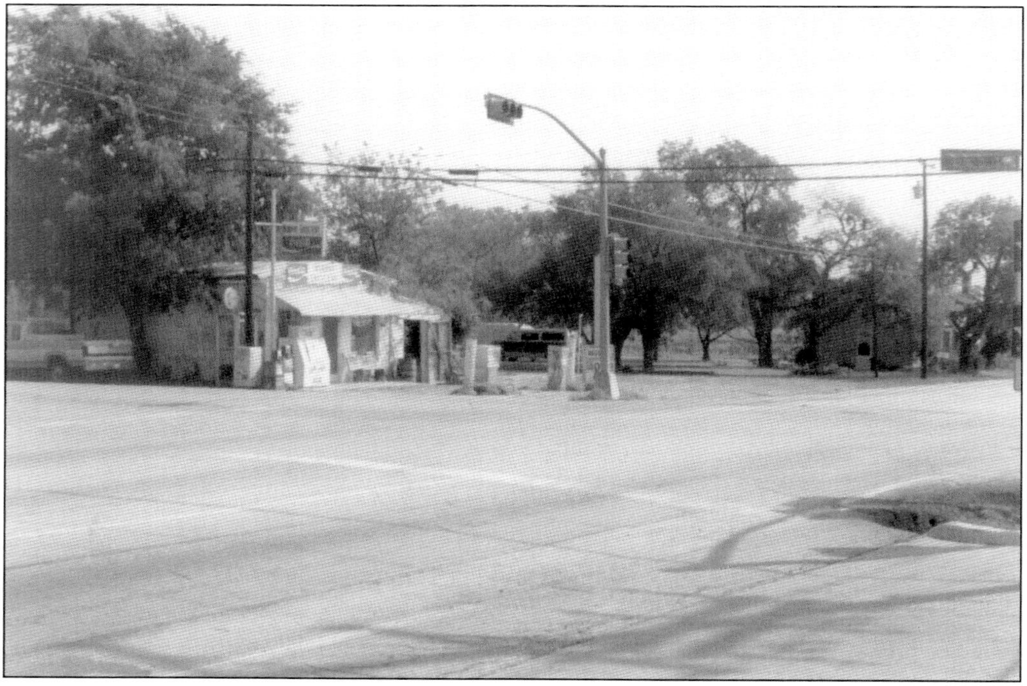

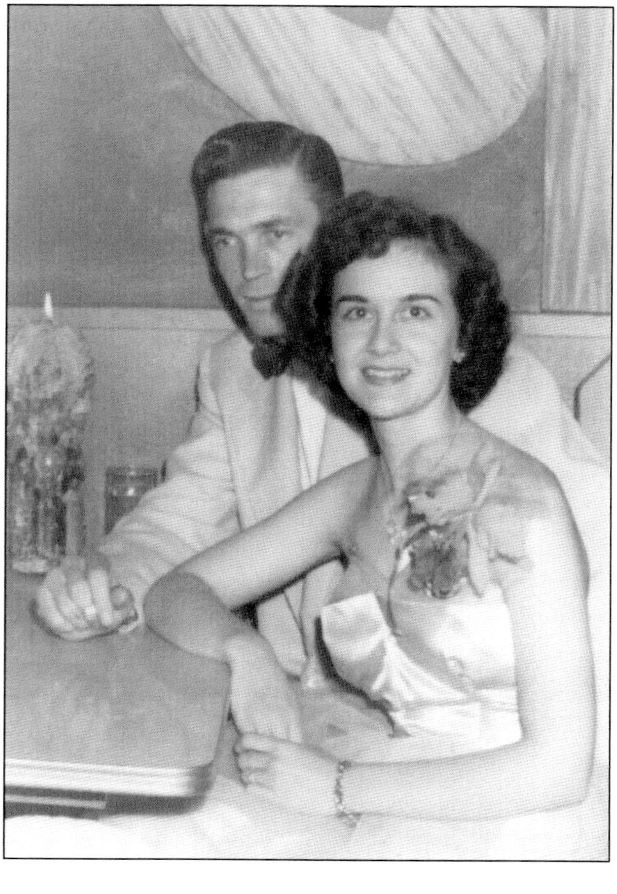

Murphy Grocery. The Murphy Grocery represented what was good about living in small-town Texas. It was a meeting place for the "Spit and Whittle Club," a group of older men or retired farmers who met to discuss the weather, solve the problems of the world, or play dominoes. The King family lived and owned the old Turner house on the east side of the store. (Brad Lapsley.)

Martha Ann King and Billy Ben Williams. This photograph was taken on the first wedding anniversary of Martha, daughter of Charlie and Mildred, and Billy Williams. Billy's parents were Claude Williams of Murphy and Kathleen Berryman. As a child, Billy lived on the Berryman farm, located on FM 544 near the Brigham farm. Like the Kings, the Berrymans grew cotton, corn, and maize. (Martha King Williams.)

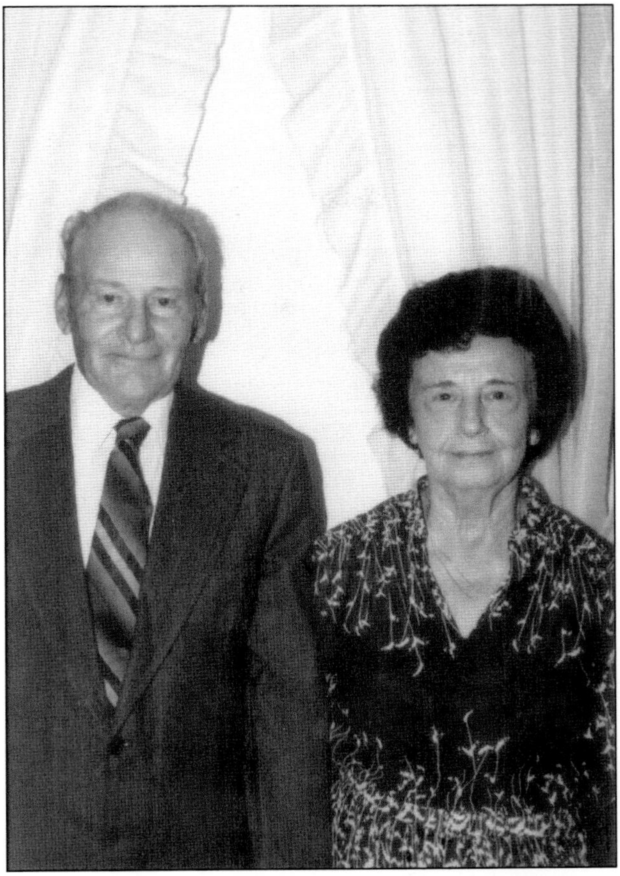

50TH WEDDING ANNIVERSARY. Noel G. Nelson and Lena Mae Yarborough were neighbors in Murphy, and both attended Murphy School. Their relationship turned from friends to sweethearts, and Rev. Milton Greer married them in 1936. They rode the train to Wichita Falls for their honeymoon and returned to the Murphy community, where Noel farmed for over 50 years. (Betty Nelson Zothiewitz.)

THE NELSON BOYS AND COUSIN LEWIS NELSON. Pictured from left to right are Joseph, Woodrow, and Noel G. Nelson, three of the 10 children born to James and Lula Pearl Nelson, and cousin Lewis Nelson. The Nelsons moved to Murphy from the Shiloh Road area and farmed the bottom lands of Rowlett Creek near Murphy. Today, this land is part of the Pecan Hollow Golf Course in Plano. (Betty Nelson Zothiewitz.)

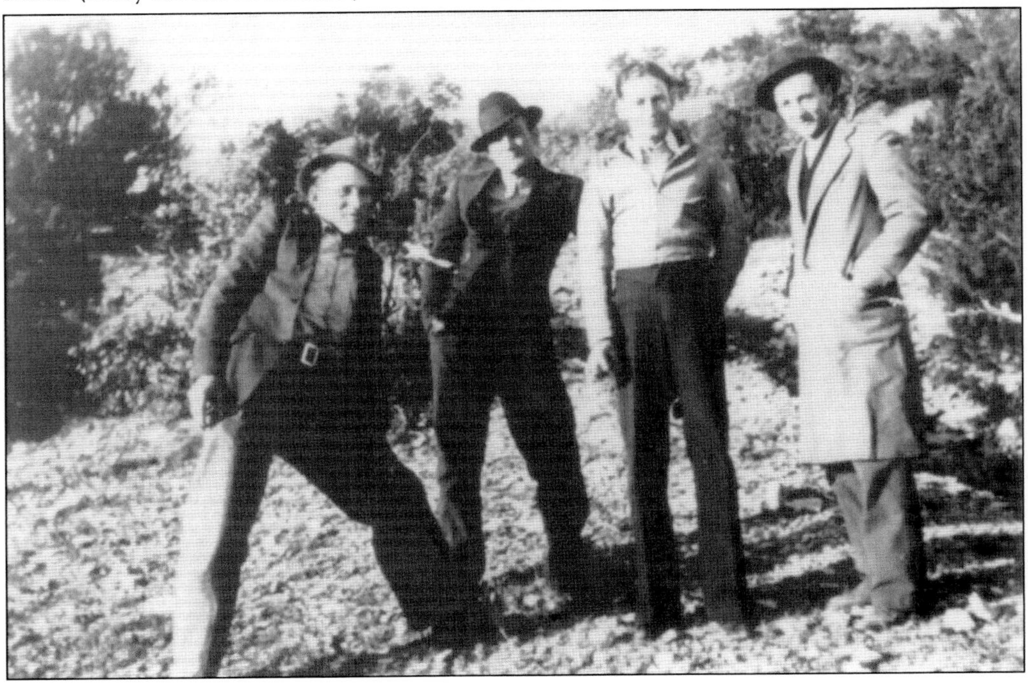

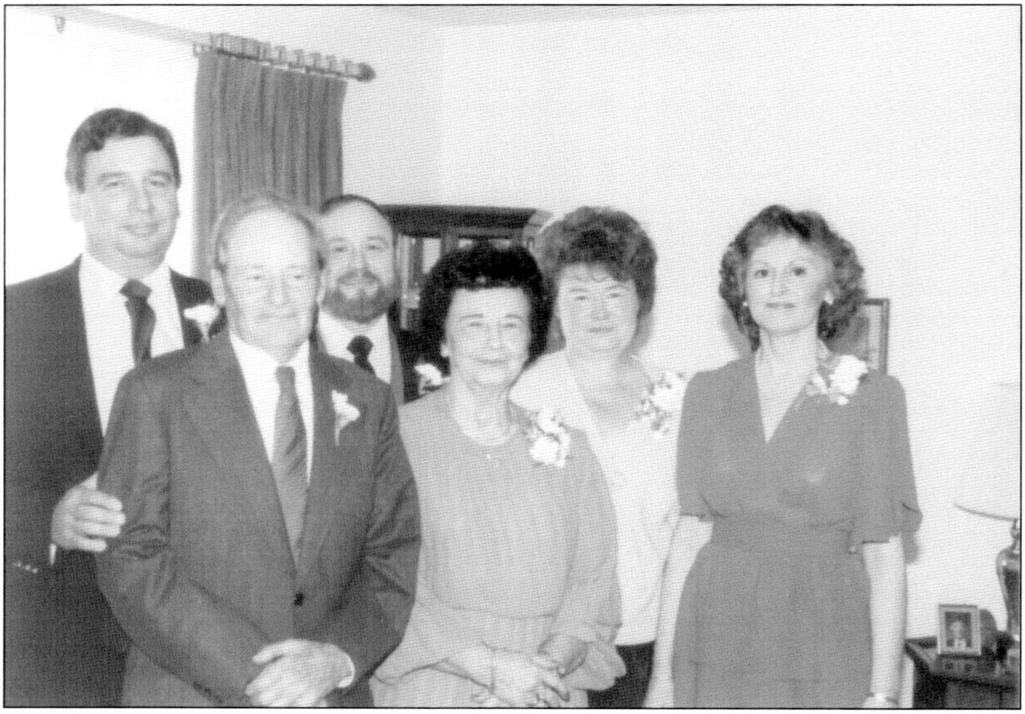

NOEL G. AND LENA MAE NELSON FAMILY. In the photograph are, from left to right, Noel Nelson Jr., Noel G. Nelson, James Nelson, Lena Mae Nelson, Patricia Nelson Bonner, and Betty Nelson Zothiewitz. As the Nelson children grew into adulthood and married, they moved into the Plano and Richardson area. Their children still reside in the area today. (Betty Nelson Zothiewitz.)

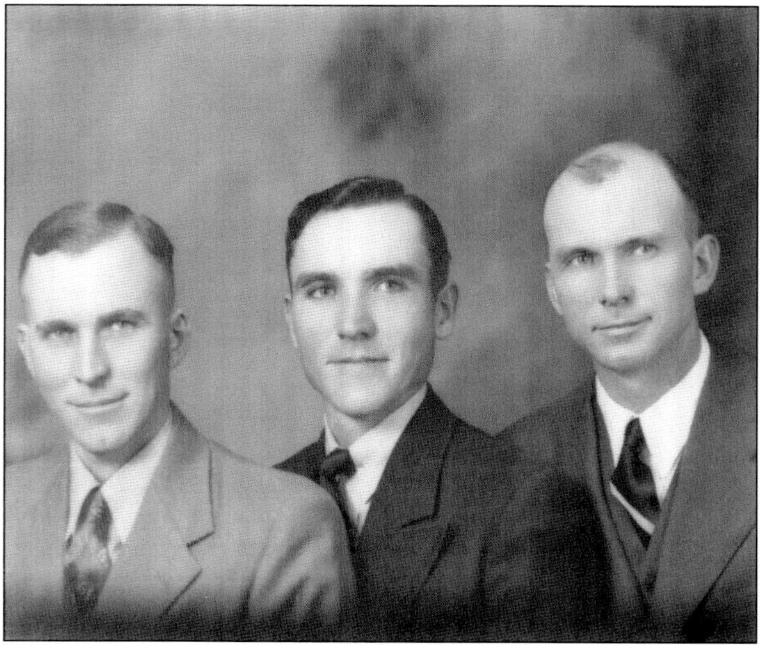

MCCREARY BROTHERS. Shown are, from left to right, Si, Robert, and Leslie, sons of Loy and Maude McCreary. They lived in the Murphy and Parker area. Leslie was well known for his encounter with a band of robbers in Murphy. He was locked in the Liberty State Bank vault in 1931 when the bank was robbed of $1,200. The Highland Park Police captured the robbers. (Joe McCreary.)

Four

PROFESSIONALS
DOCTORS, PREACHERS, AND TEACHERS

Doctors, preachers, and teachers impacted the development of the Murphy community. Little is known about Murphy's first doctor, Dr. Hunter. Early treatment was known to be primitive and dangerous, and early physicians were often ill-trained surgeons from military service. Dr. Dewitt Pardue, a doctor during the Civil War, practiced in Murphy. D. William King and Dr. Saxon Fuqua came to Murphy in 1879 and charged half the usual fee of $5 to encourage business. From 1880 to 1890, there were three doctors living in Murphy. Riding a mule from Plano, Dr. Henry Dye also treated patients. Competition was tough, and doctors supplemented their income by trading, teaching, and farming.

Preachers were significant contributors in the community. The Baptists, Presbyterians, Methodists, and Christians or Disciples of Christ were denominations that built sanctuaries in Murphy. The Presbyterians met in private homes and were the first denomination to organize. Churches did not have services every Sunday, and they shared their building with other groups of circuit-riding preachers. Parishioners had strict rules regarding working on Sunday, dancing, and card playing. R.R. Dunlap was one of the earliest Presbyterian ministers, as was S.M. Wilkins. Baptist preachers included H. Ed Calahan and Ben Snider. James M. Parker and A.C. Moyer were the first Methodist preachers.

Just as the earliest churches were in homes, so were schools. Classes were later held in the meetinghouse and run by the preacher. William Pegues was the first recorded teacher. The Maxwell family started a school in 1857. Prof. R.R. Dunlap taught a five-month school for $31.25 per month. W.P. Gully charged only a 20¢-per-day tuition. The Decatur School was located along Maxwell Creek and FM 544. It was a one-room white clapboard school where Dorothy Murphy King attended from 1868 to 1878. Some Murphy students attended the Barlough School, and by 1900, schools were built on Murphy Road. A white frame three-story building was erected first. A redbrick school followed in 1924, and the yellow brick WPA school was built in 1939. Some of the earliest teachers included H. Ed Calahan, J. M. Dunlap, Martin W. Gentry, Eliza Wilkins, and Dr. Dewitt Pardue.

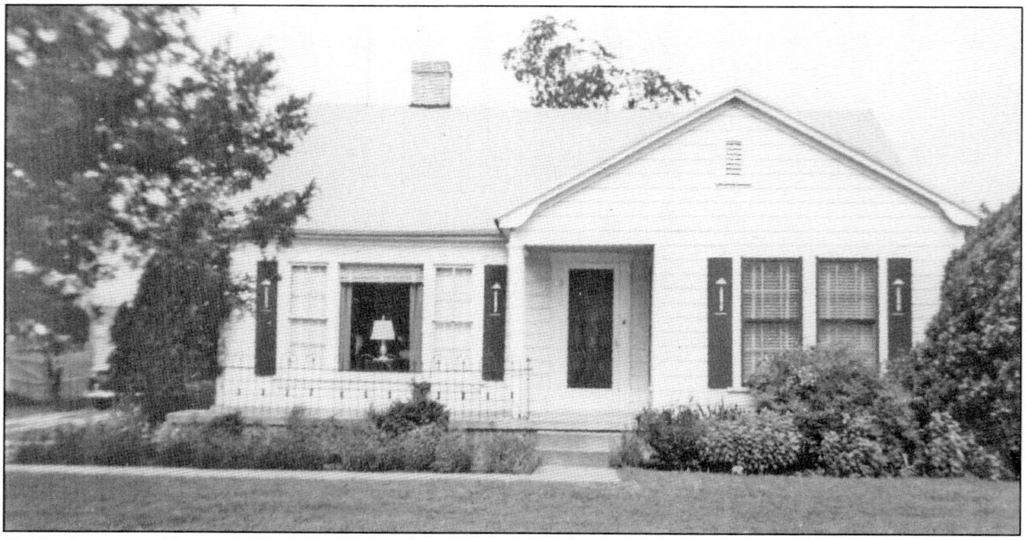

W.O. Jr. and Flora Daniel Home, c. 1950. Shown in this photograph is the Daniel home on North Murphy Road where Jimmy and Ceilia Daniel grew up. The home was conveniently located next door to the Murphy School and across the street from the gin and Daniel Implement Company. Today, the house still sits on North Murphy Road. (Jim Daniel.)

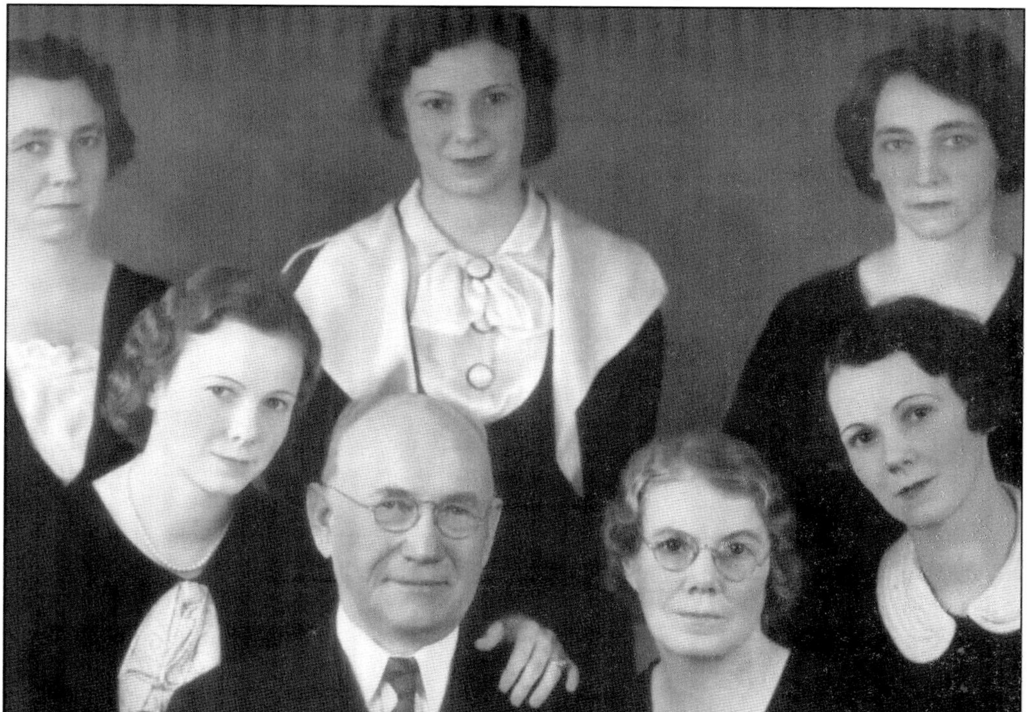

Dr. Miller Family. In the photograph are, from left to right, (standing) Lena Mae Ingram, Maxine Carpenter, and Winnie McEntee; (sitting) Helen Brooks, Dr. Dennis and Ruth Miller, and Mary Ruth Crockett. Family, faith, and medicine were Dr. Miller's life. Dr. Miller's first wife, Rebecca Olinger, died and left him two daughters, Lena and Winnie. He later married Ruth Rossetter of Murphy. They had three daughters. (Carmen Carpenter Haggard.)

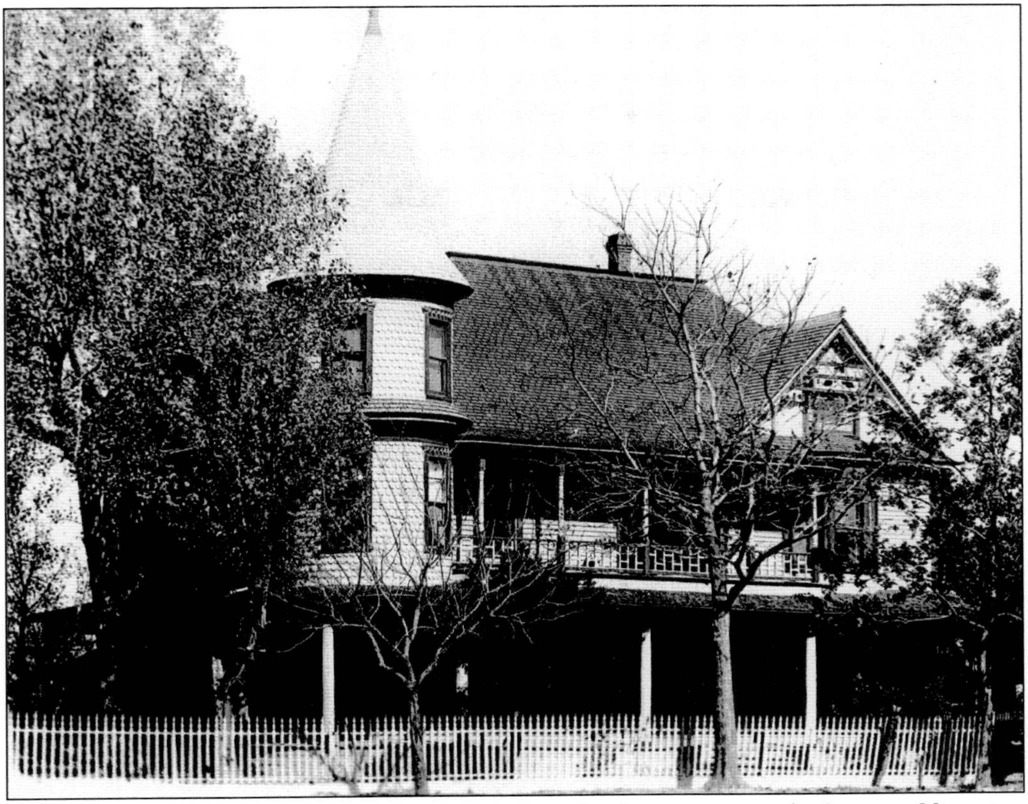

Miller Home. Murphy children often referred to this house as a castle. It was a Victorian house with a turret rising above the roof and a veranda circling around the entire house. Dr. Miller and Rebecca bought this house when they married because it reminded him of the Rice house in Plano. When this house burned, Dr. Miller moved north on Murphy Road. (Carmen Carpenter Haggard.)

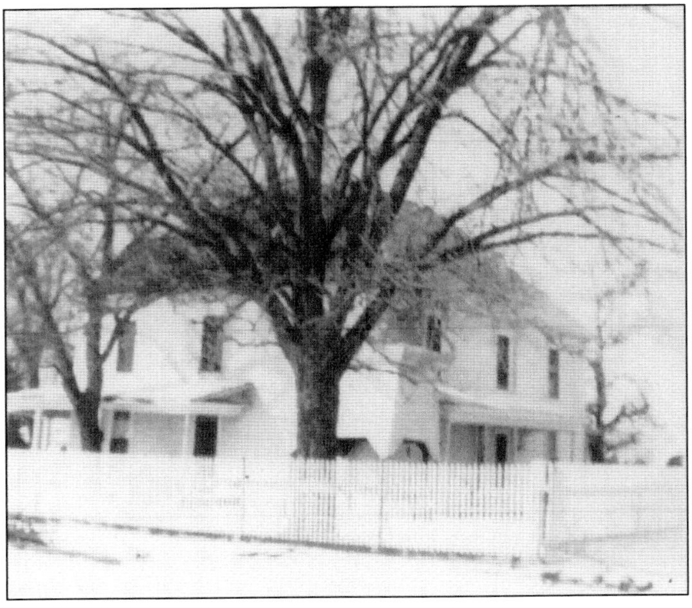

Dennis and Ruth Miller Home. This view shows the back of the home on Murphy Road south of Southfork Ranch. After the death of Dr. Miller and Ruth, the house was given to Helen Brooks. The Millers owned much land in Murphy, and R.E. Carpenter farmed their land. Today, the Kimbrough Stadium Complex sits on part of the land once owned by the Millers. (Clint Haggard.)

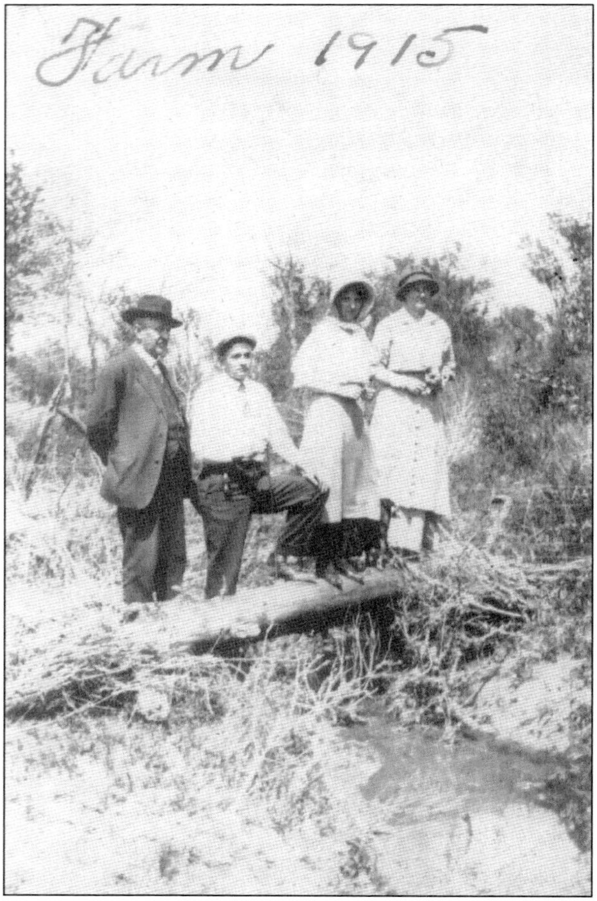

MURPHY, 1915. Pictured are, from left to right, Dr. William, Bo, Nelle, and Dorothy King. William Murphy gave the Murphy farm to his daughter Dorothy, who married Dr. William King. The Kings lived on the Murphy farm in the house originally owned by James T. Murphy. The house had several additions, and the front of the house was used as examining rooms. (Dessie Haker.)

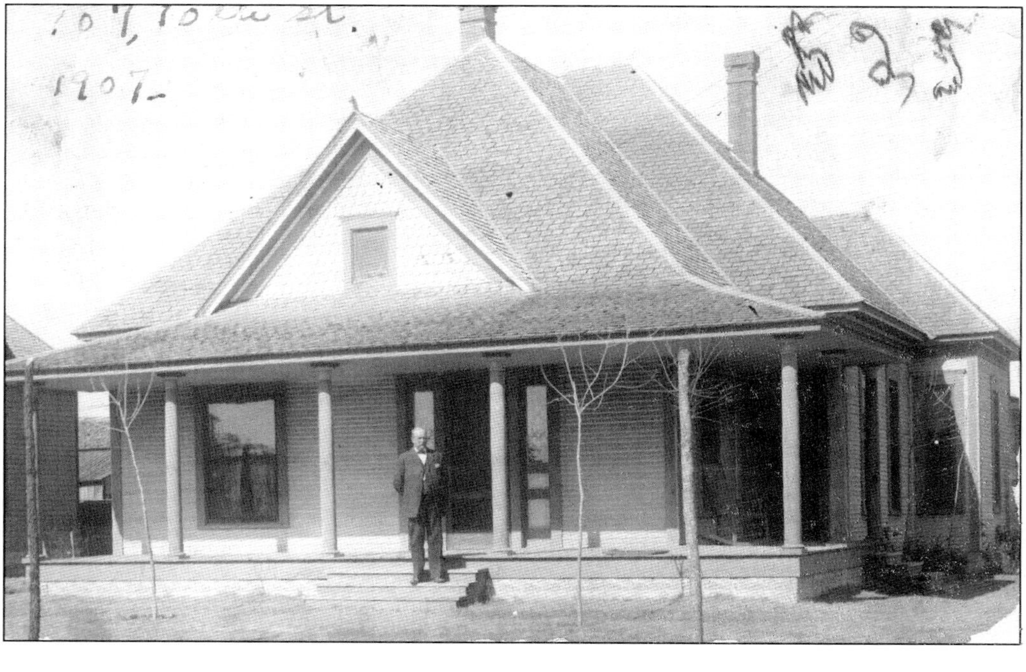

DR. WILLIAM KING. Doctoring in Murphy was competitive, which forced Dr. King to charge half the usual fees for delivering babies. Scandal and a costly trial over an abortion brought financial woes, and by the early 1900s, Dr. King relocated to South Oak Cliff. The family kept the Murphy farm, visiting on weekends and holidays. In this photograph, Dr. King stands in front of his Oak Cliff home. (Dessie Haker.)

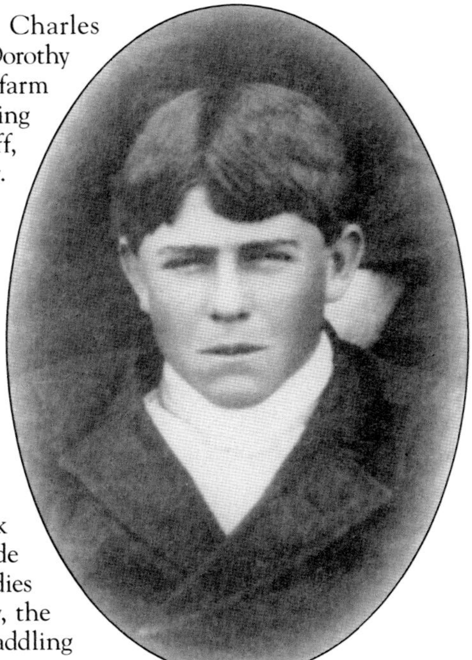

Charles Bohannon King. Nicknamed "Bo," Charles Bohannon King was the only son of Dr. William and Dorothy King. He loved to hunt with a rifle on the Murphy farm and, sadly, was killed in a hunting accident while hunting with a friend. Before the move to South Oak Cliff, Bo and his sister Nelle attended school in Murphy. (Dessie Haker.)

Nelle King, 1905. Nelle (right) and her friend are pictured riding horses while searching for persimmons. She often made trips to Wylie and Plano on horseback to fill customer prescriptions for her father. Nelle rode sidesaddle because it was not appropriate for young ladies to ride straddling a horse. Since she fell repeatedly, the Kings had a special split skirt made for her to ride straddling the horse. (Dessie Haker.)

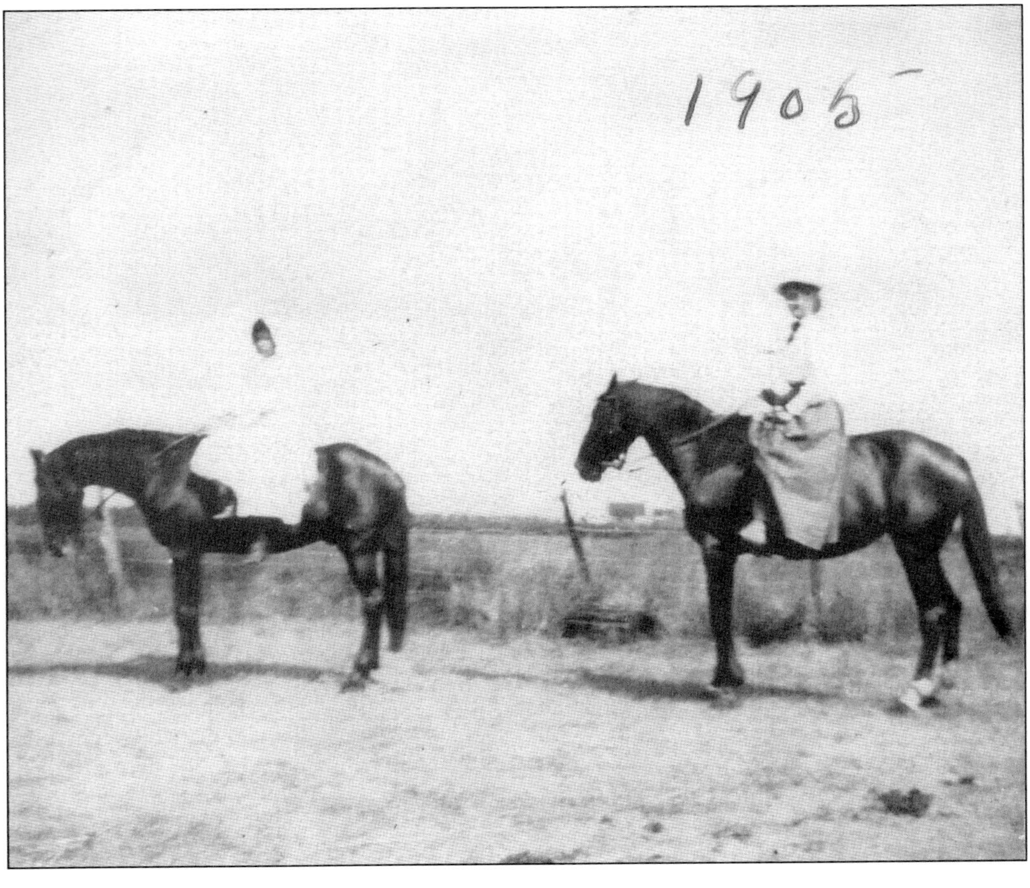

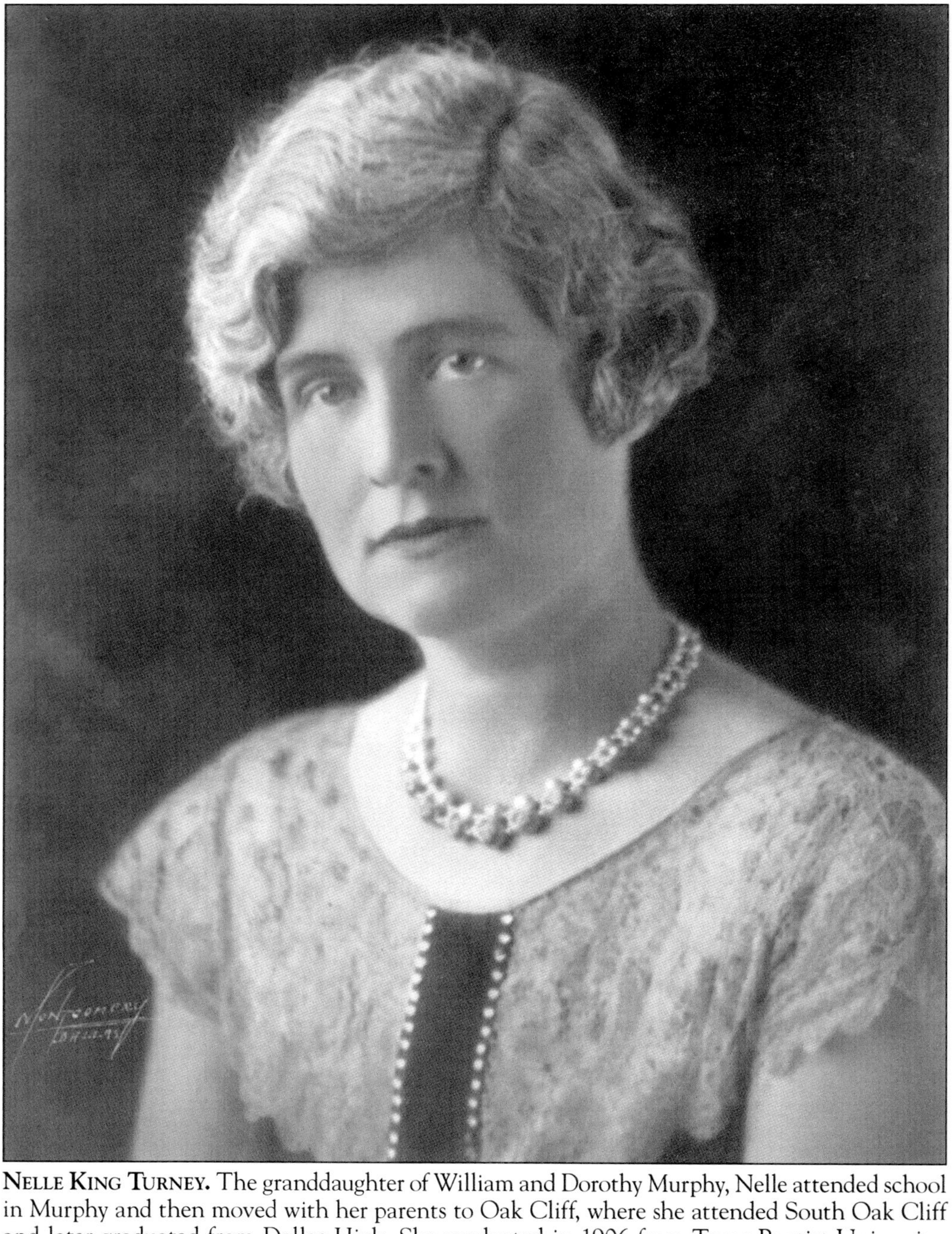

Nelle King Turney. The granddaughter of William and Dorothy Murphy, Nelle attended school in Murphy and then moved with her parents to Oak Cliff, where she attended South Oak Cliff and later graduated from Dallas High. She graduated in 1906 from Texas Baptist University, where she was on the swim team and debate team. On September 30, 1909, she married Lee Frith Turney. They returned to live on the Murphy farm. Nelle loved music, and she and Lee had one of the first Victrolas with Victor records. She kept an extensive index of all of her records, which included classical, jazz, and popular songs of the period. The Turneys entertained in their Murphy home and often held dances. Rugs were removed from the two front rooms, and couples danced to the records. They both enjoyed horseback riding, golf, and vacationing at their cottage in Buena Vista. (Dessie Haker.)

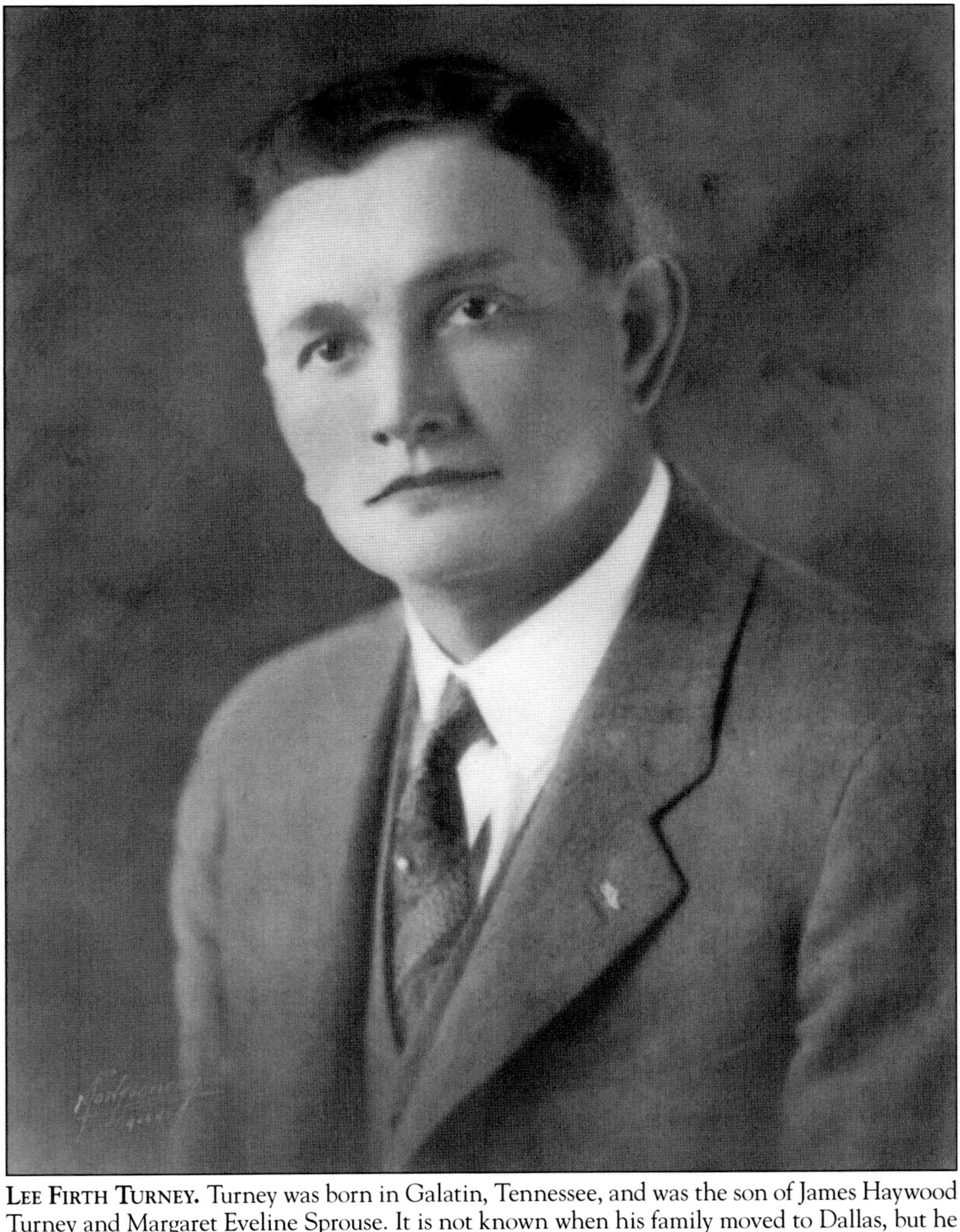

Lee Firth Turney. Turney was born in Galatin, Tennessee, and was the son of James Haywood Turney and Margaret Eveline Sprouse. It is not known when his family moved to Dallas, but he lived in Dallas when he met Nelle King. During World War II, he worked at Southern Aircraft in Garland. Most of his working years were spent as a salesman of both cars and trucks. He was a sales manager for Studebaker, Plymouth, Lee Filgo Automobiles, and Bond Equipment Company. Turney was a Mason and pioneer member of Tannehill Masonic Lodge and Kella Temple Shrine for 46 years. The Turneys attended the First Christian Church in Plano, but he enjoyed nature and said his "church" was the world around that God created. He was known to be a gentle man who was attuned to his wife's needs in her later years as she became disabled with Parkinson's Disease. They did not have children. (Dessie Haker.)

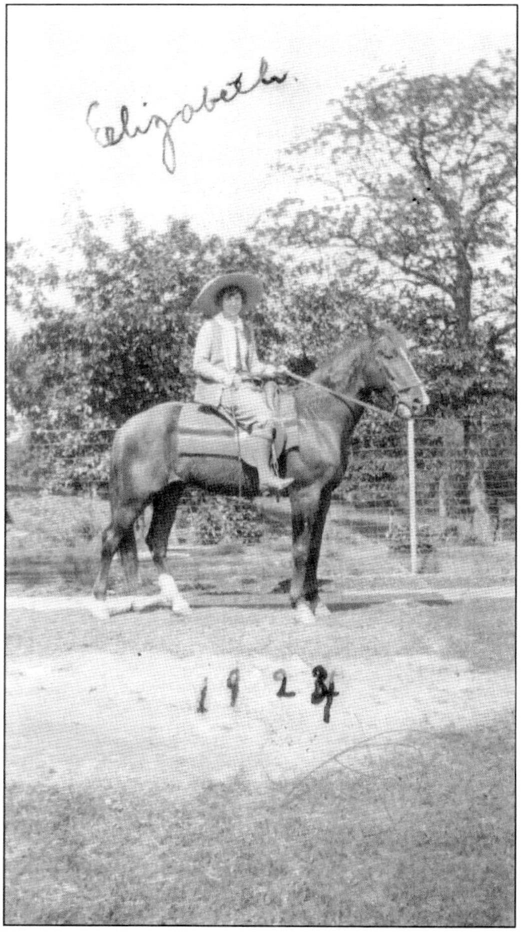

MEXICAN JOSEPH, 1924. The Kings were avid horse racing devotees, and they enjoyed visiting the Murphy farm, where they bred racehorses, as did C.C. Gregory and others in neighboring Parker. The horses were not only raced in Collin County but also in big events in downtown Dallas. Elizabeth, Nelle King's friend, is pictured on Mexican Joseph at a race in Tulsa, Oklahoma. (Dessie Haker.)

DECATUR SCHOOL, 1894. Nelle King, granddaughter of William and Dorothy Murphy, attended the Decatur School from 1868 to 1878. It was located along Maxwell Creek, and the teacher was A.J. Berryman. The first school in Murphy was a log building on the Maxwell property. Other Murphy students attended the Wilkins School, which was later moved to Corinth in Parker. The students in the picture are unidentified. (Dessie Haker.)

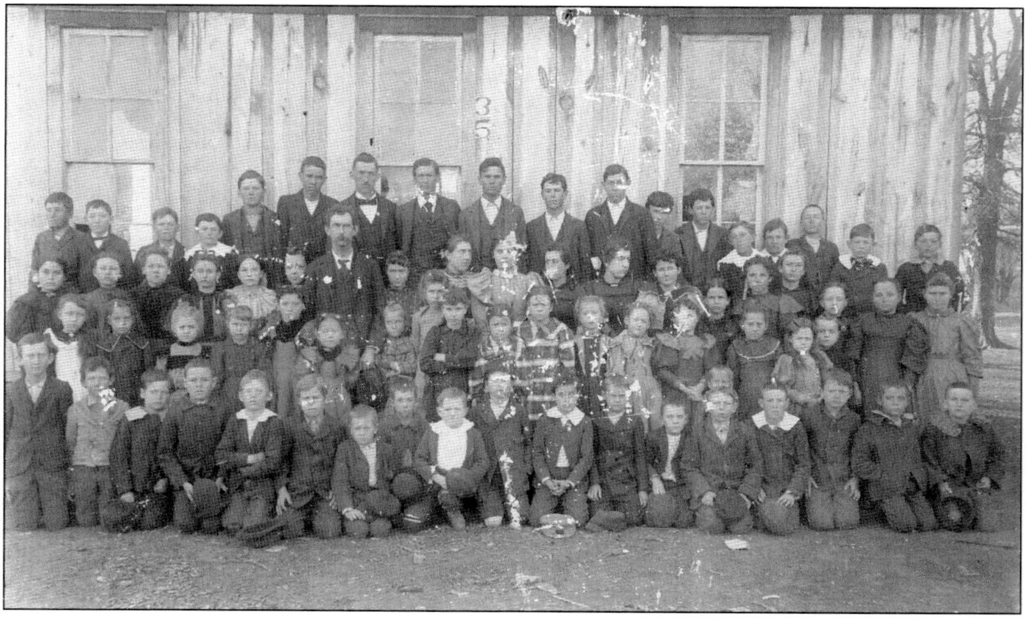

Edgar Steele Boyd. In 1898, Edgar Boyd, known by his middle name "Steele," came to Texas and settled in the Pleasant Valley area. In 1905, he and his wife moved to a 100-acre farm north of the Decatur-Maxwell-Murphy Cemetery. They used the good soil to grow cotton and sold enough cotton to pay for the farm and buy a car by 1919. (S. Michael Boyd.)

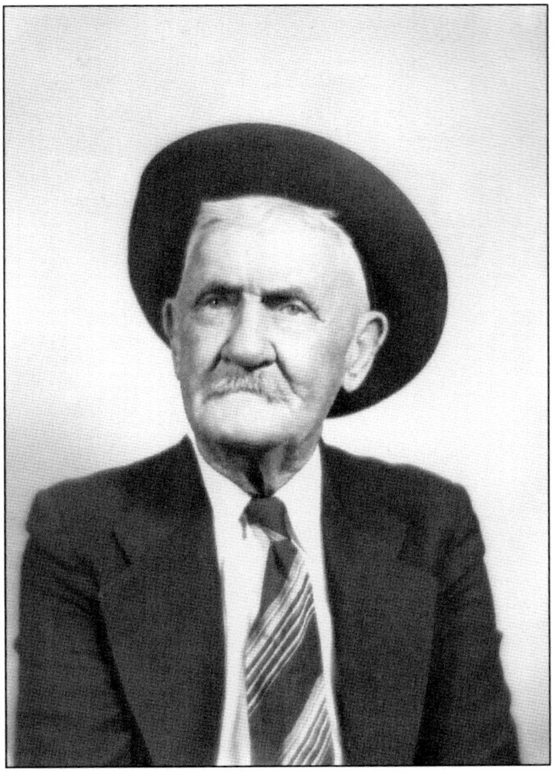

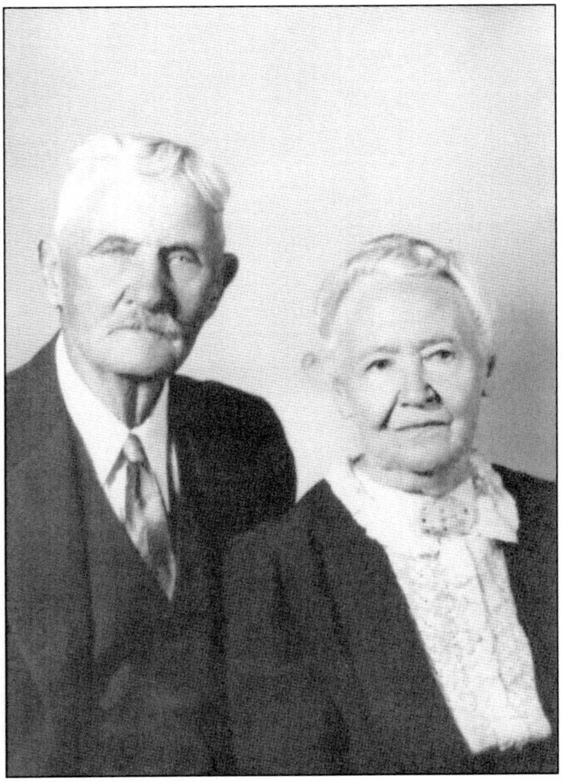

Steele Boyd and Margaret Jane Kidd Boyd. Boyd married Margaret, known as "Maggie," in 1890. He farmed land where Murphy Middle School sits today. Their sons were Vernon and Thurman, who died within a week of each other with the measles, Edgar Glen, and James Boyd. Daughters Edna and Evangeline also died young. Maggie's father, William Kidd, came to live with the Boyds in 1905. (S. Michael Boyd.)

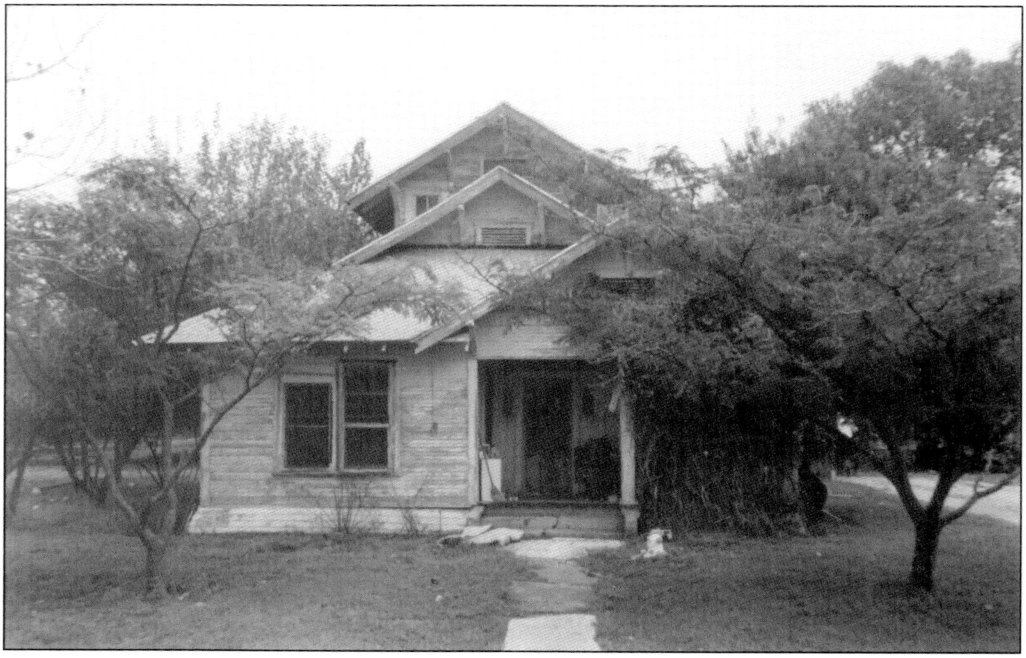

Steele and Maggie Boyd Farmhouse, 2000. Steele Boyd remembered his grandfather William Kidd hunting crows with a 12-gage shotgun on the Boyd farm. This photograph shows the old farmhouse as it looked before it was destroyed in 2000 to make way for Murphy Middle School and Kimbrough Stadium. (S. Michael Boyd.)

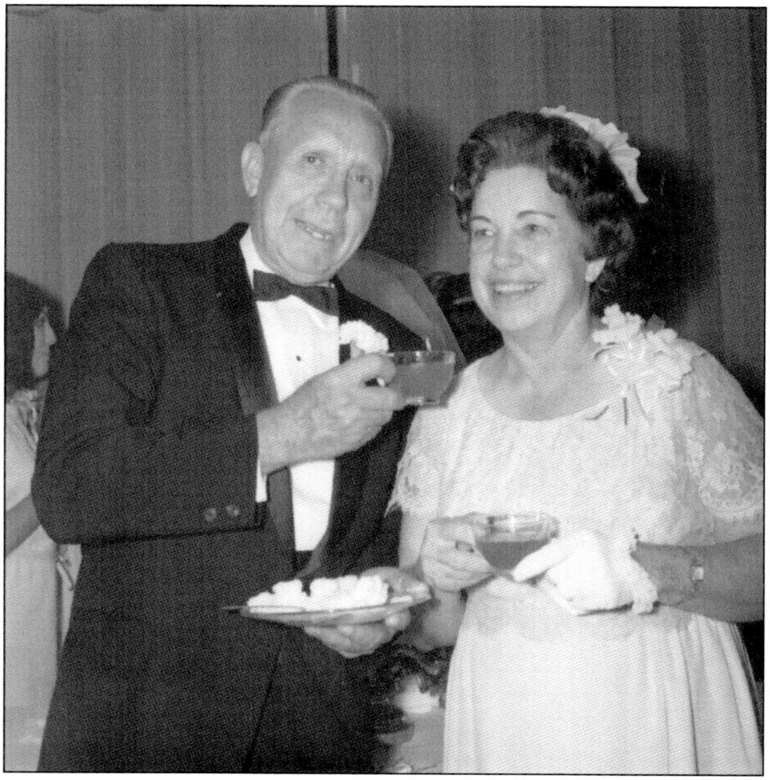

Edgar Glen Boyd and Nora Harris Boyd. "Ed," as he was called, was born in Murphy in 1908. He went to Murphy School, graduated from the 10th grade in 1925, and finished the 11th grade in Plano the next year. Ed returned to teach in Murphy from 1934 to 1937. He married Nora Harris on September 12, 1930. They were married for 65 years. (S. Michael Boyd.)

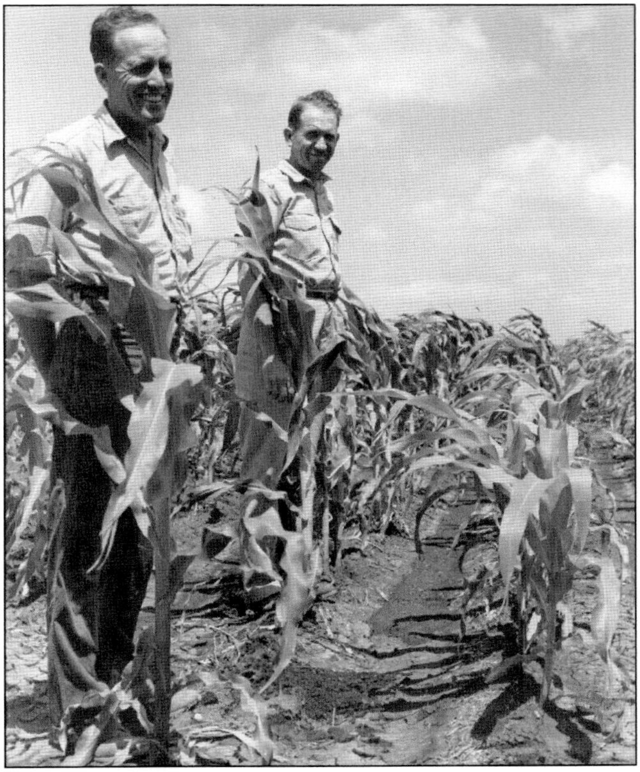

CORN CROP, 1946. W.O. (left) and Max Daniel demonstrate the difference between the fertilized corn on the left and the unfertilized corn on the right. The Daniel brothers experimented with different seeds and fertilizers trying to improve production. They were involved in the American Agriculture Movement and represented area farmers in Washington, DC. (Inez Daniel.)

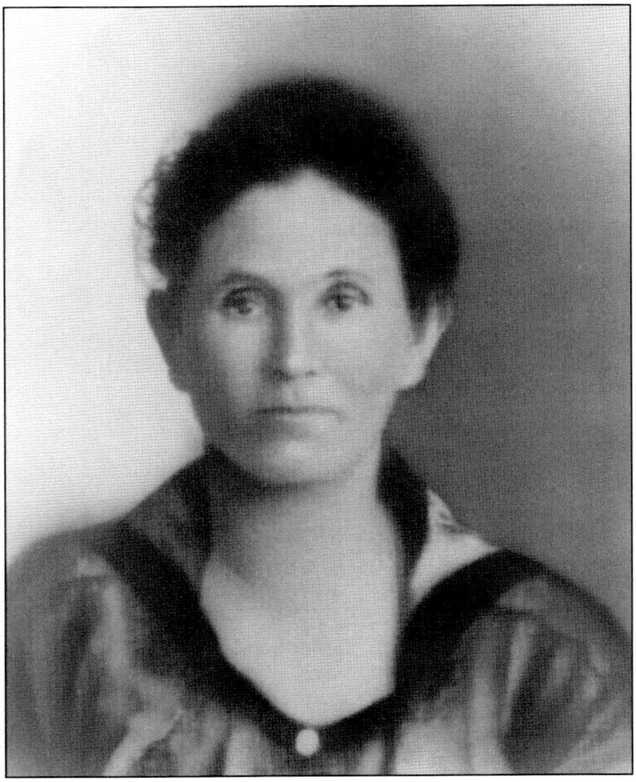

EUGENIA WARD. Sarah Eugenia Ward Gregory and her family lived in Murphy. Her mother was Sarah V. Ward, and her father was Civil War veteran Armstrong Fairbanks Ward. Eugenia married Clairborne Christopher Gregory on June 17, 1888. Their home place was located west of the current Southfork Ranch. (Ema Jean Christian.)

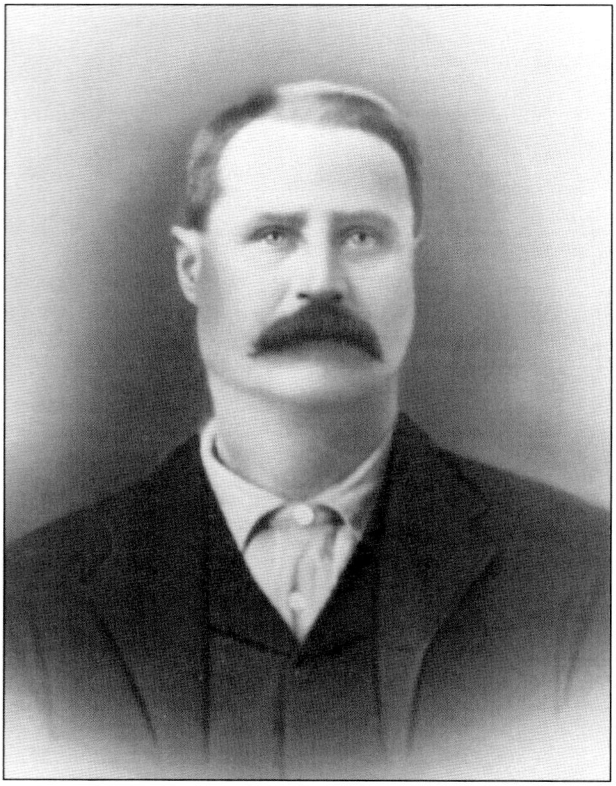

C.C. Gregory. Clairborne Christopher Gregory and his wife, Eugenia, grew cotton, corn, and grain on more than 1,000 acres of farmland in the Parker, Murphy, and Wylie communities. He lost most of the land except the Parker farm as a result of the Great Depression. (Ema Jean Christian.)

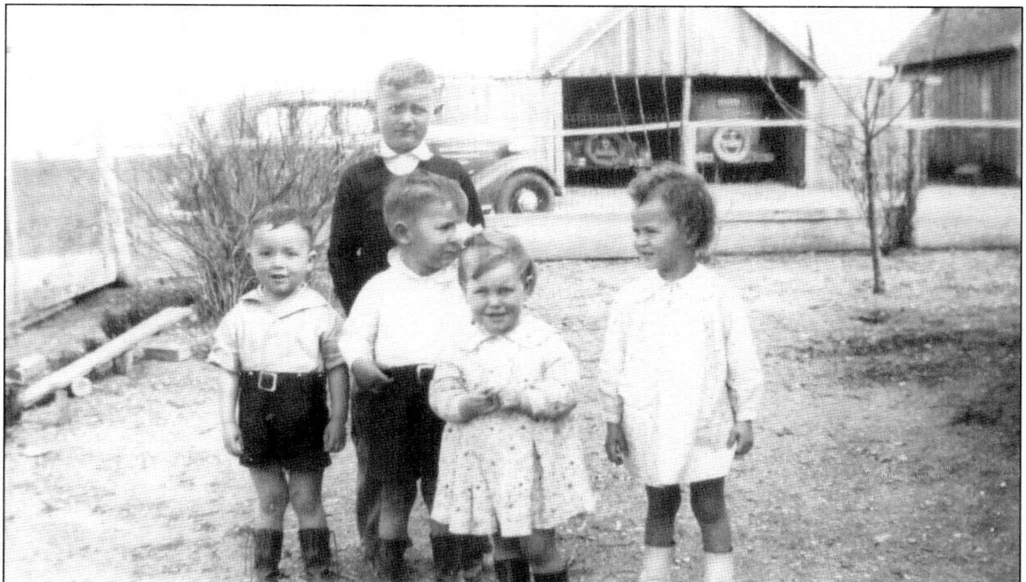

Grandchildren. The following grandchildren of C.C. and Eugenia Gregory are pictured, from left to right: Jackie Aldridge, John Henry Turner, Sammy Turner, Ema Jean Gregory, and Janie Marie Gregory. The grandchildren grew up on surrounding farms in the Murphy and Parker communities. They loved to spend time playing together in the barn at grandpa and grandma Gregory's farm. (Ema Jean Christian.)

1915 TEXAS STATE FAIR. Aldridge Dillihay (left) and Cecil Gregory (right) posed as cowboys at the fair. In 1890, the first Texas State Fair and Dallas Exposition focused on agriculture and attracted more than 35,000 visitors. By 1917, the fair drew more than one million visitors. (Ema Jean Christian.)

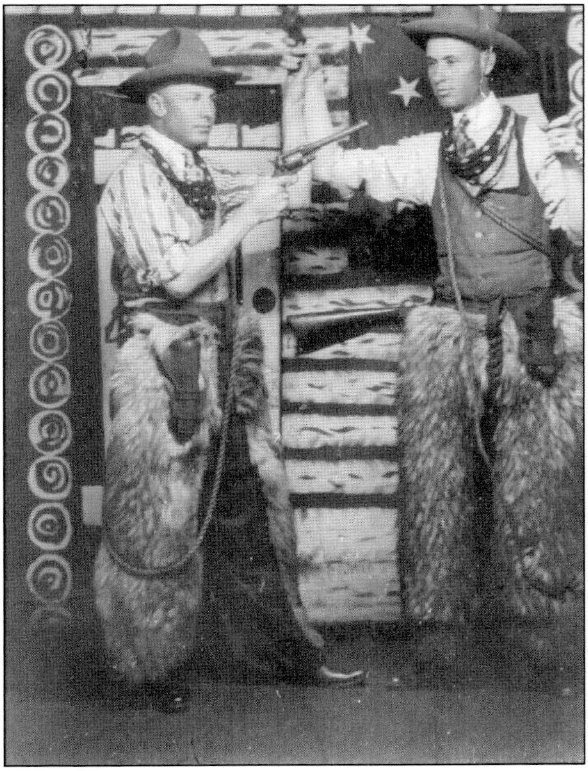

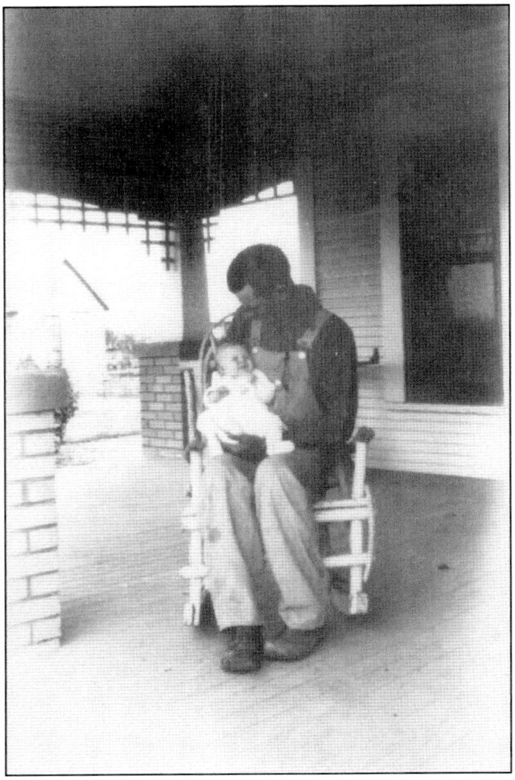

FATHER AND DAUGHTER, 1933. Cecil Clayton Gregory and Ema Jean Gregory are seen sitting on grandpa Gregory's front porch. Sitting on the porch was a pleasant break and favorite pastime for hardworking farmers. As a young woman, Ema recollected that she had fun attending the Bud Abbott and Lou Costello movies shown in the Murphy School's gym. (Ema Jean Christian.)

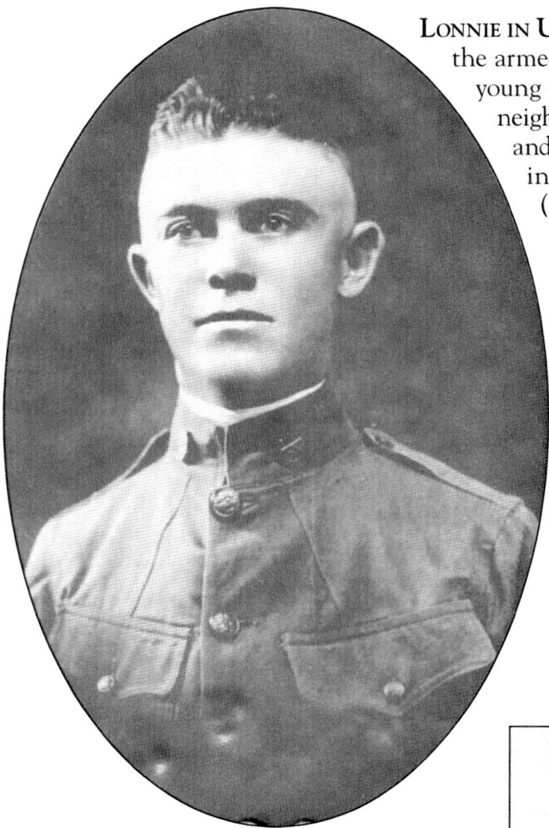

Lonnie in Uniform. Lonnie Edward Christian served in the armed forces in France during World War I. As a young child, he lived on Dublin Road. His closest neighbors were the Donihoo, Salmons, Kirkwood, and Palmer families. The children attended school in Murphy after the Dublin School closed. (Kenneth Christian.)

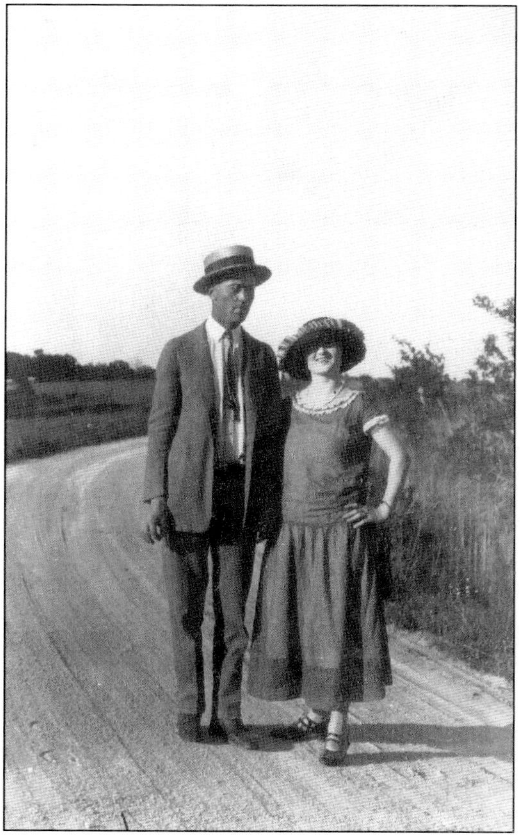

Courting Days. Soon after World War I ended, Lonnie returned home and met Elizabeth Maggie Southwood in Murphy. She was called "Jack" because her father wanted a son as a first child. A spirited young girl, she quit school during the ninth grade because, she said, "If all the school had to offer was Algebra, then they could just have it." (Kenneth Christian.)

Courting in Lonnie's Car. In this photograph, Lonnie and Cora are dressed for a date in the latest style. Few young people in Murphy had a car after the war ended. They loved to dance, and many dances in Murphy were held at the train depot, where the musicians played tunes from the platform. The couple won many waltz contests. After marrying, they moved to the Parker community. (Kenneth Christian.)

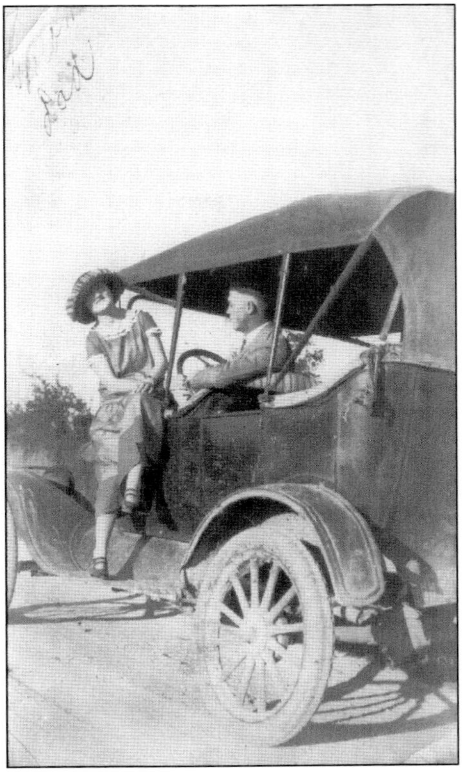

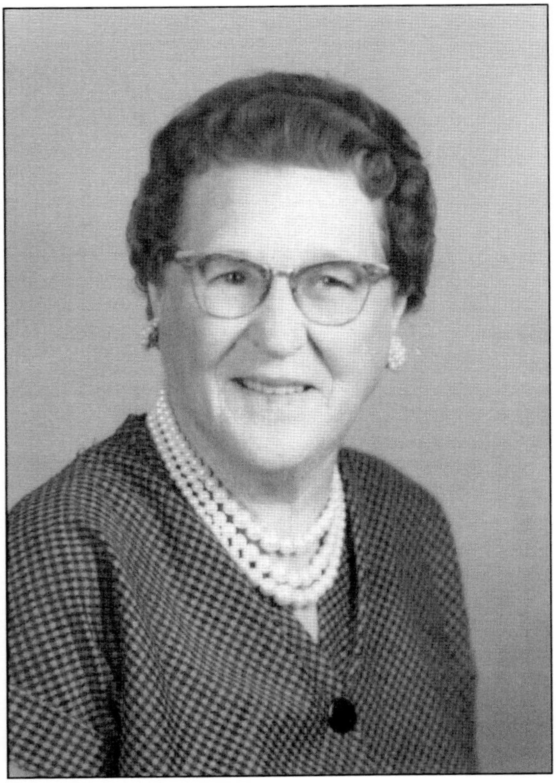

Cora Southwood. Jack Christian's mother was Cora Laura Daffron, from the Plano area. Cora's father, Elmer Southwood, was a farmer in Murphy. The Southwood family rode the train from Murphy to Plano each Saturday so the family could shop in the city. The train fare was 10¢ per person. (Kenneth Christian.)

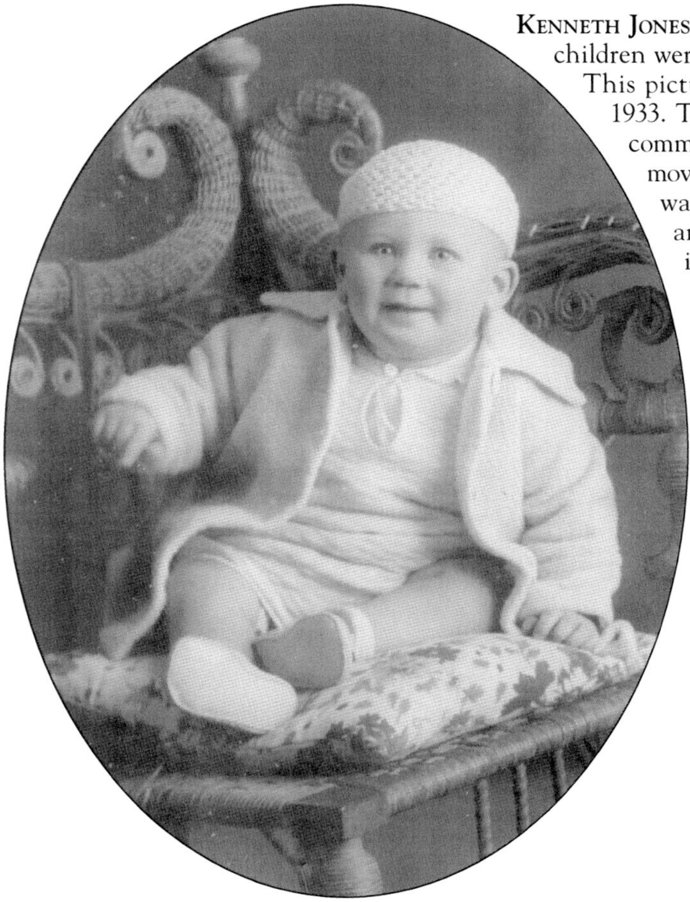

KENNETH JONES CHRISTIAN. Lonnie and Jack's children were Curtis, Kenneth, and Paula. This picture of Kenneth was taken in 1933. The family lived in the Parker community until the 1940s and then moved to the Shepard ranch, which was located on present-day Park and Preston Roads, to help run it. (Kenneth Christian.)

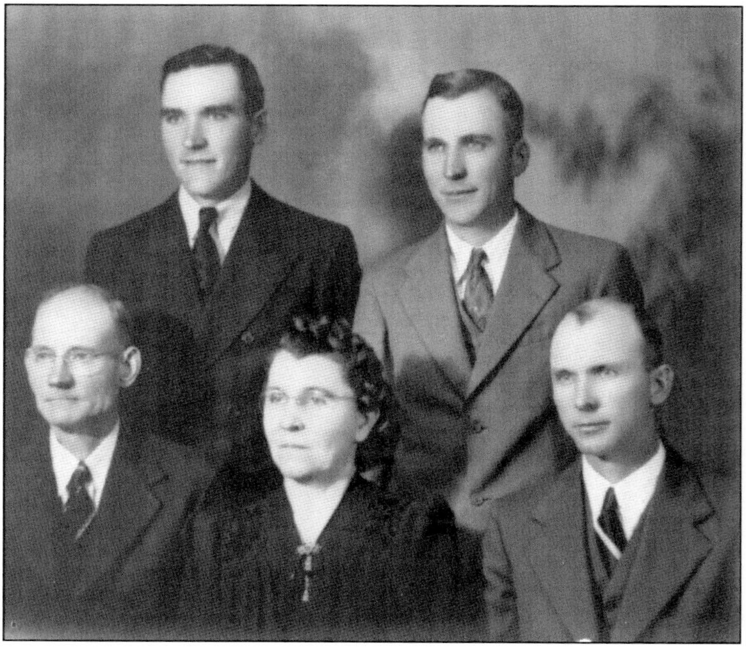

MCCREARY FAMILY. Mallory "Loy" McCreary and Lular "Maude" Stinson were married on February 3, 1907. They grew cotton and grain. Loy also managed a gin and seed house north of the railroad tracks. They had three sons and two daughters named Martha and Maude who died in infancy. Shown in the family photograph are, from left to right, (sitting) Loy, Maude, and Leslie; (standing) Robert and Si. (Zada McCreary Nicholson.)

CONDITION OF

LIBERTY STATE BANK

MURPHY, TEXAS

AS MADE TO THE COMMISSIONER OF BANKING AT THE CLOSE OF BUSINESS, SEPT. 29, 1931

RESOURCES		LIABILITIES	
Loans and Discounts	$16,458.64	Capital Stock	$15,000.00
Other Bonds	13,055.75	Surplus Fund	2,250.00
Customer's Bonds	9,000.00	Undivided Profits	4,099.80
Building, Fur. & Fix.	2,755.00	Deposits	44,656.76
Cash,	5,540.97	Cashier's Checks	7,101.00
Due from Banks	34,818.81	Customer's Bonds	9,000.00
Other Resources	478.39		
TOTAL	$82,107.56	TOTAL	$82,107.56

LESLIE McCREARY, Cashier

LIBERTY STATE BANK POSTCARD. Customers were given postcards showing the resources and liabilities at the close of business on September 29, 1931. Leslie McCreary was the cashier, and Dr. Dennis Miller was the bank president. The bank opened in 1922 and closed in 1932. The First National Bank of Plano acquired it. (Zada McCreary Nicholson.)

CONDITION OF

LIBERTY STATE BANK

MURPHY, TEXAS

AS MADE TO THE COMMISSIONER OF BANKING AT THE CLOSE OF BUSINESS, SEPT. 30, 1932

RESOURCES		LIABILITIES	
Loans and Discounts	$ 8,398.86	Capital Stock	$15,000.00
U. S. Bonds, 4th. Liberty	15,000.00	Surplus Fund	2,250.00
Commercial Paper	5,000.00	Undivided Profits	1,512.77
Customers' Bonds	9,000.00	Cashier's Checks	122.13
Banking House	1.00	Customers' Bonds	9,000.00
Furniture and Fixtures	1.00	Deposits	49,883.58
Overdraft	.35		
Cash in Banks	40,046.16		
Other Resources	321.11		
TOTAL	$77,768.48	TOTAL	$77,768.48

LESLIE McCREARY, Cashier

BALANCE POSTCARD, SEPTEMBER 30, 1932. This balance was recorded before the bank closed its doors after 10 years on November 3, 1932. The previous bank in Murphy was the Guaranty State Bank, which opened on April 16, 1919, and voluntary liquidated on April 7, 1921. The First State Bank in Wylie, Texas acquired it. (Zada McCreary Nicholson.)

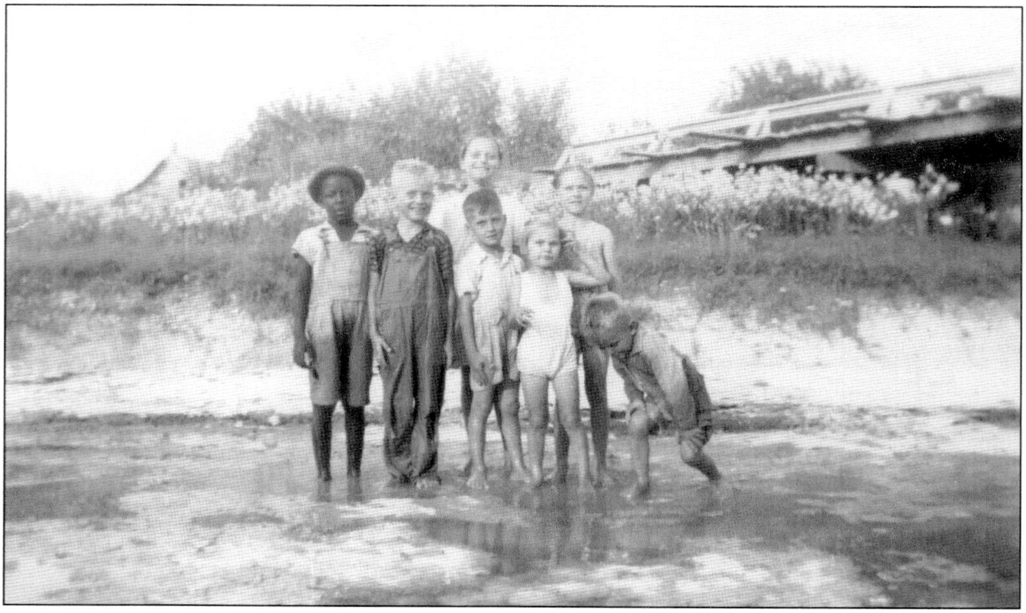

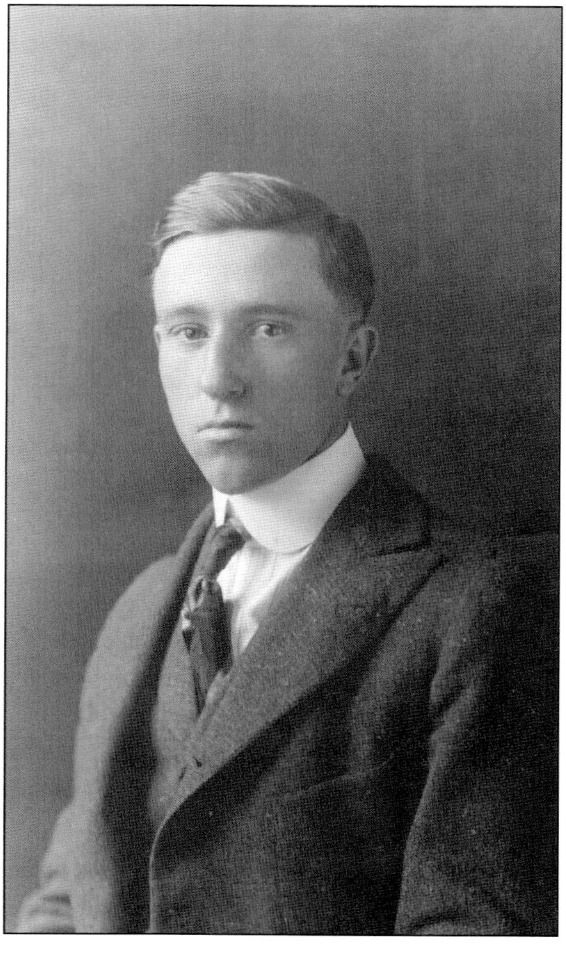

PLAYING ON MAXWELL CREEK. Pictured are, from left to right, Billy ?, Joe McCreary, his four cousins, and his little brother Gerald, who loved to play in Maxwell Creek along Murphy Road and McMillen Drive. Joe remembered there were no school buses, and the students had to walk to and from the Murphy School. They would hurry home to play in the creek. (Joe McCreary.)

GRADUATION PICTURE. Albert C. Taylor attended the Murphy School through the 10th grade and then completed his education in Plano in 1914. He was a member of the debate team and the Wildcat football team, where he earned the nickname "Jackrabbit." He was quite a character and he once rode a cow from Murphy to Plano. (Barbara Taylor Bennie.)

COMMENCEMENT INVITATION, 1909. This invitation belonged to Mary Taylor. Graduation was an important event in Murphy. Families dressed in their best attire and came to commencement to honor their graduate. Around 1880, Collin County began to finance and support area schools that were overseen by the county superintendent of schools. Prior to this time, families operated schools in churches and private homes. In the 1930s, Texas implemented strict regulations for education requirements. Rural schools with small enrollments and limited finances experienced difficulties. For the next 30 years, small districts began to close and were consolidated into larger school districts. Murphy School closed in 1950 along with eight other rural schools and joined Plano Independent School District. (Both, Barbara Taylor Bennie.)

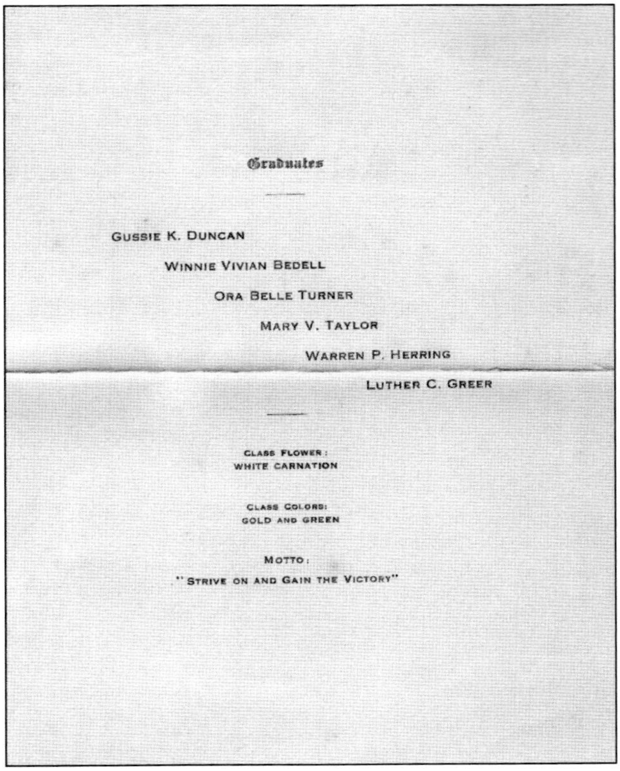

Graduates

GUSSIE K. DUNCAN

WINNIE VIVIAN BEDELL

ORA BELLE TURNER

MARY V. TAYLOR

WARREN P. HERRING

LUTHER C. GREER

CLASS FLOWER:
WHITE CARNATION

CLASS COLORS:
GOLD AND GREEN

MOTTO:
"STRIVE ON AND GAIN THE VICTORY"

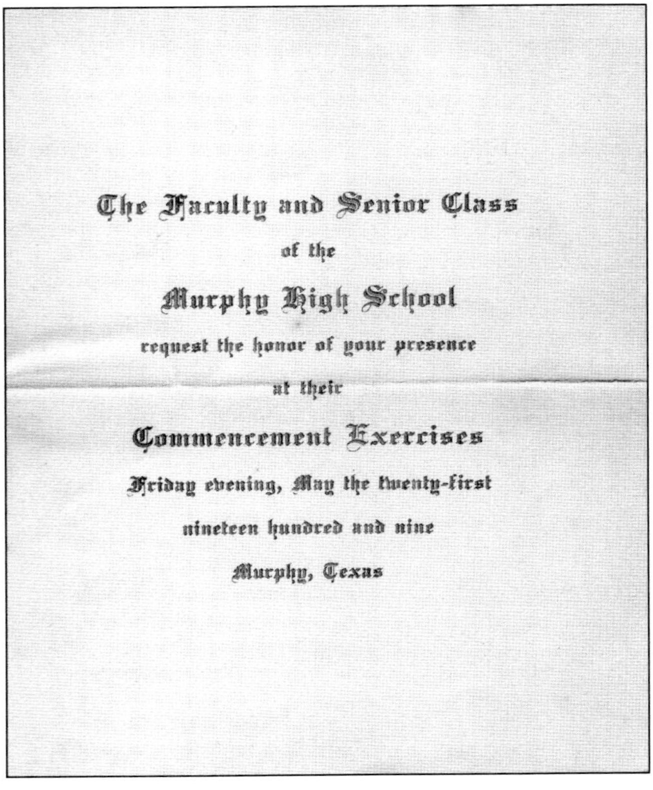

The Faculty and Senior Class

of the

Murphy High School

request the honor of your presence

at their

Commencement Exercises

Friday evening, May the twenty-first

nineteen hundred and nine

Murphy, Texas

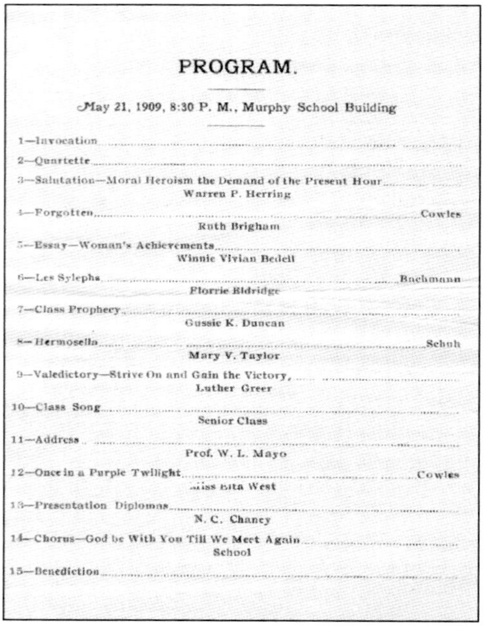

PROGRAM.

May 21, 1909, 8:30 P. M., Murphy School Building

1—Invocation

2—Quartette

3—Salutation—Moral Heroism the Demand of the Present Hour
Warren P. Herring

4—Forgotten .... Cowles
Ruth Brigham

5—Essay—Woman's Achievements
Winnie Vivian Bedell

6—Les Sylephs .... Bachmann
Florrie Eldridge

7—Class Prophecy
Gussie K. Duncan

8—Hermosella .... Schuh
Mary V. Taylor

9—Valedictory—Strive On and Gain the Victory,
Luther Greer

10—Class Song
Senior Class

11—Address
Prof. W. L. Mayo

12—Once in a Purple Twilight .... Cowles
Miss Eita West

13—Presentation Diplomas
N. C. Chaney

14—Chorus—God be With You Till We Meet Again
School

15—Benediction

Commencement Program. Six students, Gussie Duncan, Winnie Bedell, Ora Belle Turner, Mary Taylor, Warren Herring, and Luther Greer, graduated from the Murphy School on May 21, 1909. The graduation took place in the school gymnasium on the stage in view of parents and friends from the community. (Barbara Taylor Bennie.)

Murphy School Report Card, 1916–1917. This photograph shows the report card that Elizabeth "Lizzie" Southwood received from the Murphy School. Her fifth-grade teacher was Winnie Bedell, who also attended the school in Murphy and graduated in 1909. Lizzie was promoted to sixth grade on May 3, 1917. (Kenneth Christian.)

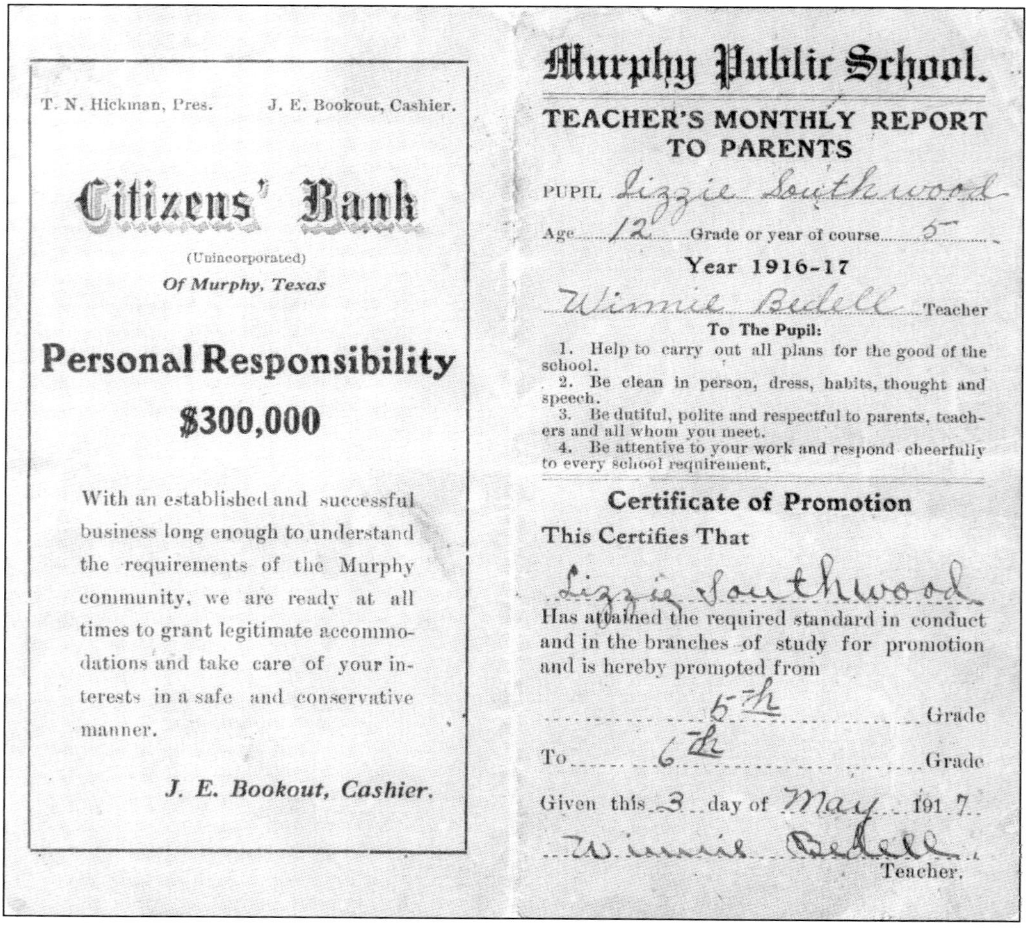

T. N. Hickman, Pres. J. E. Bookout, Cashier.

Citizens' Bank

(Unincorporated)

Of Murphy, Texas

Personal Responsibility

$300,000

With an established and successful business long enough to understand the requirements of the Murphy community, we are ready at all times to grant legitimate accommodations and take care of your interests in a safe and conservative manner.

J. E. Bookout, Cashier.

Murphy Public School.

TEACHER'S MONTHLY REPORT TO PARENTS

PUPIL Lizzie Southwood

Age 12 Grade or year of course 5

Year 1916-17

Winnie Bedell Teacher

To The Pupil:

1. Help to carry out all plans for the good of the school.
2. Be clean in person, dress, habits, thought and speech.
3. Be dutiful, polite and respectful to parents, teachers and all whom you meet.
4. Be attentive to your work and respond cheerfully to every school requirement.

Certificate of Promotion

This Certifies That

Lizzie Southwood

Has attained the required standard in conduct and in the branches of study for promotion and is hereby promoted from

5th Grade

To 6th Grade

Given this 3 day of May 1917.

Winnie Bedell
Teacher.

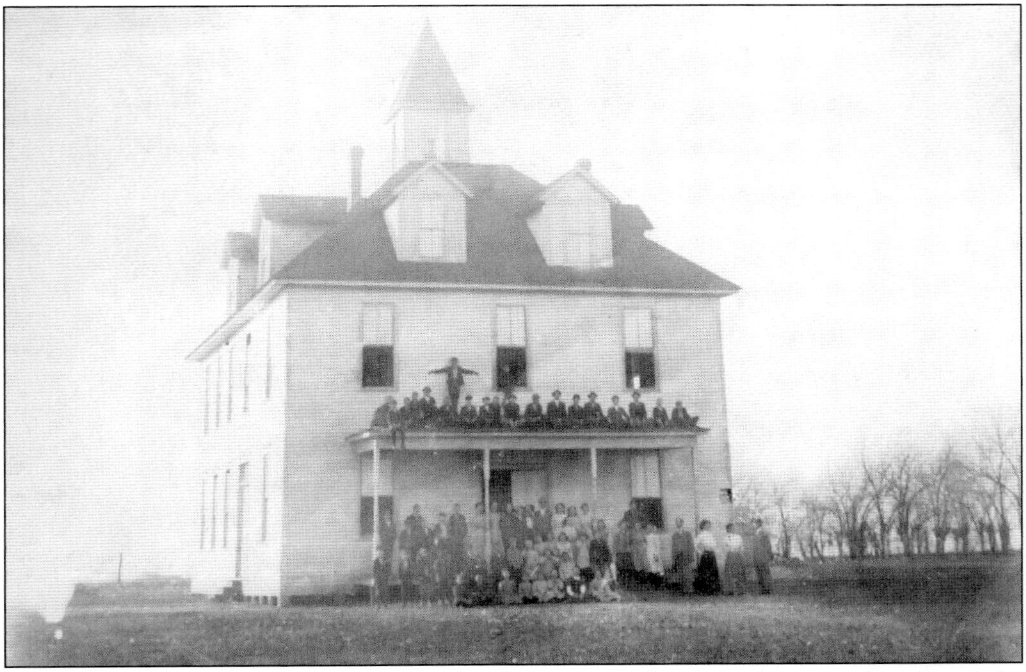

Murphy High School Students, 1919. In 1885, an acre of state land was purchased, and the Decatur School was relocated to the land on Murphy Road. The school day was from 8:00 a.m. to 5:00 p.m., and the school term ranged from four to seven months. The Decatur School was replaced by the white two-story frame building pictured above. This school housed students in all grade levels. (S. Michael Boyd.)

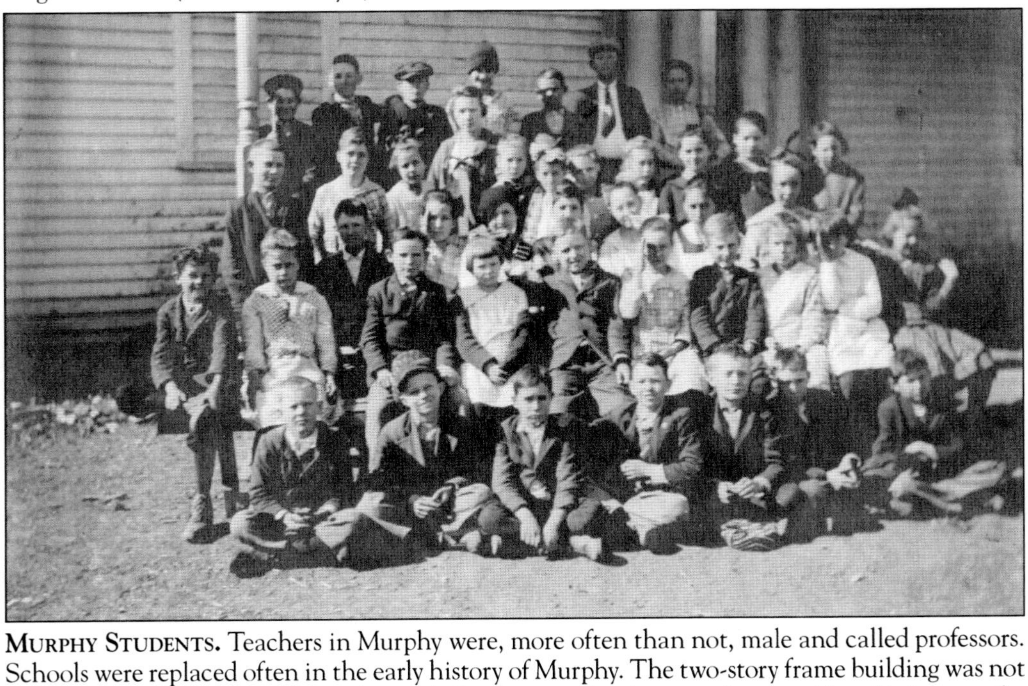

Murphy Students. Teachers in Murphy were, more often than not, male and called professors. Schools were replaced often in the early history of Murphy. The two-story frame building was not well kept and was eventually condemned. Students in the photograph are unidentified except for Edgar Glenn Boyd, who is third from the left in the first row. (S. Michael Boyd.)

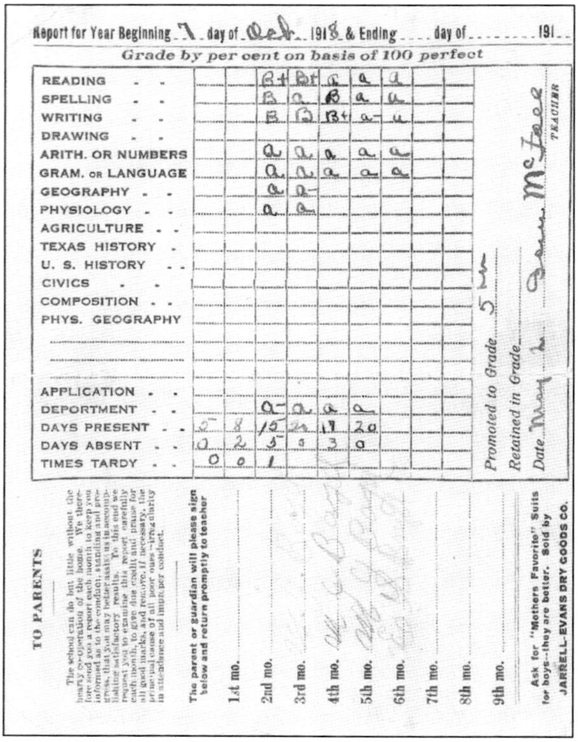

Edgar Boyd's Fourth-Grade Report Card. This photograph indicates Ed Boyd was promoted to the fifth grade. Report cards were issued monthly to students. Classes offered included reading, spelling, writing, geography, physiology, and arithmetic or numbers. The superintendent of Collin County schools was Homer Edwards, and Sam McFall was the teacher. Discipline was strict, and grades were given for conduct. Outhouses were located behind the school with separate sides for each sex. During recess time, students cracked black walnuts with a rock or played a quick game of basketball on the front lawn or football on the back lawn behind the school. By 1933, teachers were paid about $30 per month. Sometimes the money ran out before the term ended, and schools either closed early or teachers were given vouchers to be cashed. (Both, S. Michael Boyd.)

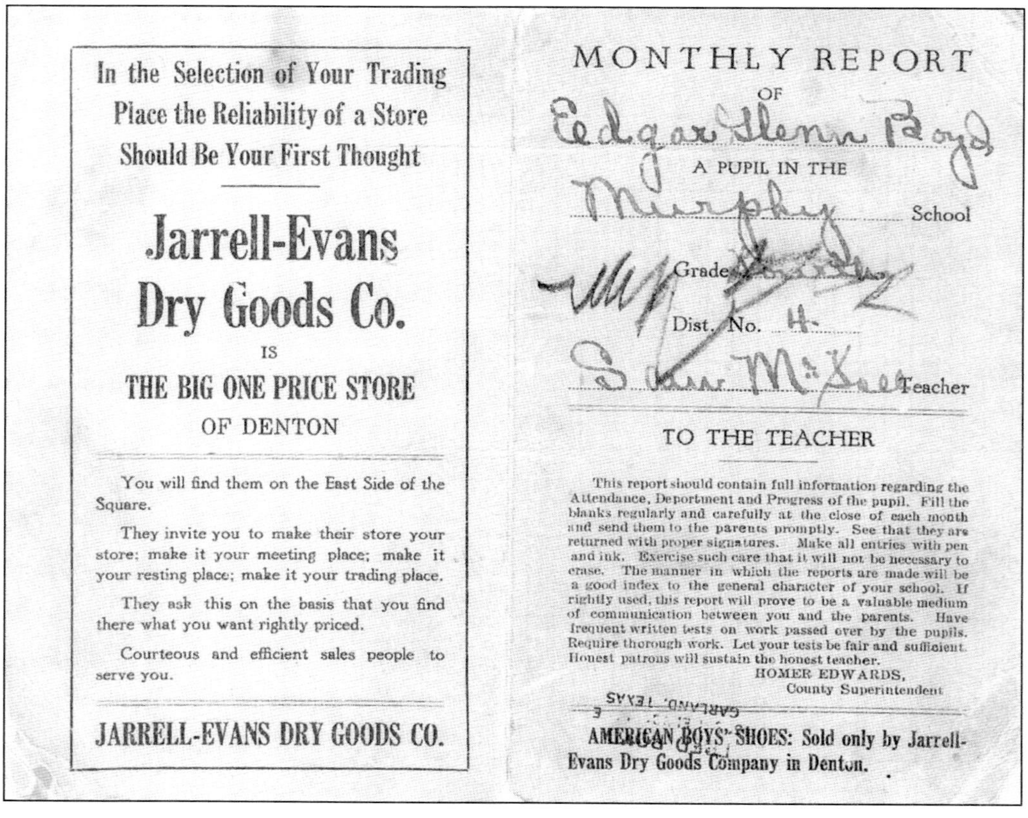

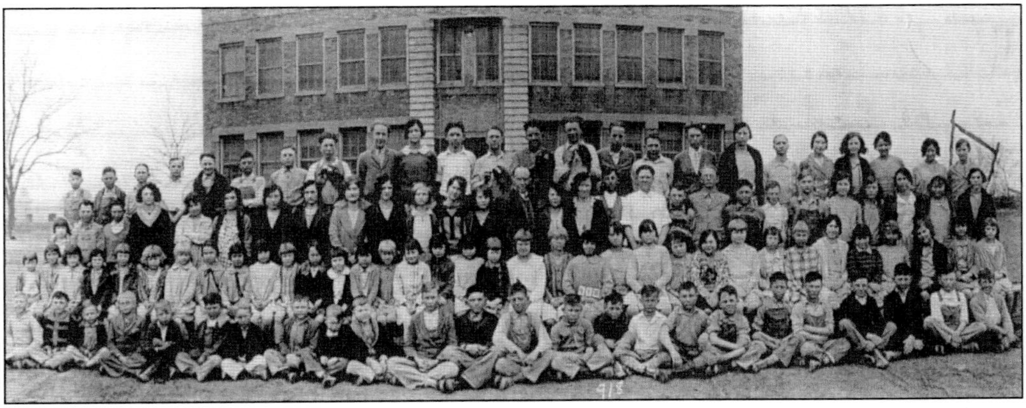

OLD RED SCHOOL. Joe McCreary remembers sitting in the front yard of his grandparents' home and watching workers remove the bricks from the redbrick school. It was during the Depression, and the bricks were removed and painstakingly cleaned to be used in other buildings. (S. Michael Boyd.)

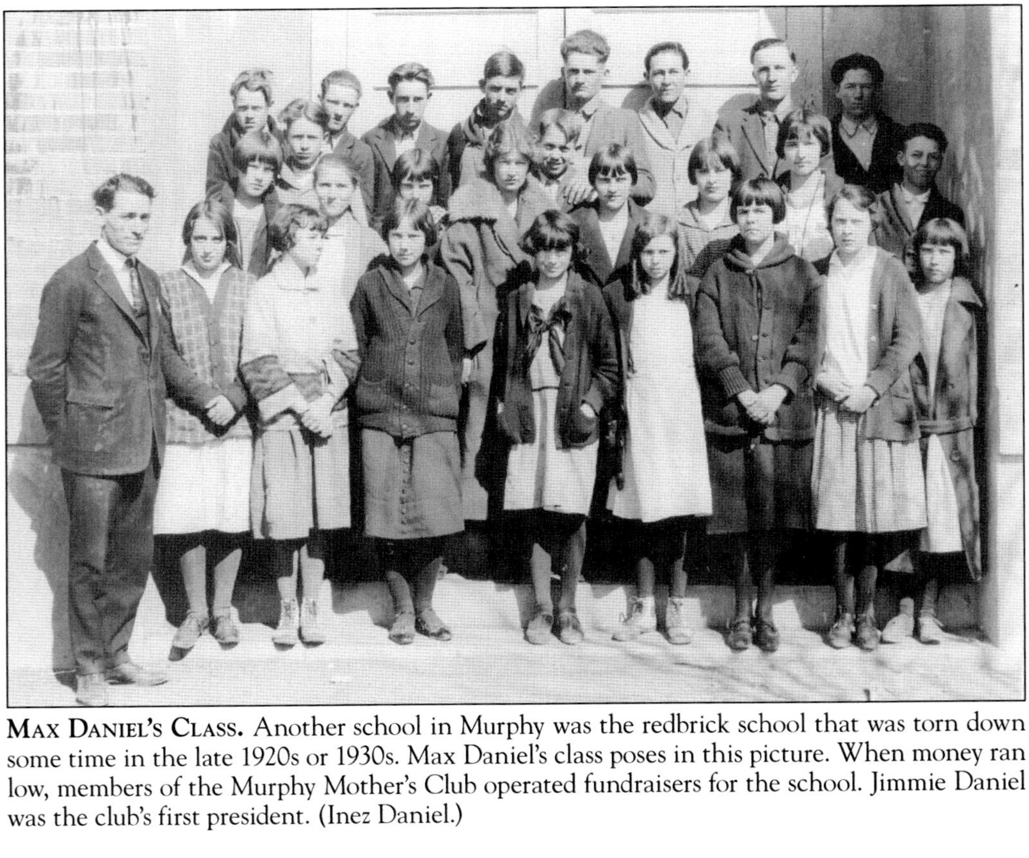

MAX DANIEL'S CLASS. Another school in Murphy was the redbrick school that was torn down some time in the late 1920s or 1930s. Max Daniel's class poses in this picture. When money ran low, members of the Murphy Mother's Club operated fundraisers for the school. Jimmie Daniel was the club's first president. (Inez Daniel.)

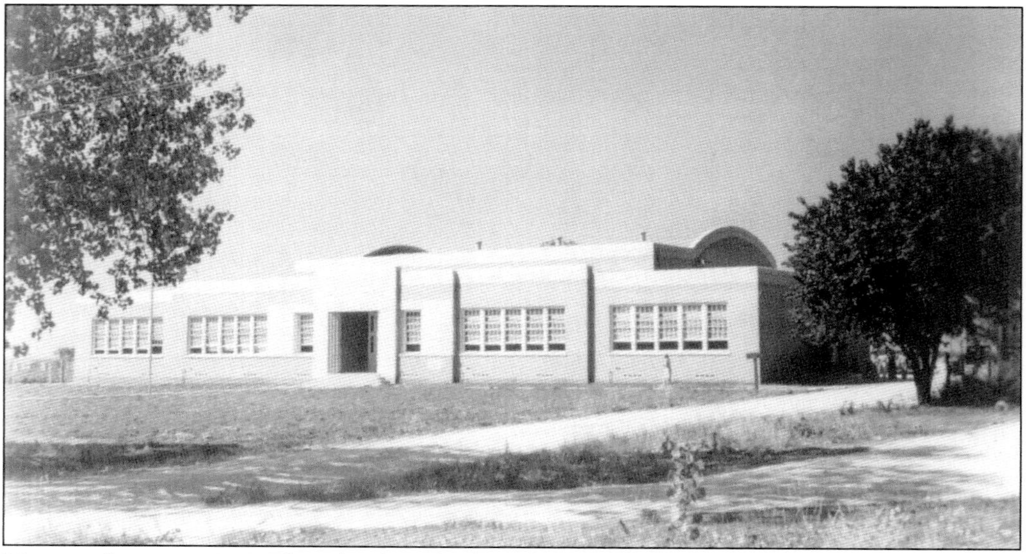

Murphy School, 1939. The school was built under the auspices of the WPA, which was a relief measure established by the US president in 1936 to give aid to the unemployed. Programs were established to build schools, and the Murphy School was built utilizing one of these programs. (Murphy City Hall.)

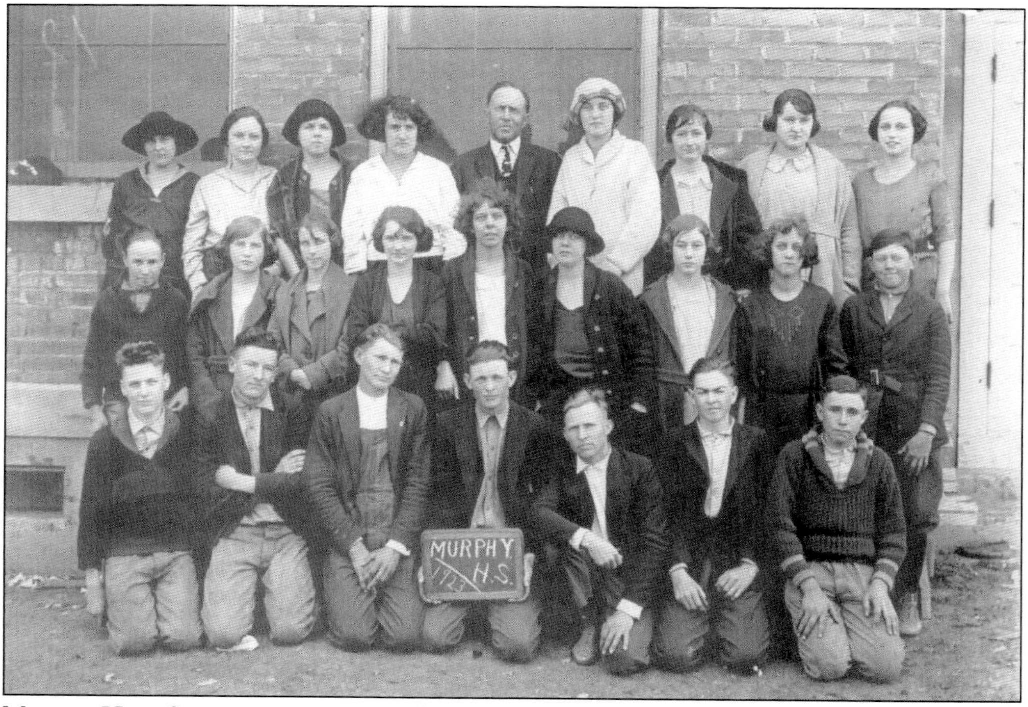

Murphy High School, 1923. Pictured are, from left to right, (first row) Charles Lynn Cockrell, Raymond Harvey, Dave Walker, Rex Strange, Willie Walker, Raymond King, and Edgar Glen Boyd; (second row) Beason Kilgore, Fannie Mae Wilson, Eula Mae Campbell, Tessie Harvey, Gussie McKinney, Alzenia McKinney, Jewel Walker, Janice Daniel, and J. Loyd Williams; (third row) Aline Moulden, ? Campbell, Mary Lou Turner, Annie Bell Bailey, teacher Joseph Robert Dickerson, Cleta Mae Cockrell, Mary Campbell, Joy Wyatt, and Ruth Back. (S. Michael Boyd.)

BASKETBALL TEAM, 1946. Although organized sports were popular, these students are unidentified. Both girls and boys played basketball in the gym of the school. Six-man football began in Murphy as early as 1938 and was played behind the school. Sunday afternoon baseball games were played in a field behind the school with teams from Sachse, Parker, and Princeton. (S. Michael Boyd.)

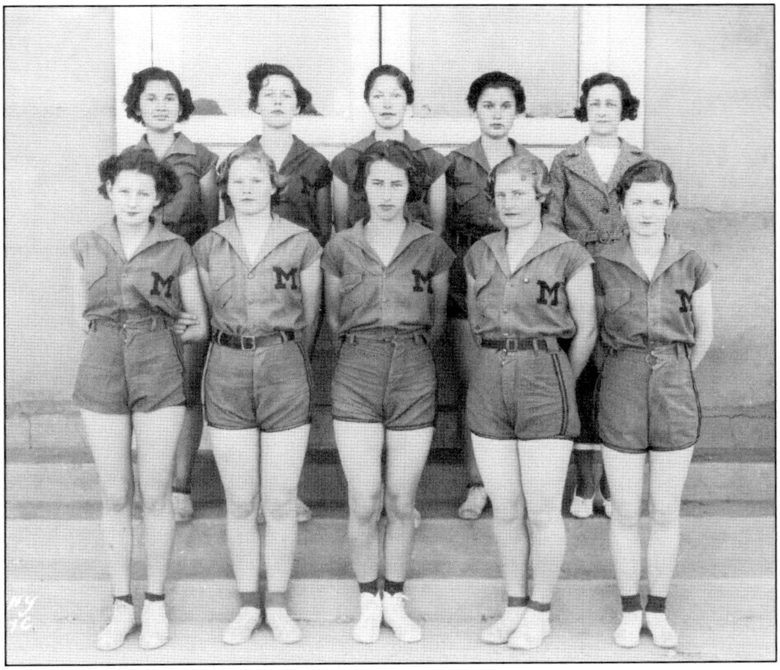

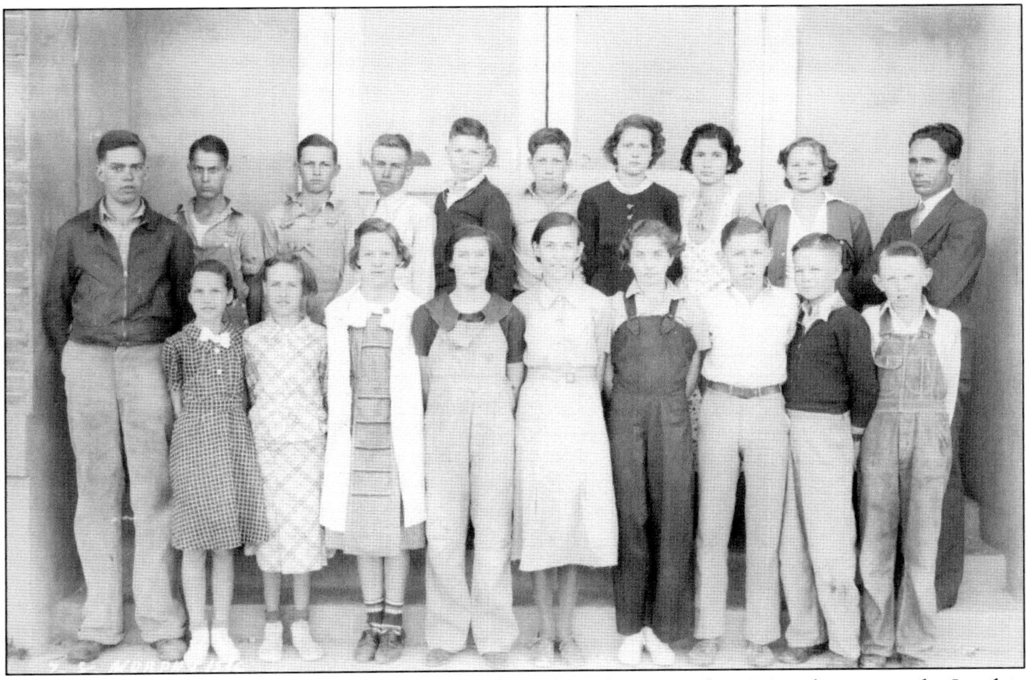

MURPHY SCHOOL STUDENTS, 1936. Edgar Glenn Boyd returned to Murphy to teach. In this photograph, he is seen posing with his students. From left to right are (first row) Naarene Ingram, unidentified, ? Moulden, two unidentified, Della Mae Holman, J.C. Greer, Pete Barnes, and Charles Williams; (second row) Thomas Brooks, Johnnie Yandell, ? Ingram, ? Geren, unidentified, Kenneth Brooks, ? Brooks, Mary Forman, ? Chumley, and teacher Edgar Boyd. (S. Michael Boyd.)

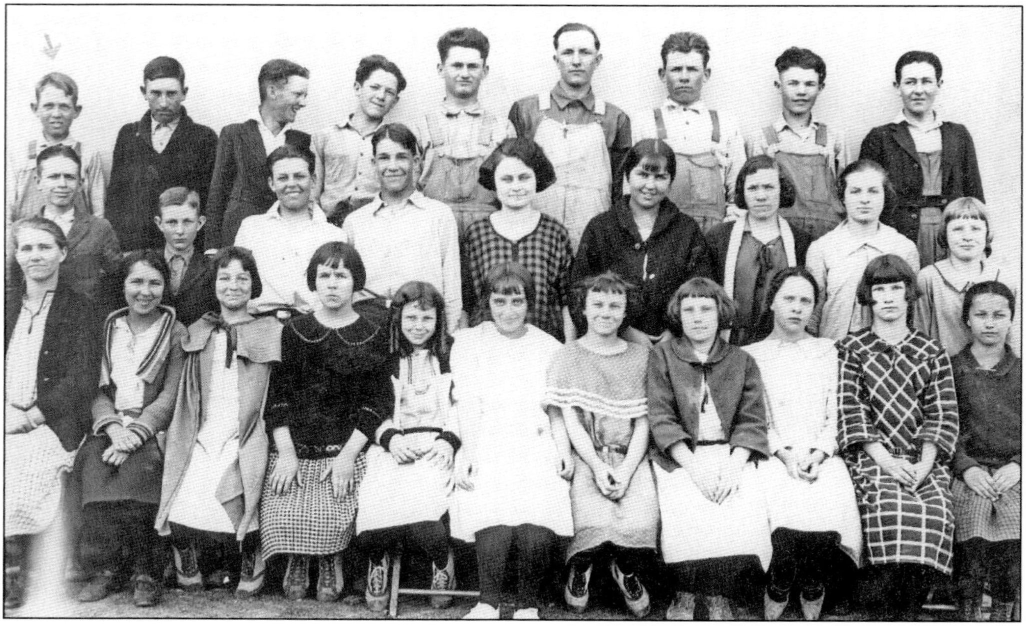

MURPHY SCHOOL, C. 1918. Max Daniel, the first person at left in the third row, is shown with students who attended the Murphy School. He helped his father, W.O. Daniel Sr., on the family farm. Children were expected to help with planting and harvesting crops. Often they attended school for only five months of the school year. (Inez Daniel.)

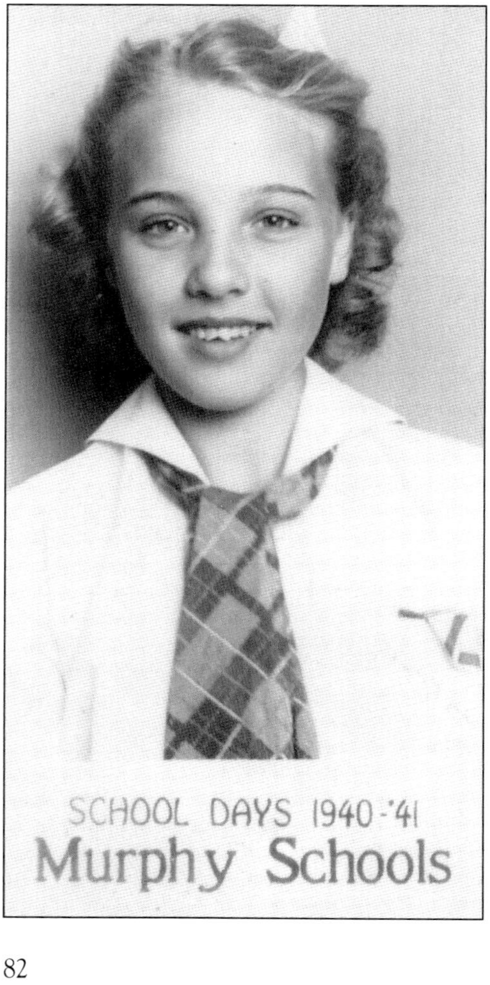

MURPHY SCHOOL DAYS, 1940–1941. Peggy Wilson Nelson started school in the redbrick building when she was five. She later attended school in the yellow brick building still standing on Murphy Road today. She remembered having diphtheria when she was in second grade. During her illness, she went to Dr. Miller, whose house sat across the street from the school. (Peggy Wilson Nelson.)

Jim Daniel. This photograph was taken of Jim in his overalls and clutching a book on the first day of school in first grade on September 14, 1942. Jim lived in the house just south of the Murphy School and walked to school each day. He attended school in Murphy until it closed, and he graduated from Plano High School and Baylor University. Later, he operated Daniel Implement Company. (Jim Daniel.)

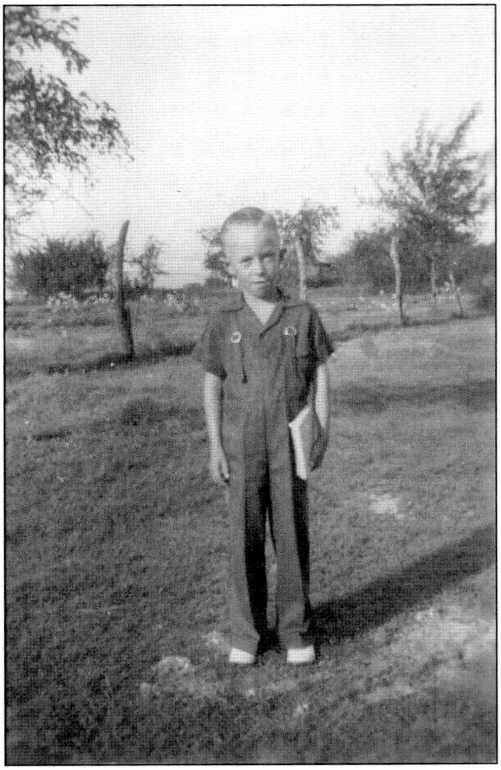

The Plano Independent School District
Board of Trustees

invites you to attend
the dedication ceremony for

Dr. Dennis Miller Elementary School
5651 Coventry
Richardson, Texas 75082

at 2:00 p.m.
Sunday, May 5, 1996

A reception hosted by the PTA
will follow immediately.

Invitation. In 1996, Dr. Miller was honored by having a school in Plano Independent School District named for him. During the dedication, his granddaughter Carmen Haggard stated it was important to remember Dr. Miller as a soft-spoken man and a devout Christian who touched the lives of his patients. The Miller family donated his manual typewriter and his ledger with the names of Murphy patients to the school. (Carmen Carpenter Haggard.)

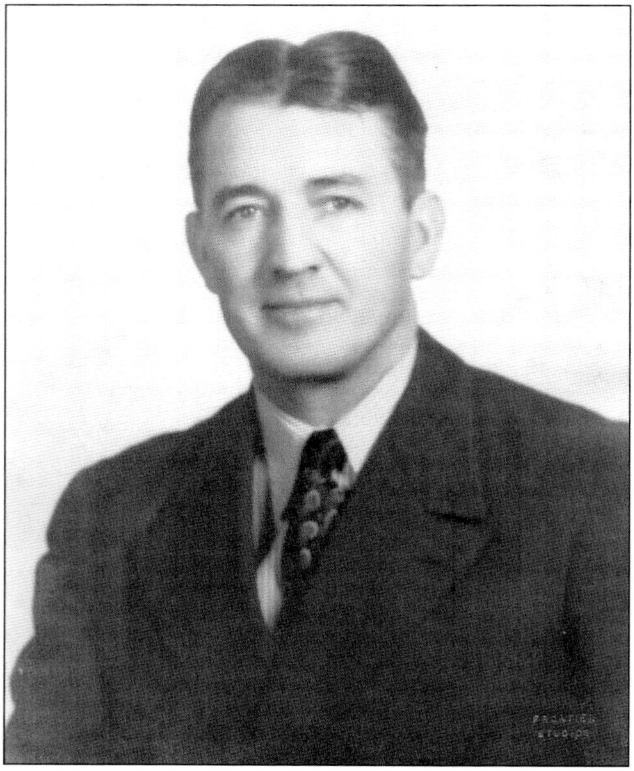

Homer Lee Adams. Born in 1903, Homer Adams was a teacher and superintendent in Murphy School for seven years before World War II. After the redbrick school was no longer safe, he applied to the government for a WPA school to be built for students. He spent four or five days drawing up plans for the Murphy School, which still stands at 200 Murphy Road today. (Grace Atherton.)

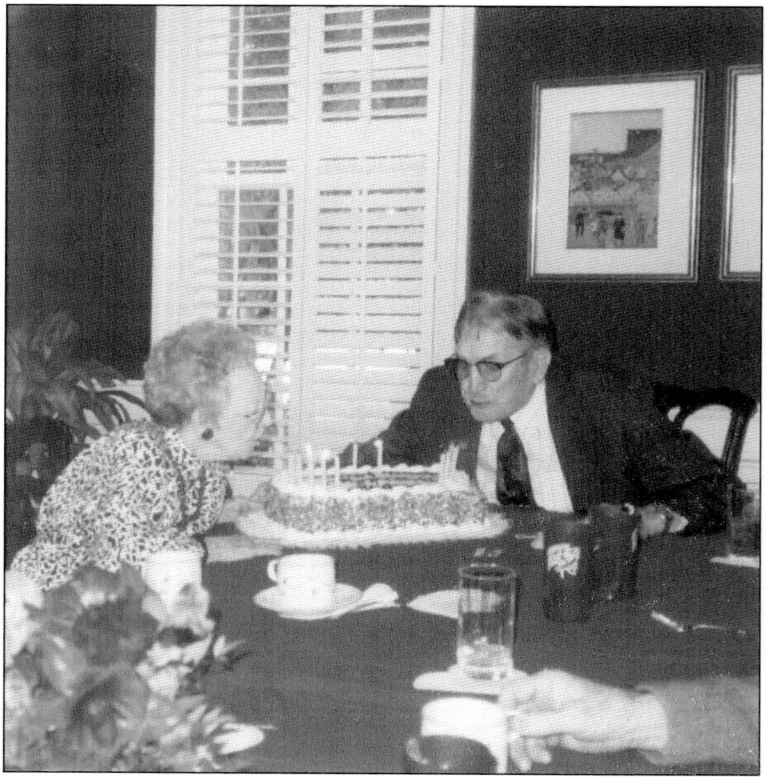

Birthday Party. After the Murphy School was completed, Adams began working for the government. He recruited workers for defense plants, like Southern Aircraft, during World War II and helped to build a hospital in McKinney for wounded soldiers. Helping others was important to Adams. As shown in this photograph, Adams and his sister Grace Atherton enjoyed family birthday celebrations. (Grace Atherton.)

Marie Allen Adams. Marie and Homer Adams met in college and were married after graduation from East Texas State in Commerce, Texas. Marie was a teacher in the Murphy School from 1934 to 1942. She taught various grades, but Bill Donihoo and Joe McCreary remembered she was their first-grade teacher at Murphy. Marie left Murphy and taught in Plano for 28 years, retiring in 1970. (Grace Atherton.)

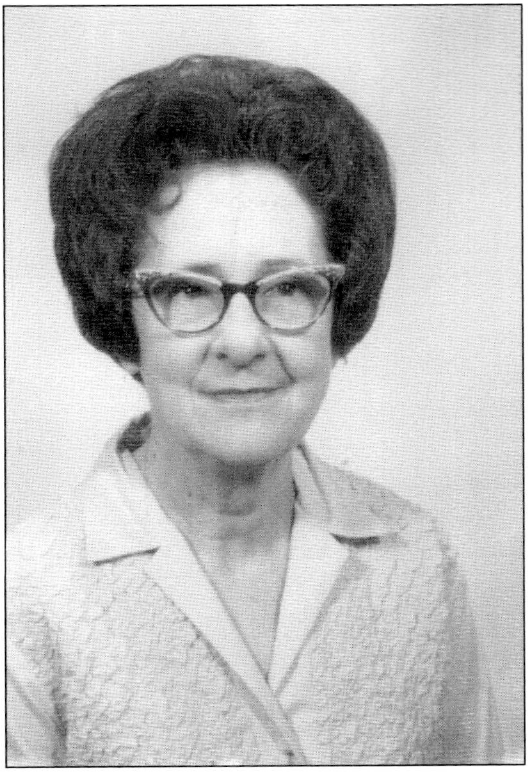

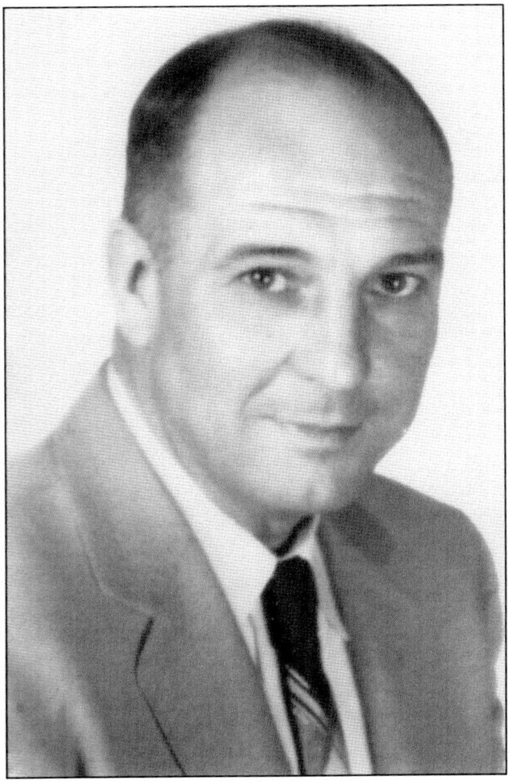

Robert "Bob" Atherton. In World War II, Bob served in France with the 49th Tank Division of the US Army. When he was discharged from service, he became the principal of Murphy School and served for two years until he moved to Wolf City. He married Grace Adams, who taught in Murphy, and they relocated to Arlington, where he was a principal and she was a teacher. (Grace Atherton.)

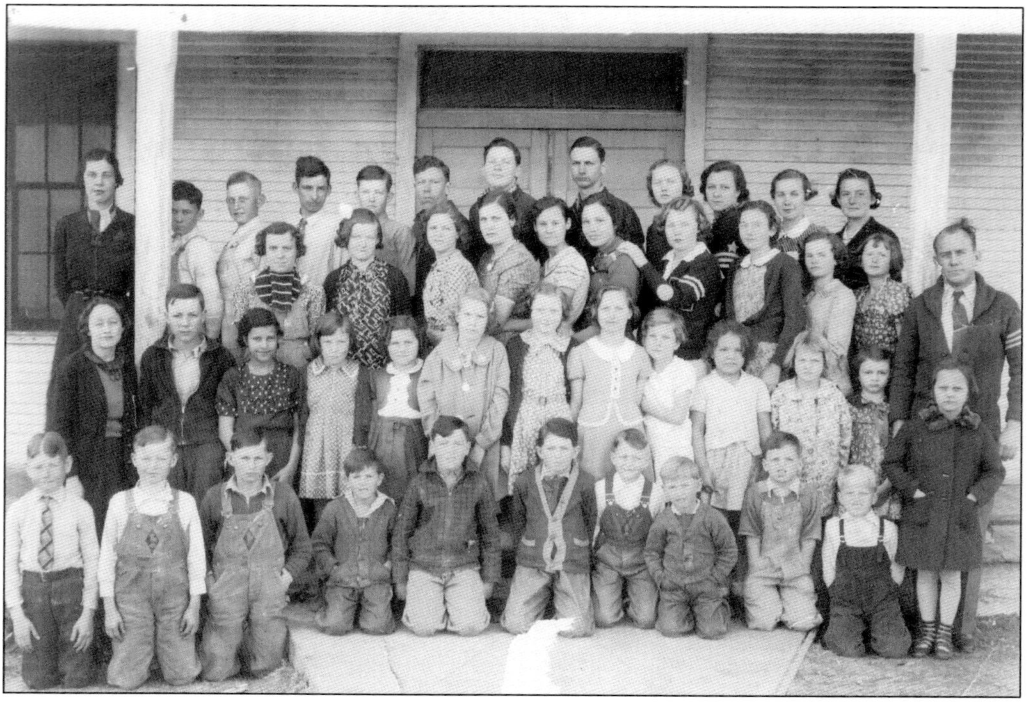

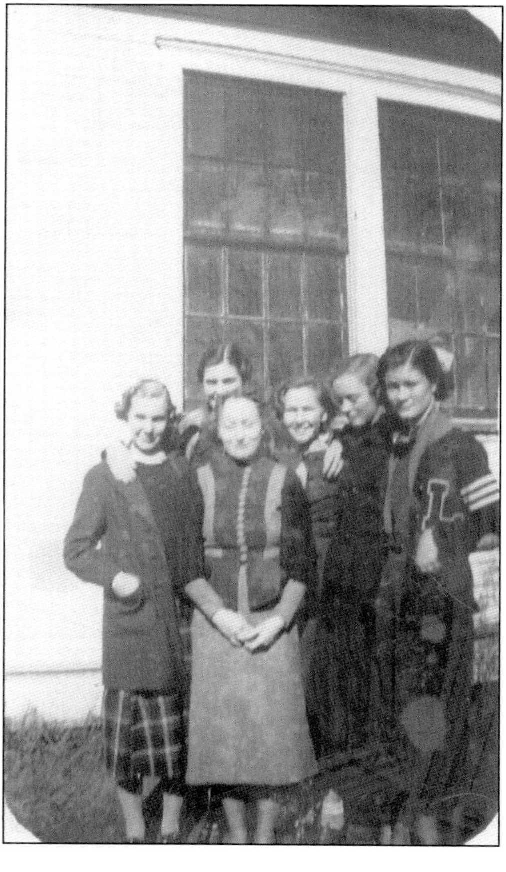

Lucas School. Grace Atherton began her teaching career in 1936 at Lucas School. She was a basketball coach and teacher from 1936 to 1945. Grace and her mother lived in Murphy on Main Street. Gas was rationed during the war, but she remembers driving a 1938 Buick to school each day. Grace is the first person on the left in the second row. (Grace Atherton.)

Lucas School Faculty, 1938. Grace Atherton is pictured second from the left with the 1936 faculty of Lucas School. In 1945, her brother Homer Adams helped her secure a job at the Murphy School, where she was paid $100 per month. She was the teacher, principal, and basketball and football coach. (Grace Atherton.)

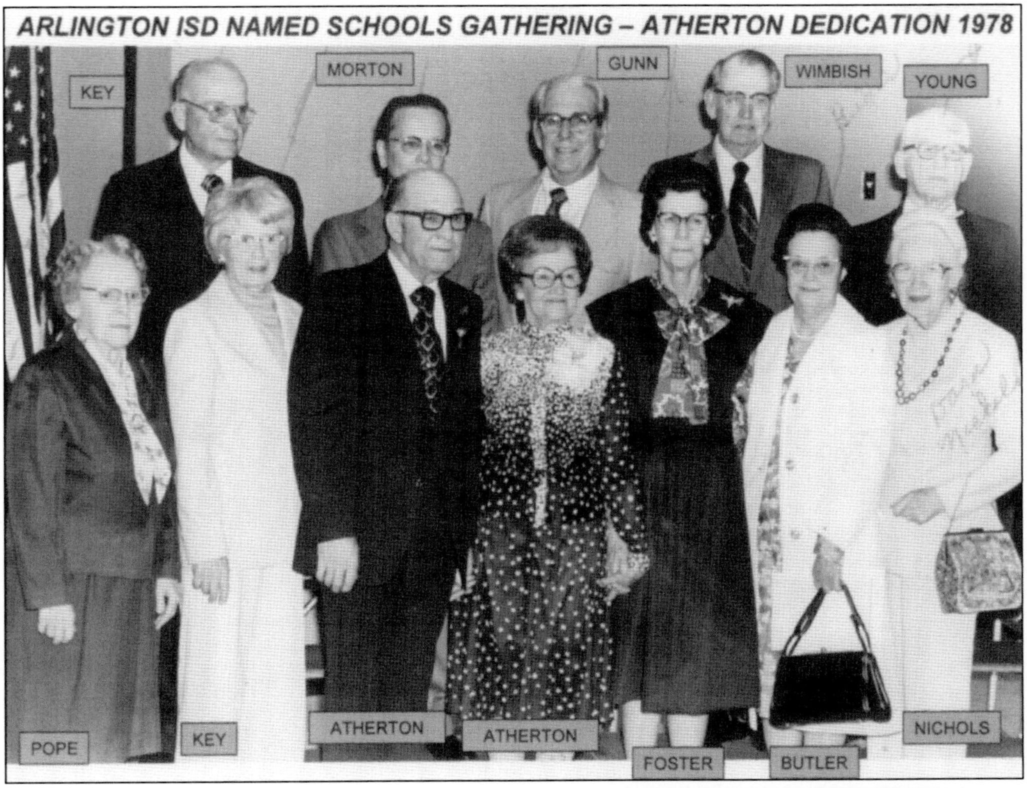

Dedication of Atherton Elementary School. Bob and Grace Atherton moved to Arlington in 1952 and joined the Arlington Independent School District. In 1978, they were honored for their dedication and service to the district by having a new school named for them. Robert served as a principal, and Grace was a teacher for 36 years. (Grace Atherton.)

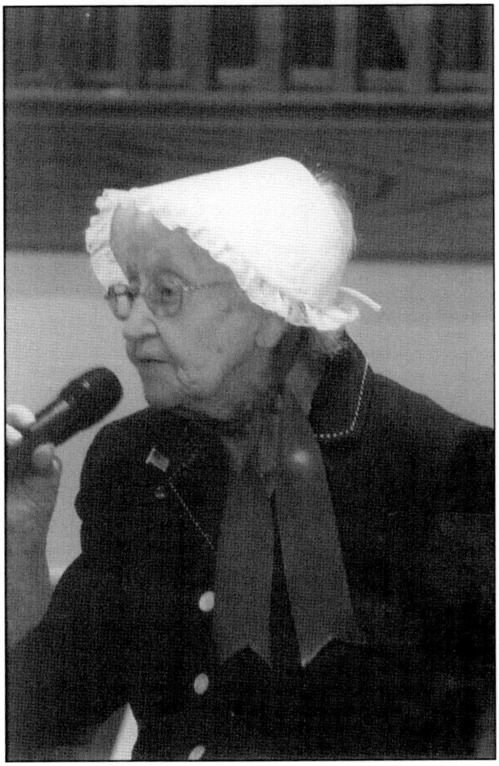

Story Time. Grace's love of teaching did not end when she retired. In 2011, at 98, she still volunteers to read stories at Atherton Elementary School. In this photograph, she is dressed as a pilgrim and reading a story about Thanksgiving. She sews her costumes and dresses in character for each story time. (Grace Atherton.)

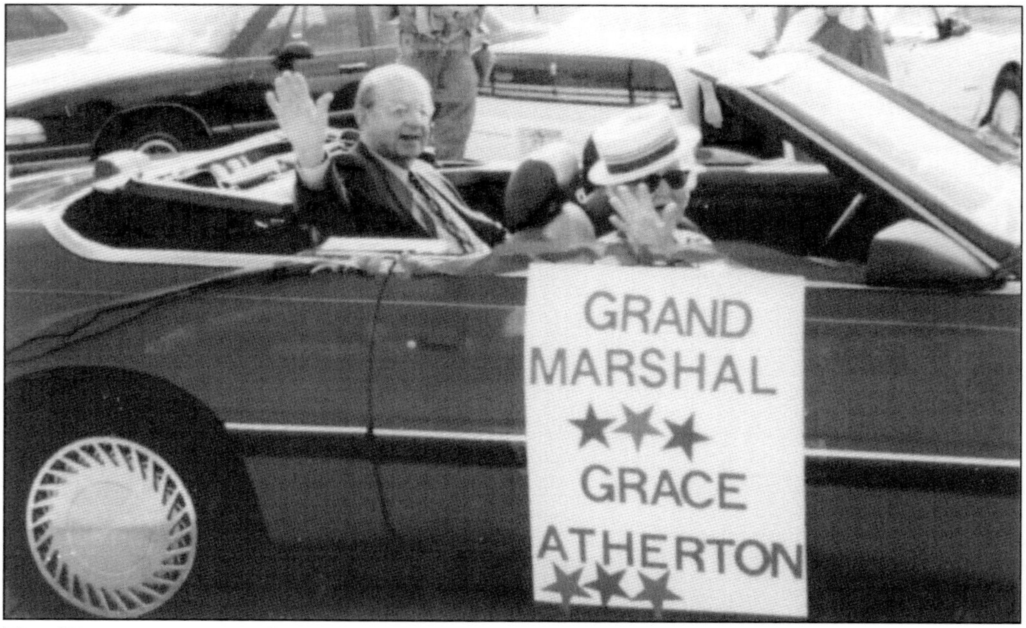

Tom Vandergriff and Grace Atherton. In 1995, Grace was grand marshal in the Fourth of July parade. Riding in the car with her was the mayor of Arlington, Tom Vandergriff. Retirement from teaching left Grace time to work in other areas. She was a longtime member of the Arlington Women's Club, where she still presents programs. (Grace Atherton.)

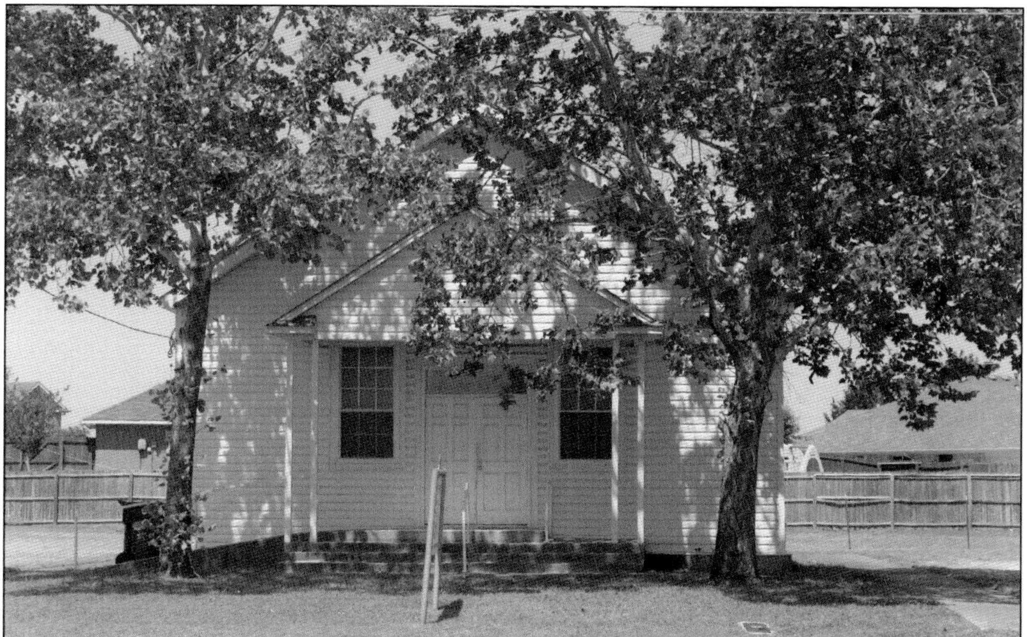

Current Church of Christ. Three churches occupied the land where the Church of Christ is now located. The first Church of Christ and Christian Church split in 1903, and the congregation removed the lumber to build a church in Sachse. The Methodists purchased the land and erected a church. When the Methodist church relocated to Wylie, it sold the church and land to the current Church of Christ. (Larry Taylor.)

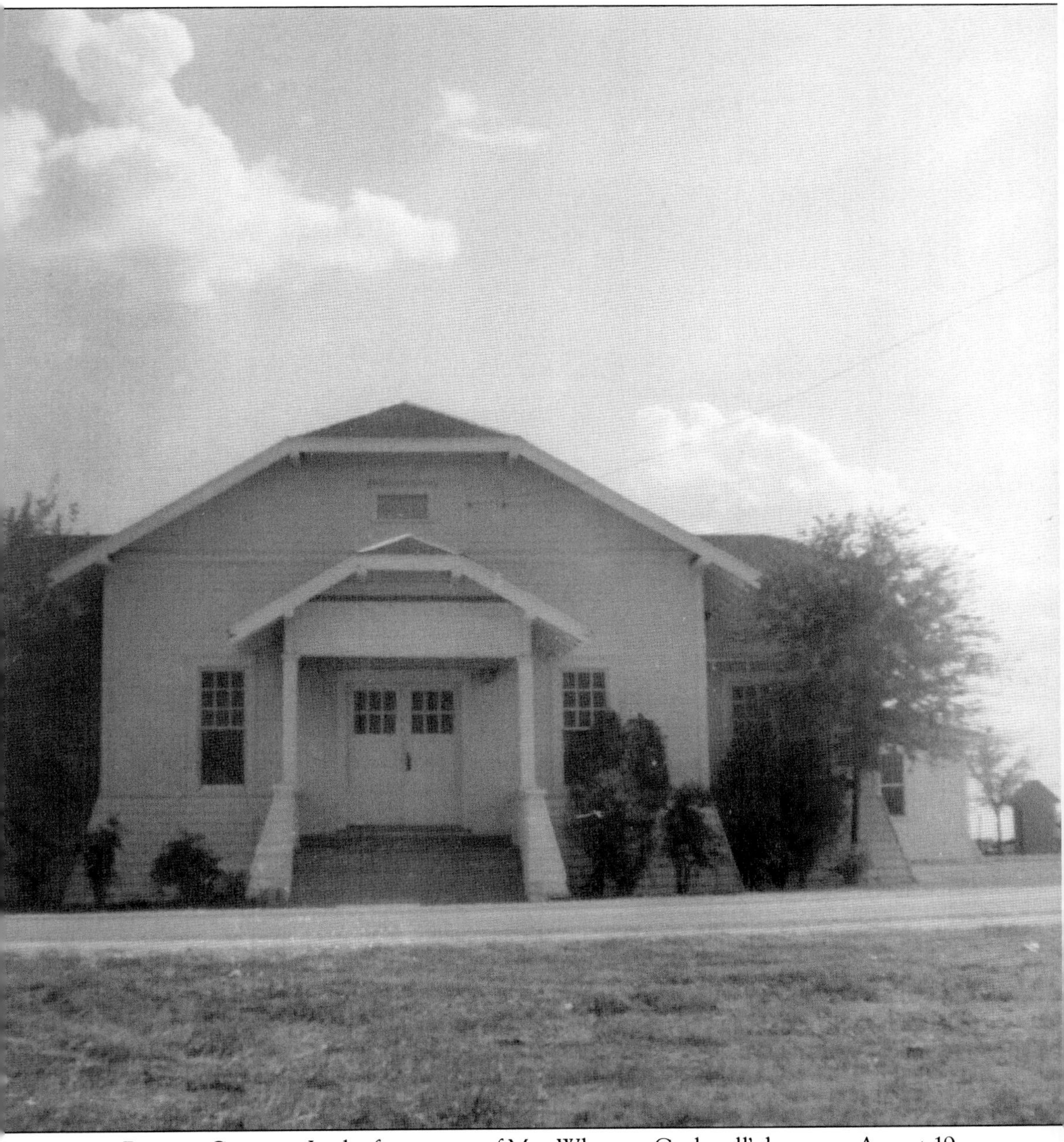

Murphy Baptist Church. In the front room of Mae Whorton Cockerell's home on August 19, 1900, the Murphy Baptist Church was organized. Meeting with her were her friends G.W. McCall, pastor of First Baptist Plano, and Bob Coleman, publisher of the *Plano Star Courier.* During the same month, the church was deeded a half-acre of land on FM 544 by Louisa E. Brown, a charter member of the church. The original building was just one rectangular room with a raised platform for the preacher to speak. In the center of the room was a large coal-burning pot-bellied stove. There was no running water, and the restroom facilities were two outhouses, one for the men and one for the women. One outhouse is visible on the right side of the photograph. The first wedding in the church took place on December 20, 1903. W.O. Daniel and Jimmie Eunice Harrison were married at the Murphy Baptist Church. (Inez Daniel.)

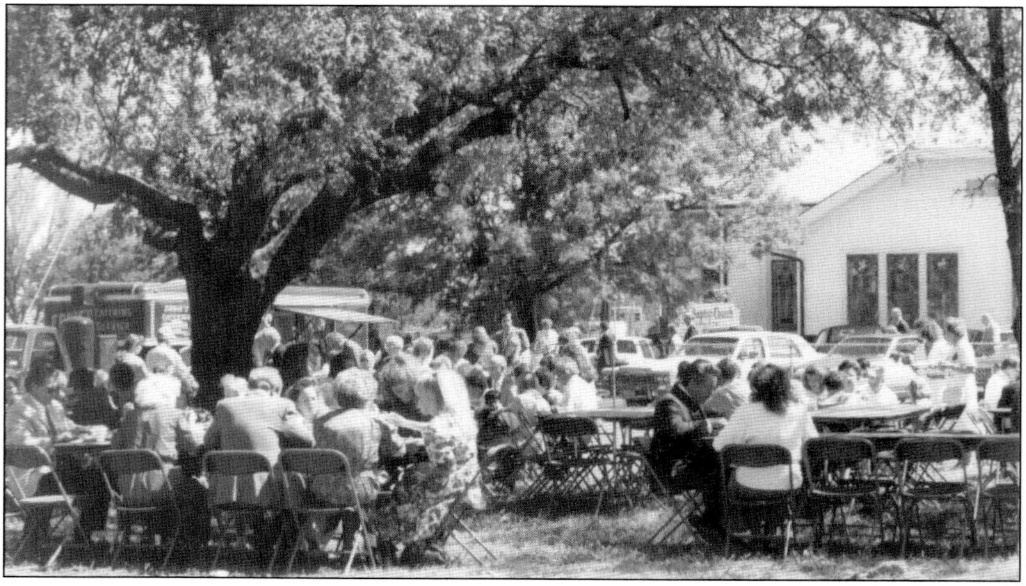

Growth of Church. Pictured is a homecoming celebration and church picnic. The church continued to grow, and by 1921, there were 296 members. By 1924, two new wings were added to the church as well as a small porch to the front entrance. In later years, beautiful stained glass windows were added to enhance the beauty of the church. (Courtesy of Inez Daniel.)

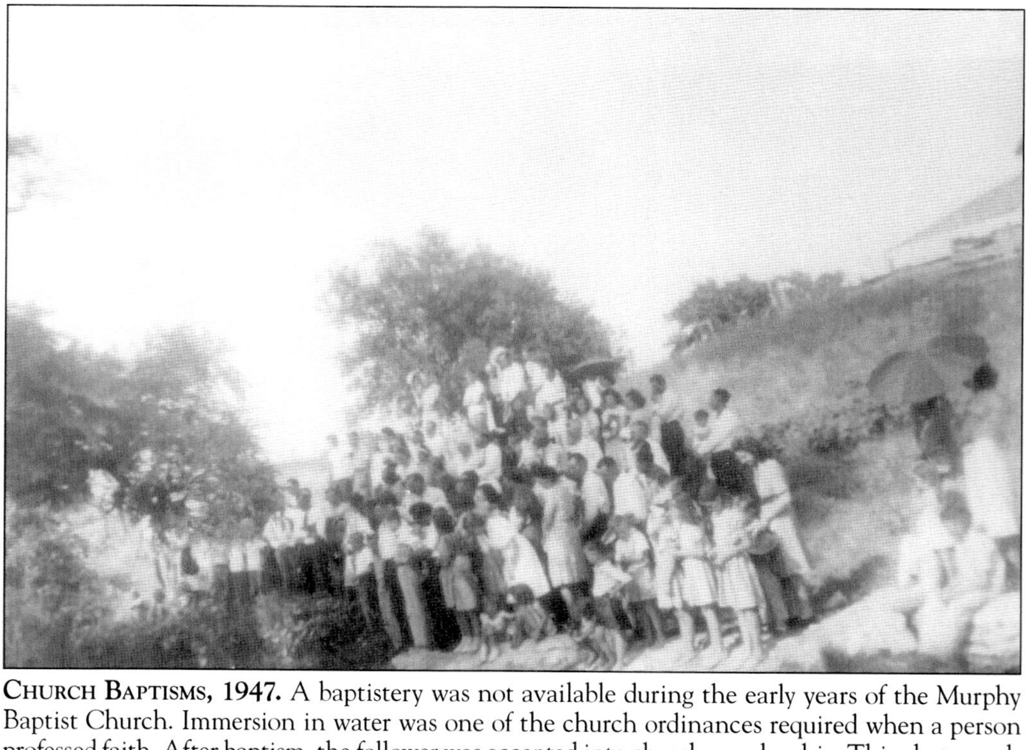

Church Baptisms, 1947. A baptistery was not available during the early years of the Murphy Baptist Church. Immersion in water was one of the church ordinances required when a person professed faith. After baptism, the follower was accepted into church membership. This photograph captured a baptism in Maxwell Creek. Pastor Bill Jenkins is standing with Millie and her two daughters. (Inez Daniel.)

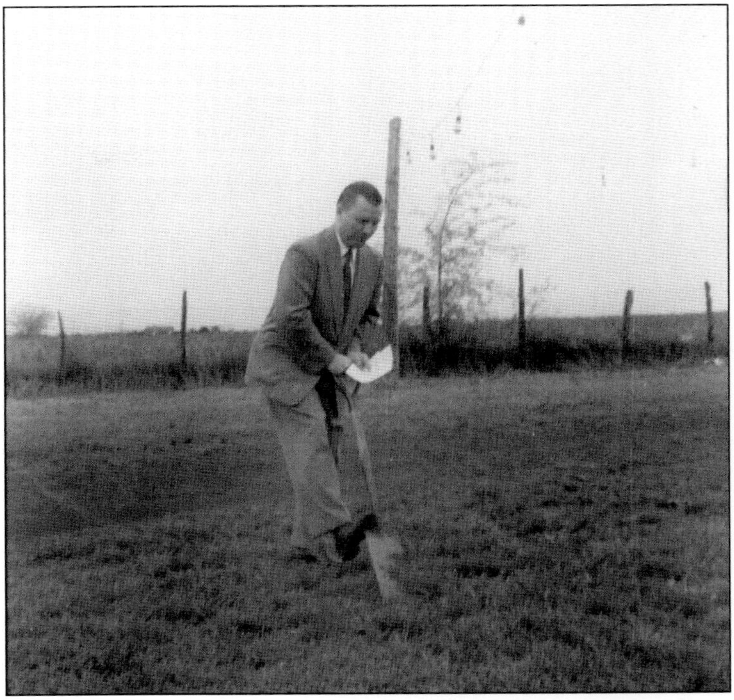

Breaking Ground. Membership of the Murphy Baptist Church dwindled during World War I, the Great Depression, and World War II. Services were held only two times a month, alternating with the Methodist church. Pastors were paid $10 per month. It was not until 1948 that the church again began to prosper and offer full-time services. Shown is Pastor Tom Ritzinger breaking ground for a new addition in April 1957. (Inez Daniel.)

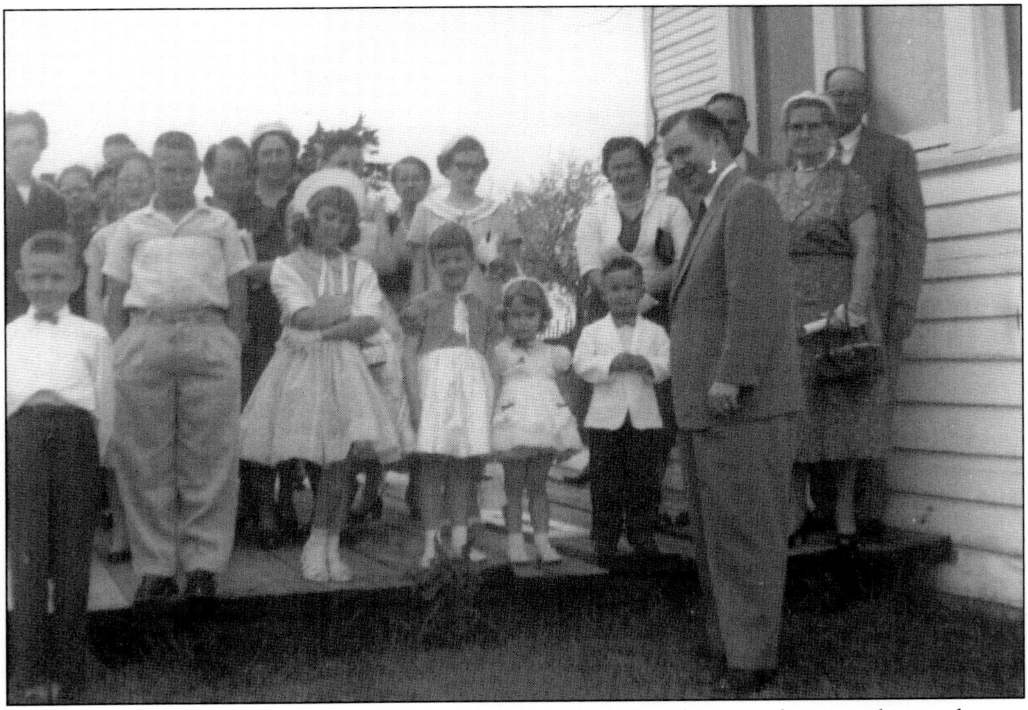

Attending the 1957 Ground-Breaking. Pictured in the photograph in random order are Madge Daniel, Randy Roller, Mary Bess Jones, Jim Ed Massey, Evelyn Lewis, Vera Roller, Brenda Dickerson, Nan Walker, Celia Daniel, Fran Roller, Shirley Massey, Cynthia Daniel, Kathy Daniel, David Massey, Norma Daniel, T.B. Ritzinger, Robert Daniel, and Mrs. and Mrs. Calmese. A catered lunch was served on the church grounds after the ground-breaking ceremony. (Inez Daniel.)

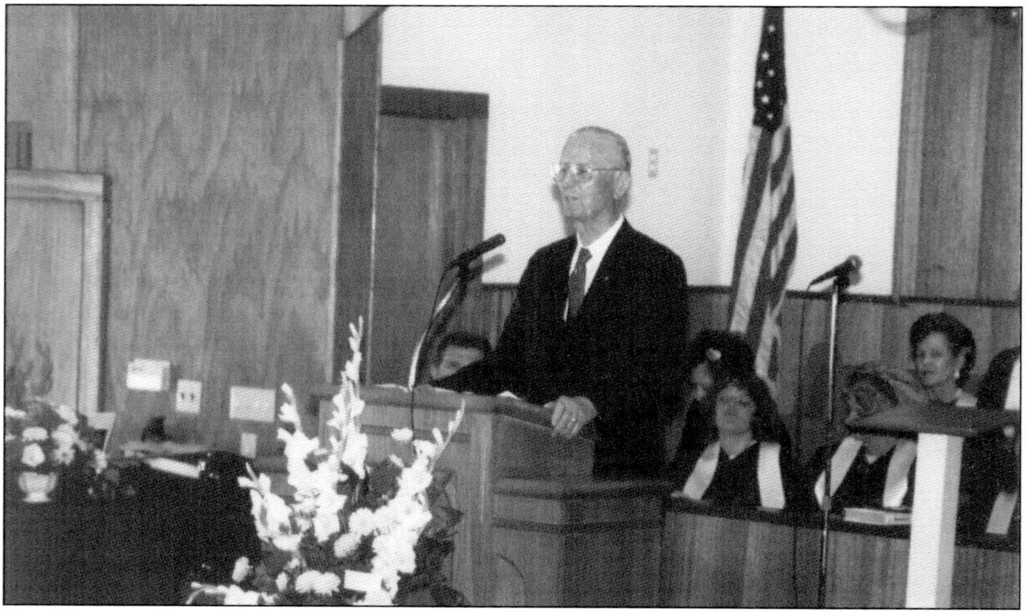

Dr. Charles Cockrell. Charles Cockrell was the son of Mae Cockrell, the founder of Murphy Baptist Church. He received strong Biblical training in the church and decided to become a minister. He attended Baylor University during the Depression and paid his way by pastoring a small church. He later served as minister of the First Baptist Church of Garland for 28 years. (Inez Daniel.)

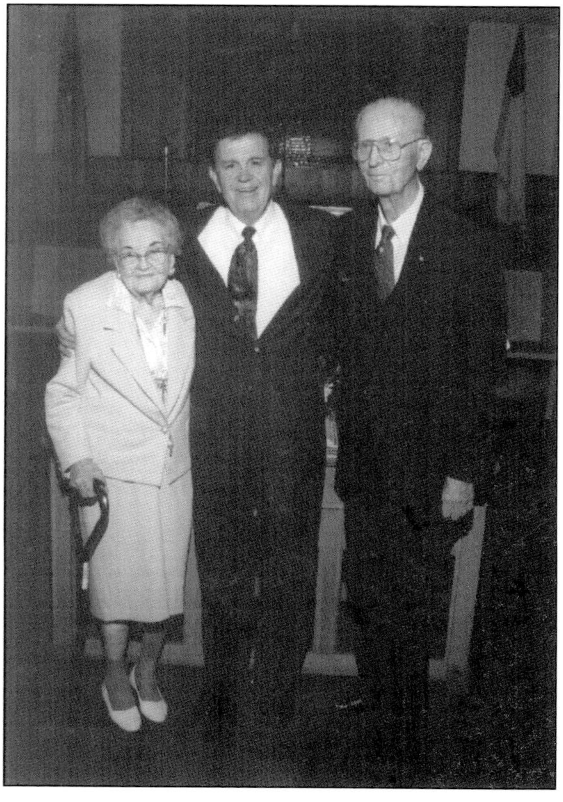

Dedication, 1989. Shown celebrating the dedication of the stained glass windows and a bell honoring W.O. Daniel are Nona Greer, Pastor John Max Cox (center), and Milton Greer. Milton and his brother Luther grew up in the congregation and became preachers. Other members who became preachers were Ernest Massey and Clay Walker. (Inez Daniel.)

EDITH BOYD STUART. Edith attended school in Murphy and taught school there before she became a missionary to China. She was a member of the Murphy Baptist Church, which was considered a training ground for the ministry. In this photograph, she is pictured with her husband, Malcolm. They served as missionaries in China, Japan, and Hawaii and reared two sons who became preachers. (Inez Daniel.)

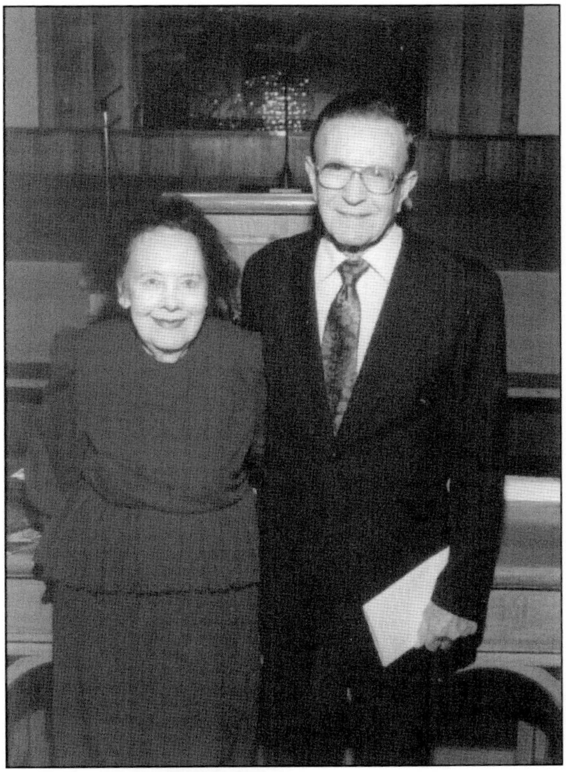

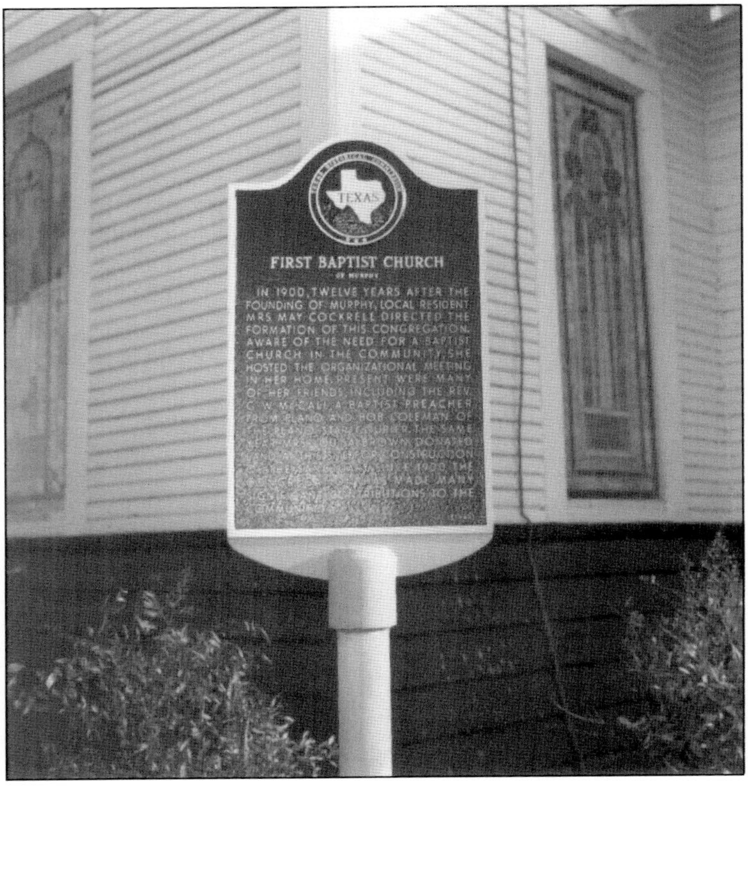

HISTORIC CHURCH MARKER. In 1979, some church members wanted to build a new church on Murphy Road; however, other members wanted to remain in the historic church. They renamed the church the First Baptist Church of Murphy. The Collin County Historical Commission dedicated a Texas Historic Marker for the congregation in 1982. The church remained at the same location until 2010. (Inez Daniel.)

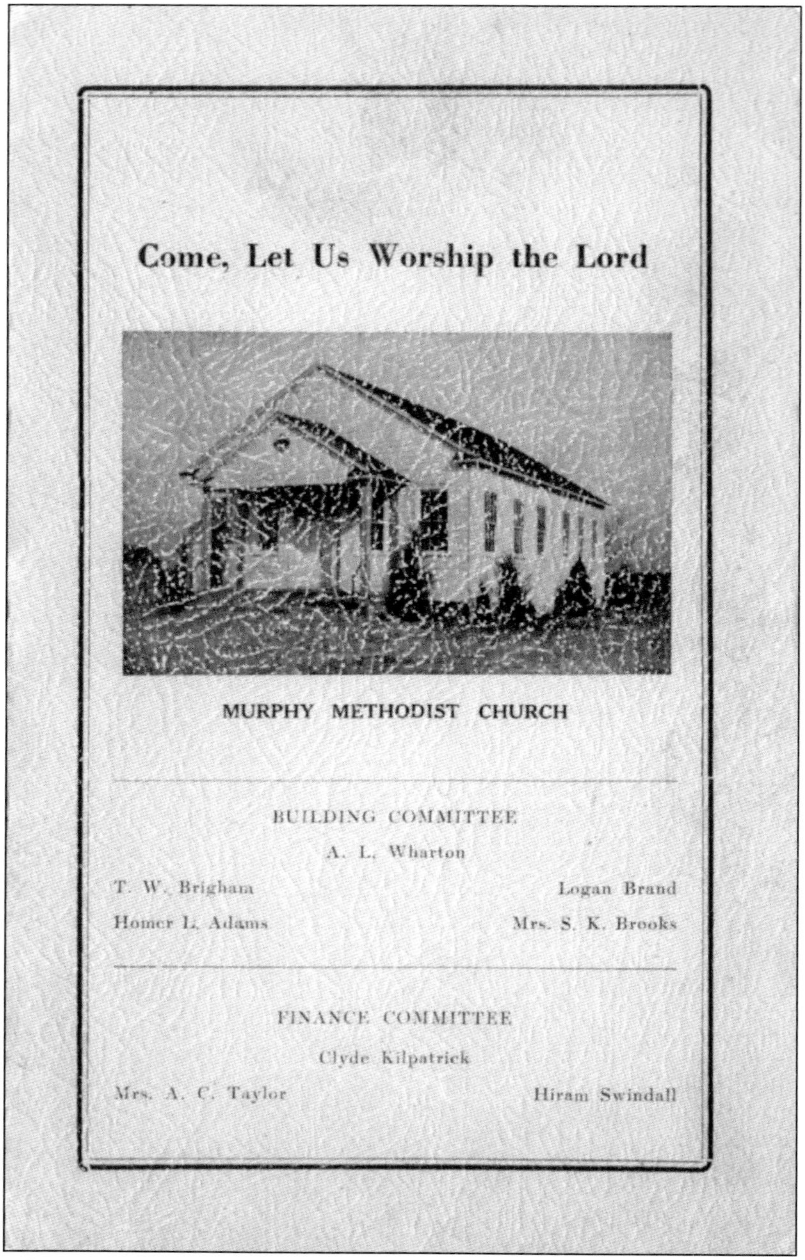
Come, Let Us Worship the Lord

MURPHY METHODIST CHURCH

BUILDING COMMITTEE

A. L. Wharton

T. W. Brigham — Logan Brand

Homer L. Adams — Mrs. S. K. Brooks

FINANCE COMMITTEE

Clyde Kilpatrick

Mrs. A. C. Taylor — Hiram Swindall

METHODIST CHURCH DEDICATION PROGRAM. The Murphy Methodist Church was first organized in 1897, and S.Z. Ball was the first pastor. The Methodist church building was erected in the same year, and Johnnie King was the first Sunday school superintendent. Prior to building the church, the Methodists met in homes. James M. Parker was one of their earliest pastors. The first Methodist camp meeting was held in 1872 at Pegues Springs on Dublin Road. People came from Murphy, Parker, and Dublin in their wagons packed with food in order to sing and worship. The meetings lasted a week, and people camped around the springs. In the 1940s, a new church was built on Murphy Road near the Murphy School. The program pictured above showed the church building, and Felix Kindel was the pastor. T.W. Brigham was listed as the church school superintendent, and Mrs. A.L. Wharton was the pianist. (Barbara Taylor Bennie.)

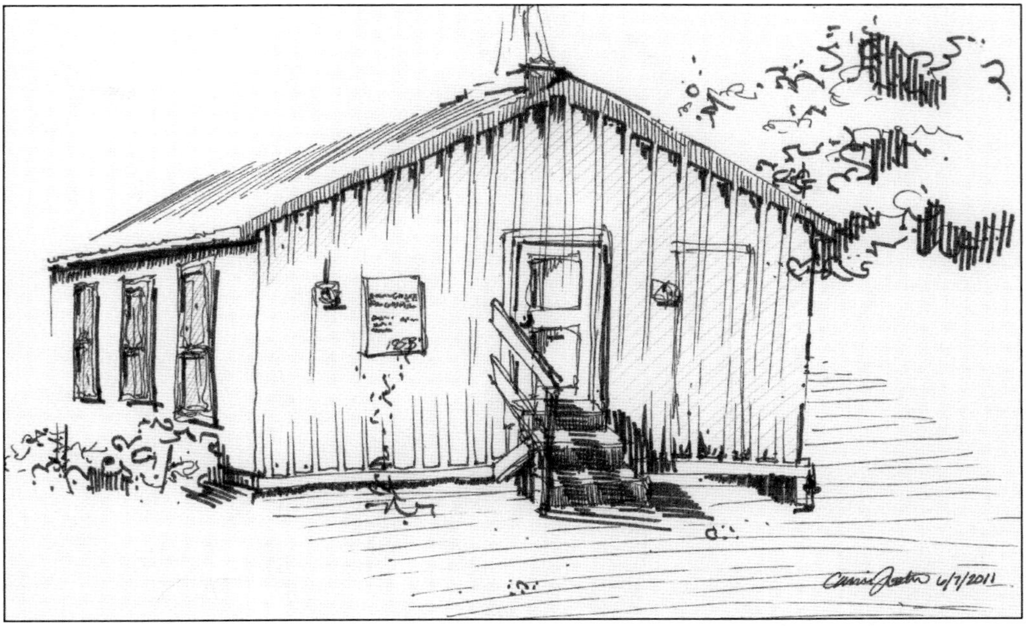

SHADY GROVE CHURCH. The first church for African Americans serving the Murphy community was started on the Berryman farm located on East FM 544 between Murphy and Wylie. In 1939, Ollie Mae Halbert, who lived on Brand Road, asked a Baptist minister from Dallas to help her organize a church for African Americans in the Murphy community. Neal Callin was the first pastor. The church burned in the 1980s. (Carrie Fisher.)

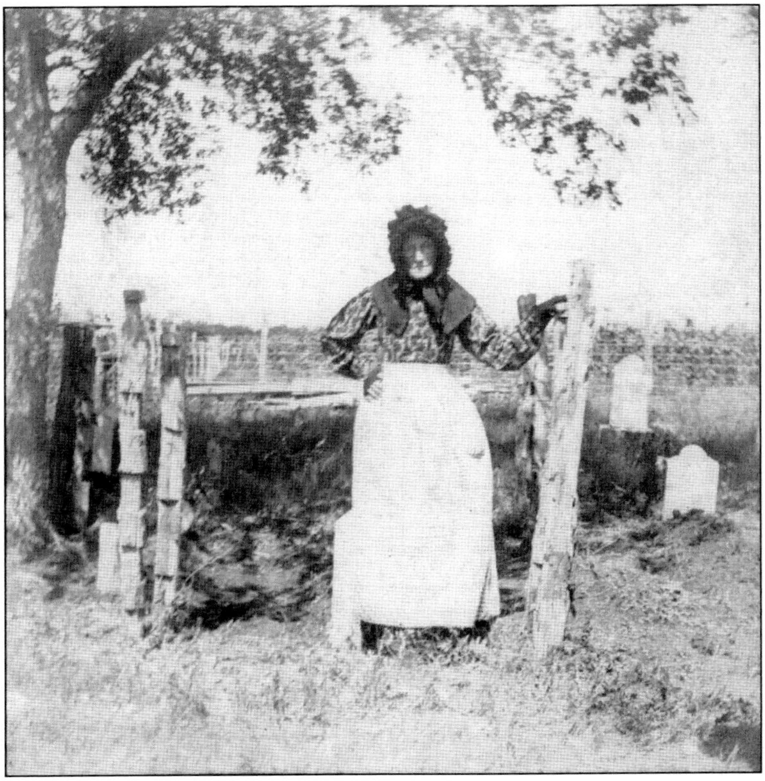

JANE MCMILLEN TAYLOR. In this photograph, Jane Taylor, in her bonnet, is cleaning the Decatur-Maxwell-Murphy Cemetery, where many of her relatives were buried. May was the time for cleaning and decorating the cemeteries in Murphy because it was between last planting and first harvest. This was a family event with singing, speeches, and prayers. Often, a picnic was held outside the graveyard. (Barbara Taylor Bennie.)

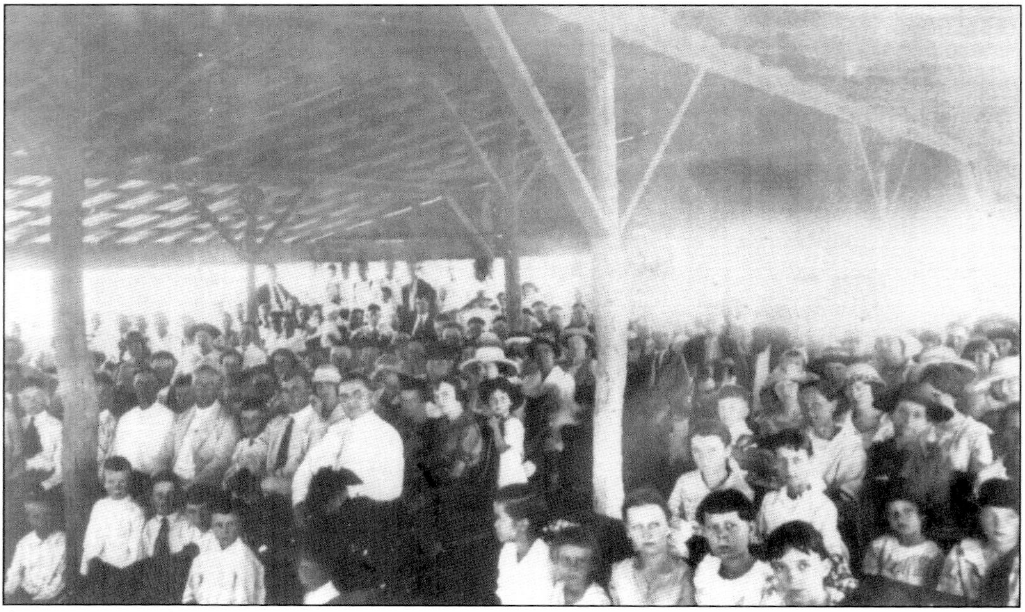

Church and Corinth Tabernacle. The Corinth Presbyterian Church was the first church organized in Murphy on August 2, 1846, in the home of Comfort Allen and Lydia McMillen. It is not known how long the church met in homes or when the first church was built, because the church records between 1846 and 1873 are missing. By 1921, when the photograph below was taken, the congregation had built a church at Corinth, north of Murphy and south of Parker Road along Maxwell's Branch. As shown in the photograph, revival meetings were often held in a tabernacle set up on the south side of the church. The meetings were crowded, and many had to sit on the ground outside the tabernacle. In 1923, the congregation built the current church on Parker Road on land donated by Clairborne Christopher Gregory and his wife, Eugenia. The church is one of the oldest in Collin County and is now 165 years old. (Both, Corinth Presbyterian Church.)

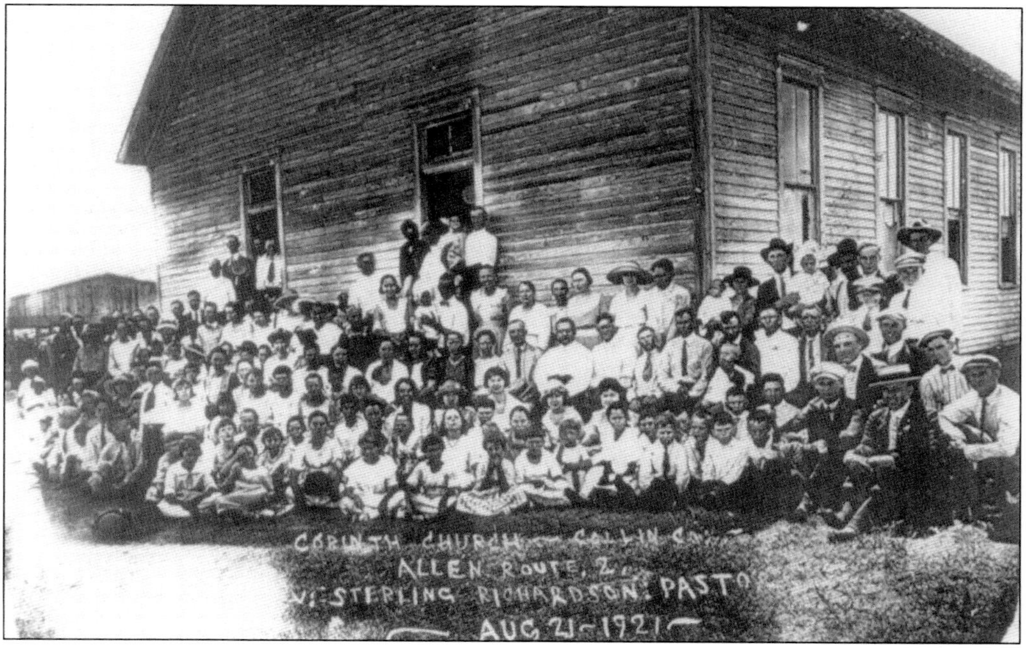

Five

Local Government
Leaders and Services

The first formal government was not organized until the 1950s; however, this did not mean citizens were not involved in politics. Early citizens were declared Democrats voting in local and federal elections. On November 7, 1877, H.D. Maxwell wrote that he "went to Presidential Election."

Some citizens of Murphy served during the American Civil War and later joined the United Confederate Veterans (UCV). The UCV, organized in 1889, was a veterans' organization for Confederate soldiers that was similar to the Grand Army of the Republic, an organization for Union veterans. Veterans from Murphy attended the UCV reunions.

Prior to organized government, Murphy was dependent on Collin County for roads and police protection. Surrounding cities provided fire protection. The first government in Murphy was established as a general law charter on February 9, 1958, with the swearing in of the newly elected officials. The first mayor was A.F. Ingram, and the first aldermen were W.O. Daniel, Mack Turner, E.L. Wright, Henry Jones, and H.A. Swindall.

In 1973, the city began to develop a master plan for growth and signed a lease on the Murphy School to remodel and use the building as a community center, fire station, and for town hall meetings. In 2003, Murphy developed a home rule charter. Roy Bentle was elected mayor, and councilmen were Michael Ashby, David Forehand, Bob Russell, David Trudeau, and Kent Bogdan.

The Murphy Volunteer Fire Department was organized in August 1973. Mayor Tom Clevenger purchased a 1949 pumper truck at an auction in Odessa, Texas. Under the direction of city councilman Cyril Poindexter, a volunteer fire department was established. The first elected officers were: Carl Davis, fire chief; Don Duncan, assistant chief; Jack Russell, captain; and Vernon Downing, secretary-treasurer. Volunteers were on call 24 hours a day, seven days a week.

The police department was formed in 1980. Fred Garwacki became the first part-time officer and used his personal vehicle to patrol the city. Ben Ferguson became a full-time officer in 1987. Dennis Perkle, another officer, resigned to become the chief of police in Parker. Garwacki was named the first Murphy police chief.

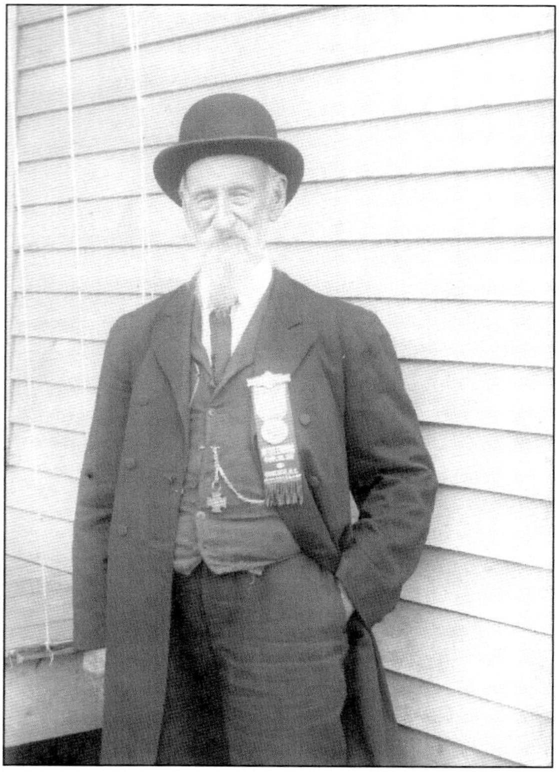

William Kidd. William Henry Kidd was born in 1831 in South Carolina. He enlisted in Jenkins's Infantry and served in the Battle of the Wilderness and the Battle of Chaffin's Farm in Virginia where he was wounded. He was proud of his service to the Confederacy and attended many of the Confederate conventions. In this photograph, he wears his Confederate Southern Cross medal. (S. Michael Boyd.)

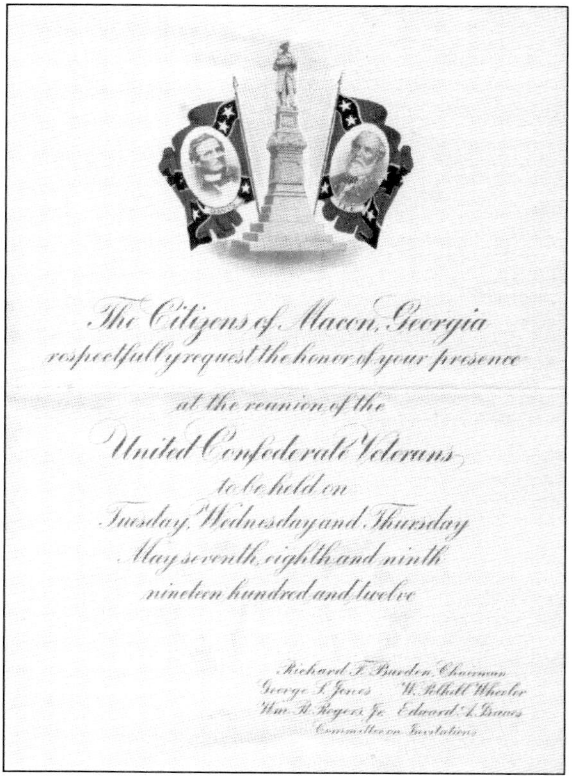

Invitation, 1912. The citizens of Georgia issued this invitation to attend the UCV convention held in Macon, Georgia, on May 7–9, 1912. The invitation was in the memorabilia of the Albert Taylor family. It was decorated with the picture of Jefferson Davis, the president of the Confederacy; the Confederate flag; and a picture of Robert E. Lee, a general of the Confederate army. (Barbara Taylor Bennie.)

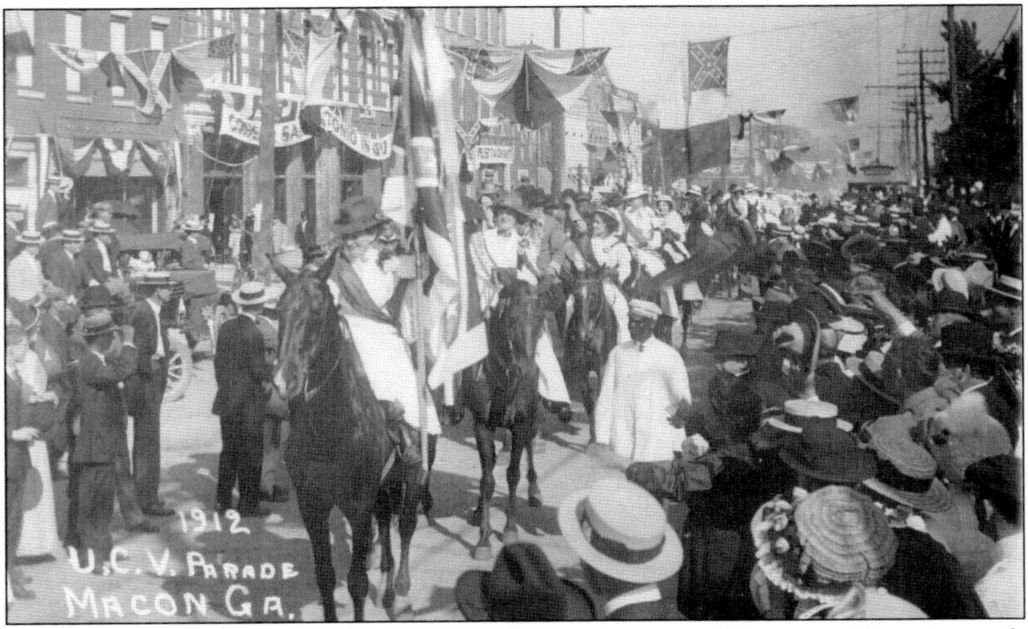

POSTCARDS OF 1912 UCV CONVENTION AND DELEGATION FROM TENNESSEE. These postcards were from the May 7–9, 1912, convention held in Macon, Georgia. UCV conventions were a time of great celebration, as shown by the parade of both women and men on horseback and seated in cars. Storefronts were decorated with flags, and citizens, dressed in their straw hats, suits, and best finery, lined the streets to enjoy the parade. This parade was led by the delegation from Tennessee. The first UCV convention was held in Chattanooga, Tennessee, from July 3 to 5, 1890. Veterans of both armies were invited to attend. The first commander-in-chief was Gen. John B. Gordon, who was a Confederate soldier, governor of Georgia, and later US senator. The organization gathered data for an impartial history of the Civil War, preserved the memories of the soldiers, and promoted the ties of friendship among the men who served. (Both, Barbara Taylor Bennie.)

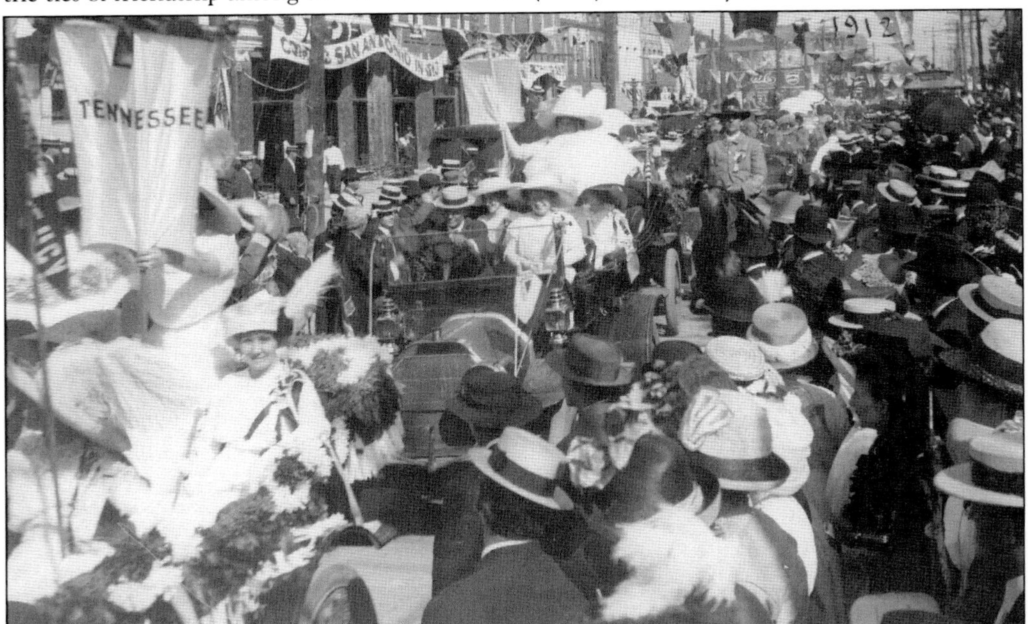

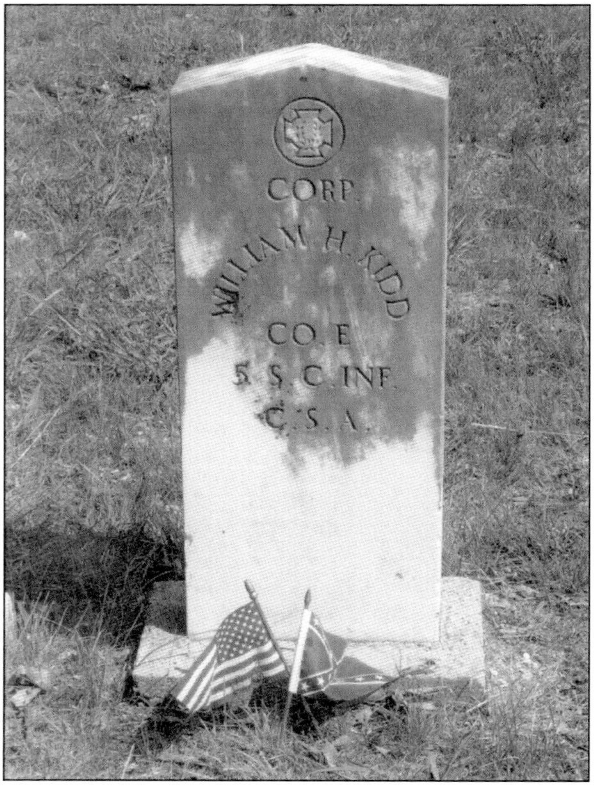

KIDD GRAVESTONE. William Kidd was a corporal in the Civil War and returned to his wife, Maggie, and three children when the war ended. He opened a store called W.H. Kidd, Groceries and Confectioneries, which he ran for over 20 years. He came to Texas in 1890 to live with his daughter Maggie Kidd Boyd. Kidd died in 1916 and was and buried in the Maxwell-Decatur-Murphy Cemetery. (Murphy City Hall.)

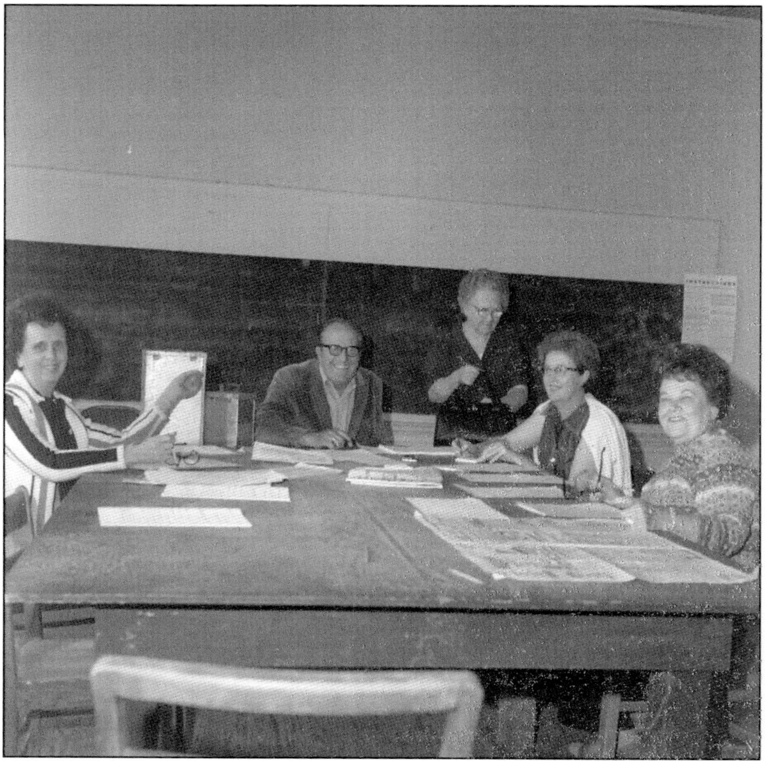

VOTING. The old Murphy School served as a voting place for citizens until the new government facilities were opened. Pictured is Madge Daniel (left), who served as the election judge for a number of years. In 1920, there were 85 male voters in Murphy. After women received the vote in 1922, there were 153 male and female voters. (Brenda Barnes Coleman.)

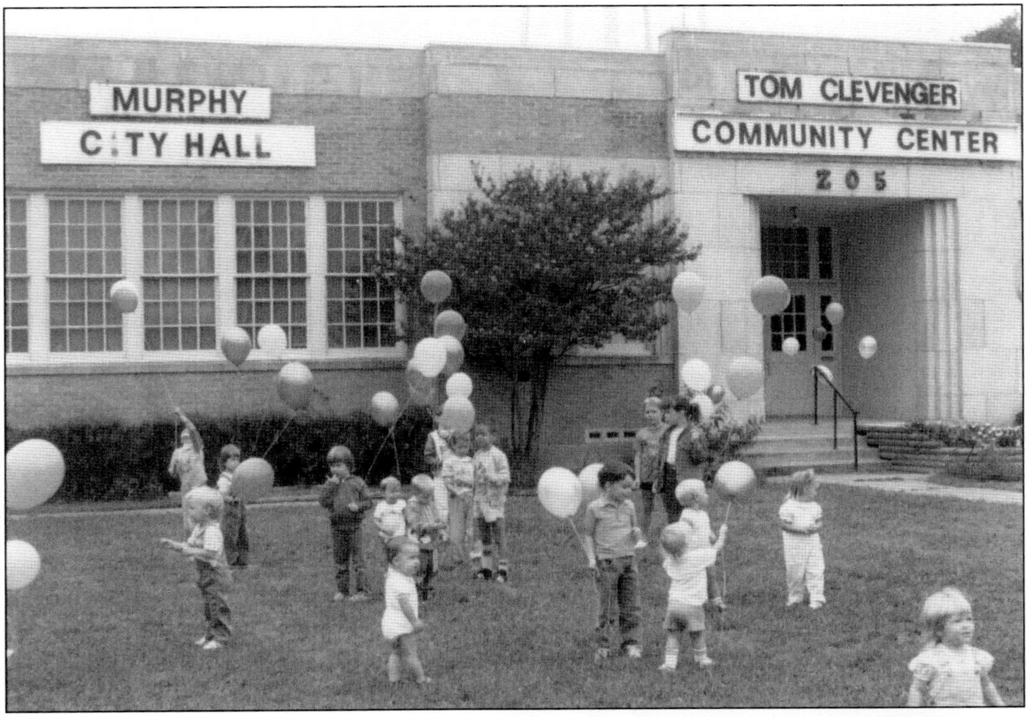

Tom Clevenger Community Center. The Murphy School, built in 1938, was one of the 1,634 schools built by the Works Progress Administration. The WPA was a national agency created by Pres. Franklin D. Roosevelt as a relief measure to increase employment during the Great Depression. The Murphy School closed in 1950 and was converted to the Tom Clevenger Community Center. (Murphy City Hall.)

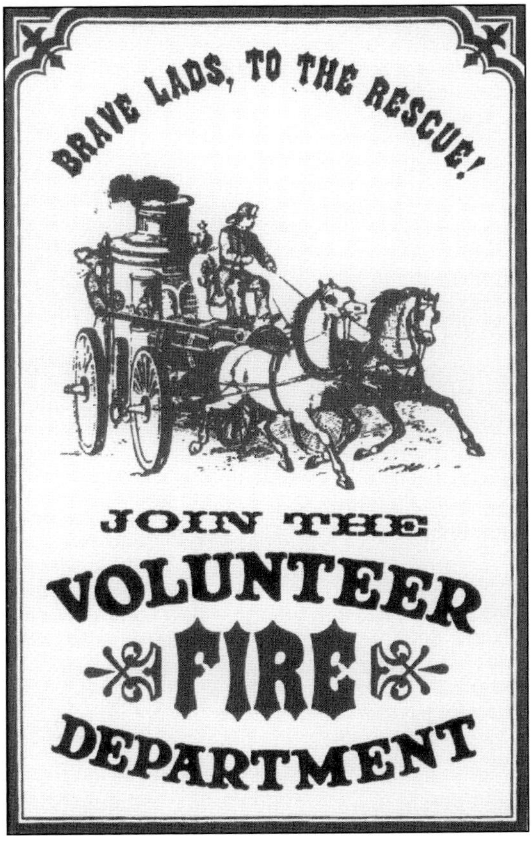

Fire Department Volunteer Emblem. After organizing in 1973, the volunteers grew in number and began training. Their first job was to convert one room of the Murphy School into a garage and fire station to house their only fire truck, Engine No. 8. In 1974, they purchased a dispatch system with three mobile units for cars and 14 monitors to use in the homes of volunteers. (Murphy Fire Department.)

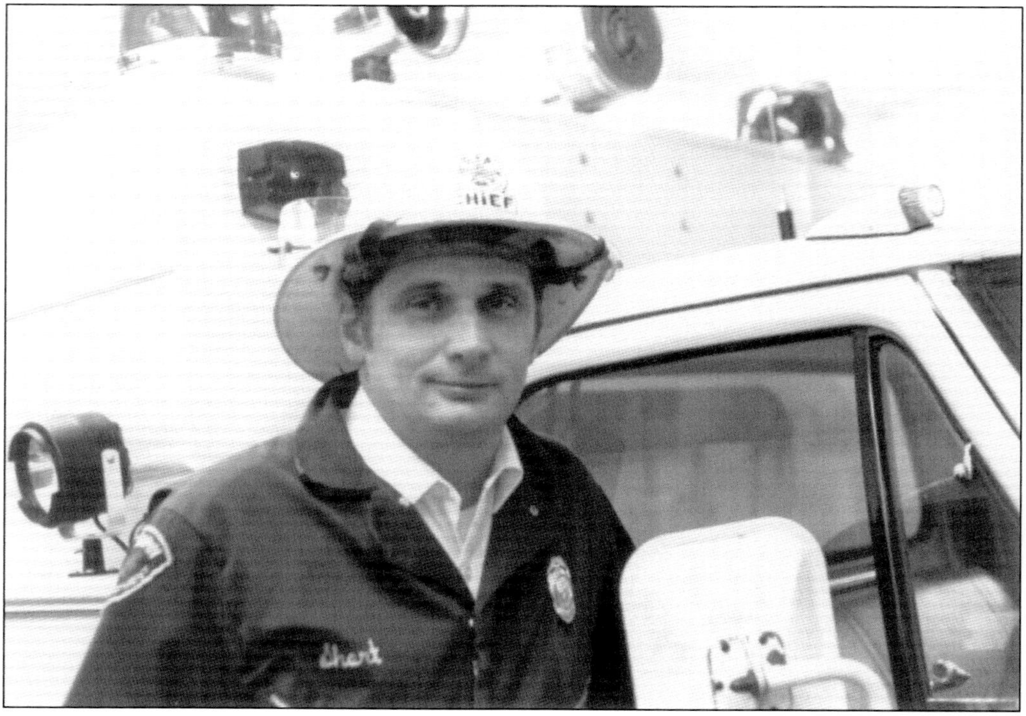

CHIEF DON SHORT. Chief Short succeeded Tim Arion and Carl Davis as chief of the volunteer fire department. In the early years, volunteers handled routine calls to extinguish brush fires. Occasionally, they were called to round-up Samson, a bull who fancied escaping from his pasture along Murphy Road. One day, a concrete truck hit Samson, and the department was called to bury the bull. (Don Short.)

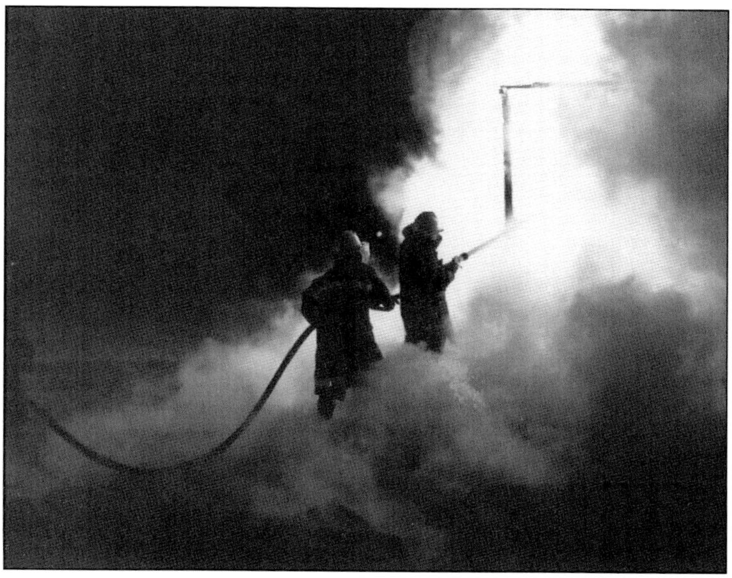

CONTROLLED BURN. Murphy city councilman Cyril Poindexter trained the first volunteers. The volunteer fire department used vacant houses, which were donated, to practice in a controlled burn environment. The old abandoned Turner house, which sat across the street from the fire station, was one such house used for training. (Murphy Fire Department.)

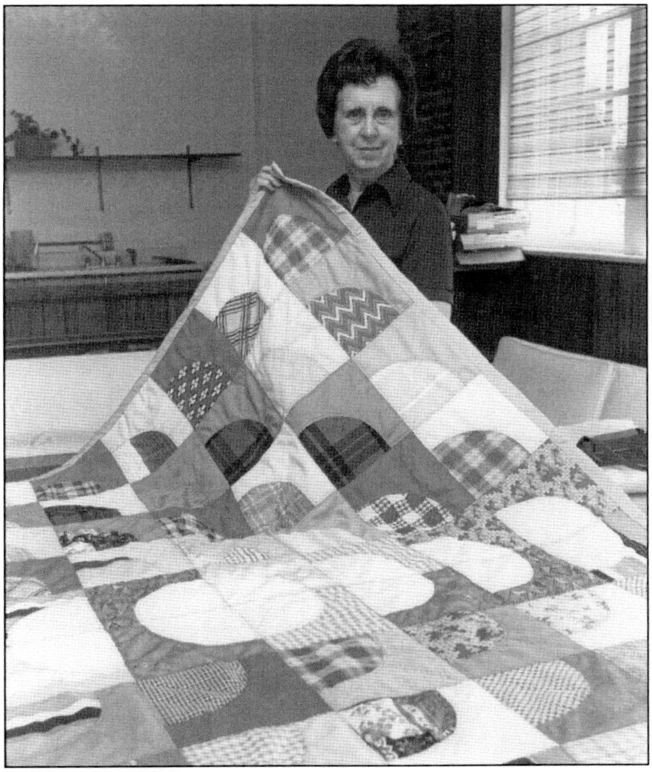

Madge Daniel. The Murphy Women's Volunteer Auxiliary was first organized in 1979 to help obtain equipment and supplies for the fire department. In this photograph, Madge Daniel displayed a quilt that was raffled off at the Murphy Fair to aid the needs of the department. By 1980, the auxiliary aided both the fire and police departments. (Inez Daniel.)

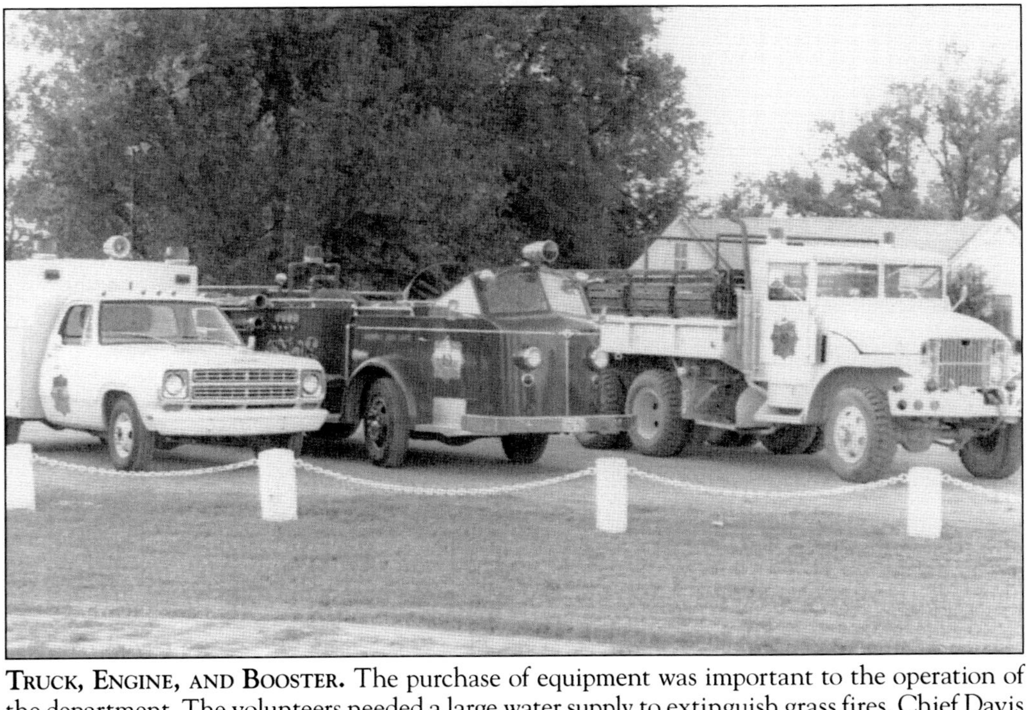

Truck, Engine, and Booster. The purchase of equipment was important to the operation of the department. The volunteers needed a large water supply to extinguish grass fires. Chief Davis purchased two army surplus military trucks. The volunteers used one for parts, and the other was modified for a booster truck. The truck was named "Ole Yeller." (Don Short.)

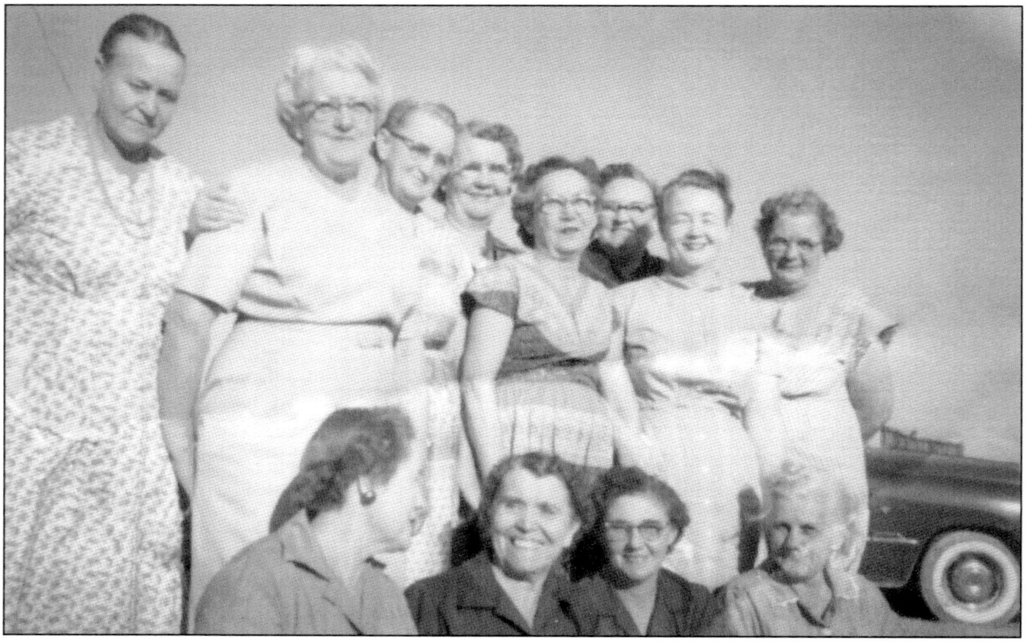

Murphy and Parker Home Demonstration Club, 1960. Home demonstration clubs began in Texas in 1912. One early effort was to organize clubs for rural girls and teach them homemaking skills, and by 1917, demonstration clubs expanded to include women. The focus during both world wars was production and food preservation. In the 1950s and 1960s, the emphasis changed to meet the needs of employed women, since fewer families lived in rural areas. The clubs focused on leadership roles and community service. Parker and Murphy women met in area homes to socialize and engage in community service. Shown above are, from left to right, (first row) Mrs. Gray, Maude McCreary, Margret Hogge, and Billie Fondern; (second row) Mrs. Williams, Mrs. Gatlin, unidentified, Mina Hogge, three unidentified, and Emma Spears. Pictured below are, from left to right, (first row) Evelyn Spears, three unidentified, and Florence Spears; (second row) Mrs. Williams, unidentified, Maude McCreary, Billie Fondern, and Margaret Hogge. (Both, Zada McCreary Nicholson.)

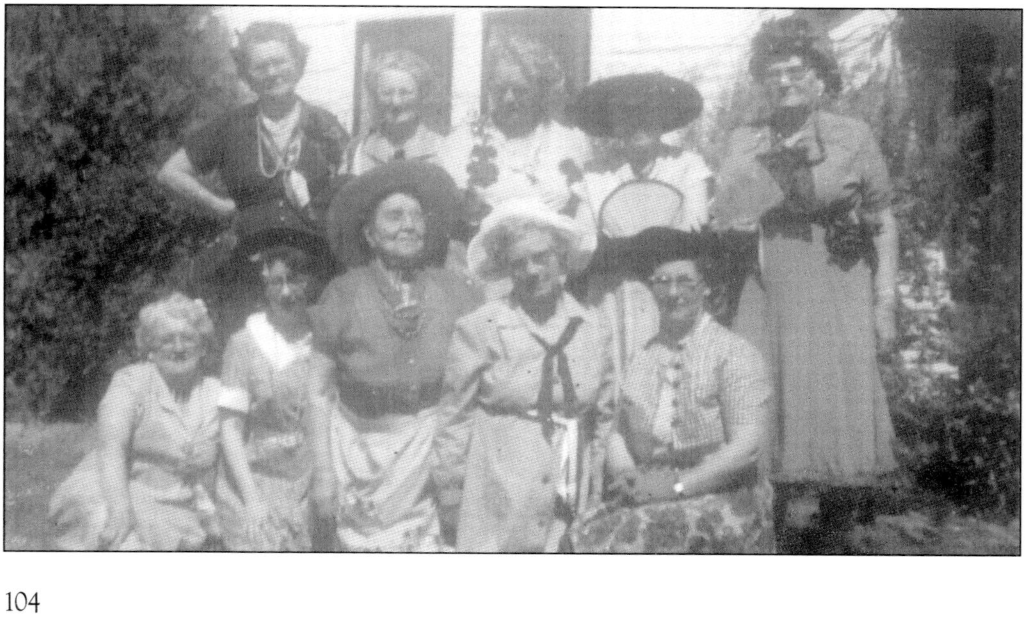

Six

MURPHY
THEN AND NOW

Settlers of the Peters Colony arrived in 1846 to find inexpensive and abundant farmland. Talk of the railroad coming began as early as 1857, but it did not arrive until 1888. From the 1880s through the 1950s, Murphy was a prosperous farming community, and the population, though small, was stable. Neighbors grew close as they helped each other. Farm equipment, horses, and mules were shared as easily as a family meal. A sense of community grew as churches and schools were built. Life in the rural community was filled with hard work, but citizens could always depend on family, friends, and neighbors. The advent of World War I, the Great Depression, and World War II brought new problems. The demand for farm mechanization and war machines increased and job opportunities in surrounding towns and larger cities led to a decrease in population.

Today, Murphy is a fast-growing suburb trying to balance the atmosphere consistent with small-town America and the demand of increasing population. New subdivisions create the need for more services, and revenue must increase to provide for the demands. Citizens want city services comparable to their neighbors in surrounding cities without raising taxes or adding additional businesses. A central business district, started in 2008, sits along the intersection of Murphy Road and FM 544. Ironically, this area is located along the same railroad route started in 1888, which necessitated building stores, gins, and a bank near the railroad depot.

The faces of pioneer families were seemingly erased from Murphy. Prairie and timber gave way to farmland. Farmland gave way to home development, and few remnants of the past exist. Gone are the gins, stores, streets, bank, onion shed, train depot, churches, and numerous other buildings that embraced the history of the community. The Murphy Baptist Church, four cemeteries, and the old Murphy School building remain.

Thomas A. Kempis said, "To-day the man is here; to-morrow he hath disappeared. And when he is out of sight, quickly also is he out of mind." Perhaps these photographs will preserve the faces and places of Murphy so the town's history is not forgotten.

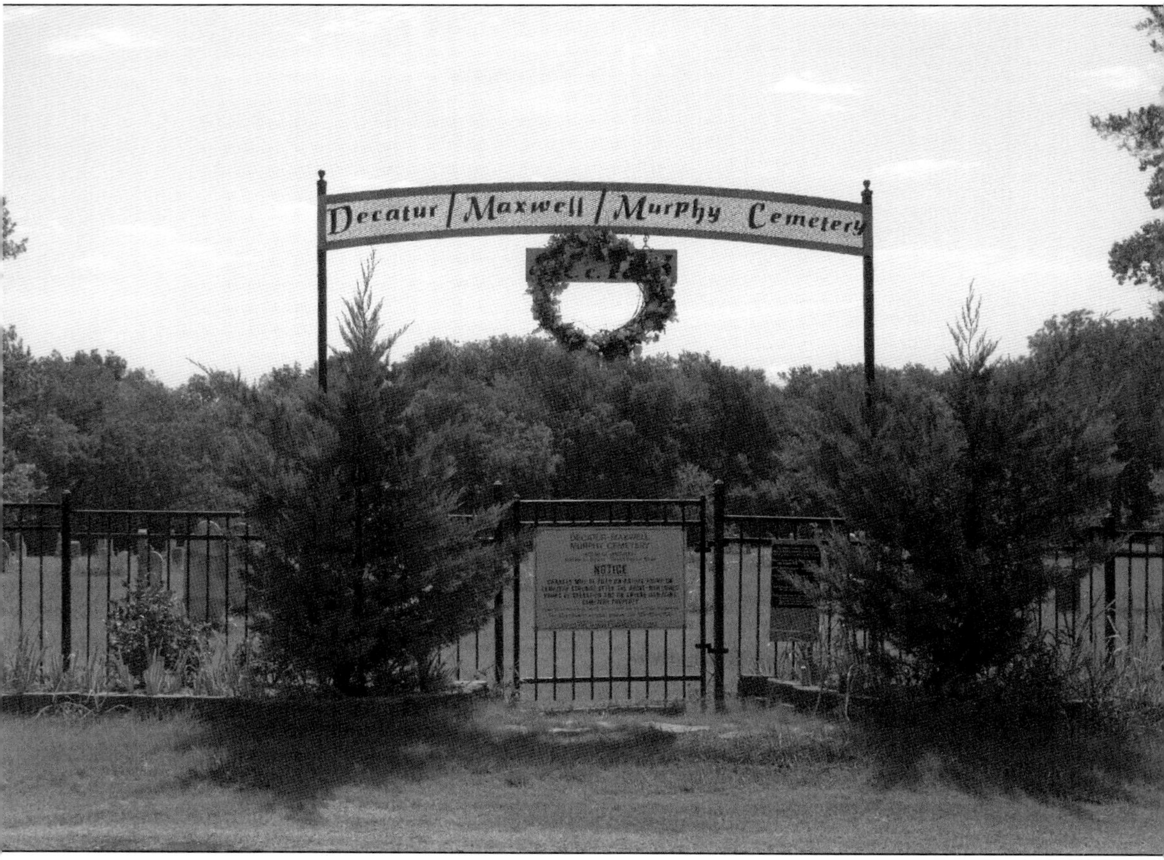

DECATUR-MAXWELL-MURPHY CEMETERY. This cemetery remains one of Murphy's most important links to the pioneers. It contains over 300 graves, and as a testament to the hard life in the early days of Murphy, one third of the graves are infants less than a year old at the time of their death. The earliest grave on record is that of Samuel McCreary in 1853. There are 15 known veterans, including the grave of a Black Hawk War veteran, a World War I veteran, a Union veteran, and 12 Confederate veterans. Today, the cemetery is well maintained by the Cemetery Association of Murphy. Each year, a Memorial Day celebration is held to honor the veterans and celebrate the history of the cemetery. Descendants of the early pioneers attend the ceremony. The photograph shows the cemetery as it is today. (Larry G. Taylor.)

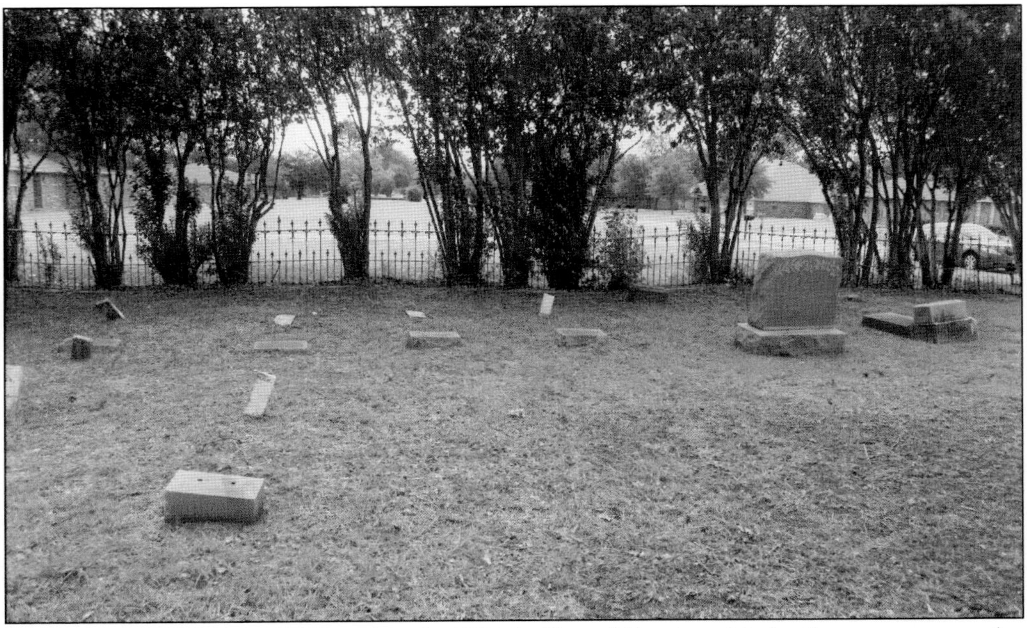

HERRING CEMETERY, 1989. Started in the 1870s by Daniel Herring, this family cemetery was also known as the Herring-Hogge Cemetery. Daniel Herring and his first wife, Mary Deck Herring, came from Illinois in 1848, as did his brothers Isaac and Sherwood. They received land grants near the Collin County–Dallas County Line, and Eli Hogge, another landholder, married Sarah Herring, the daughter of Daniel and Mary. (Brad Lapsley.)

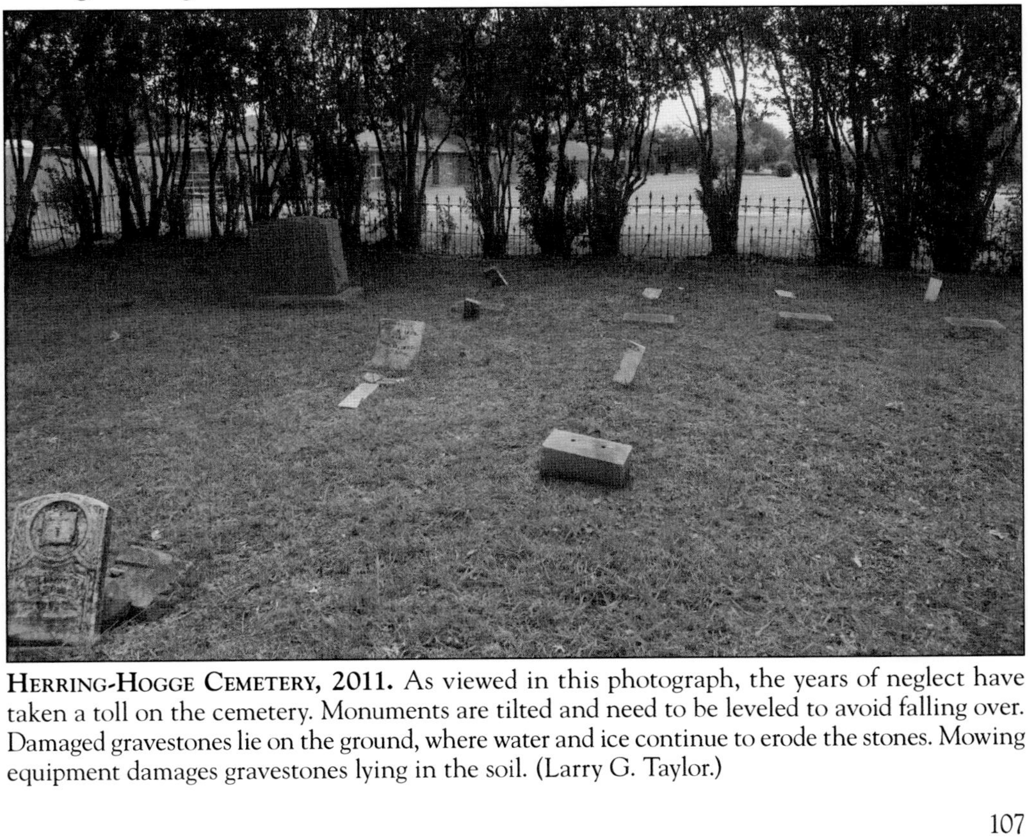

HERRING-HOGGE CEMETERY, 2011. As viewed in this photograph, the years of neglect have taken a toll on the cemetery. Monuments are tilted and need to be leveled to avoid falling over. Damaged gravestones lie on the ground, where water and ice continue to erode the stones. Mowing equipment damages gravestones lying in the soil. (Larry G. Taylor.)

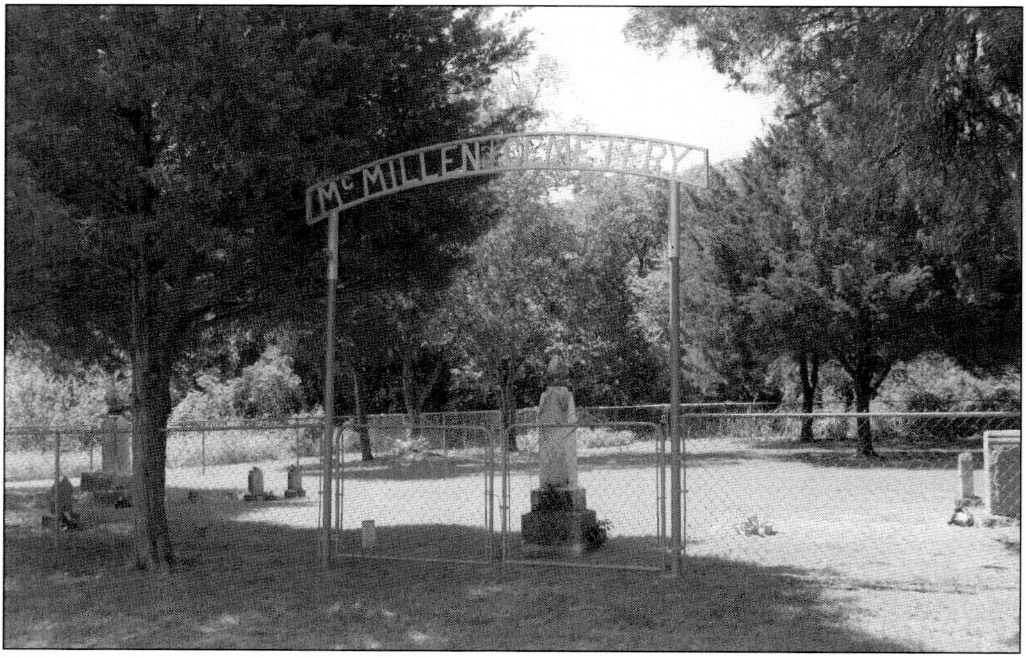

McMillen Cemetery. Comfort and Lydia McMillen deeded the McMillen Cemetery to Corinth Presbyterian Church of Parker in 1907. It is located on McMillen Road behind the McMillen High School and south of the McMillen home place. The cemetery has received the state historic cemetery designation. (Larry G. Taylor.)

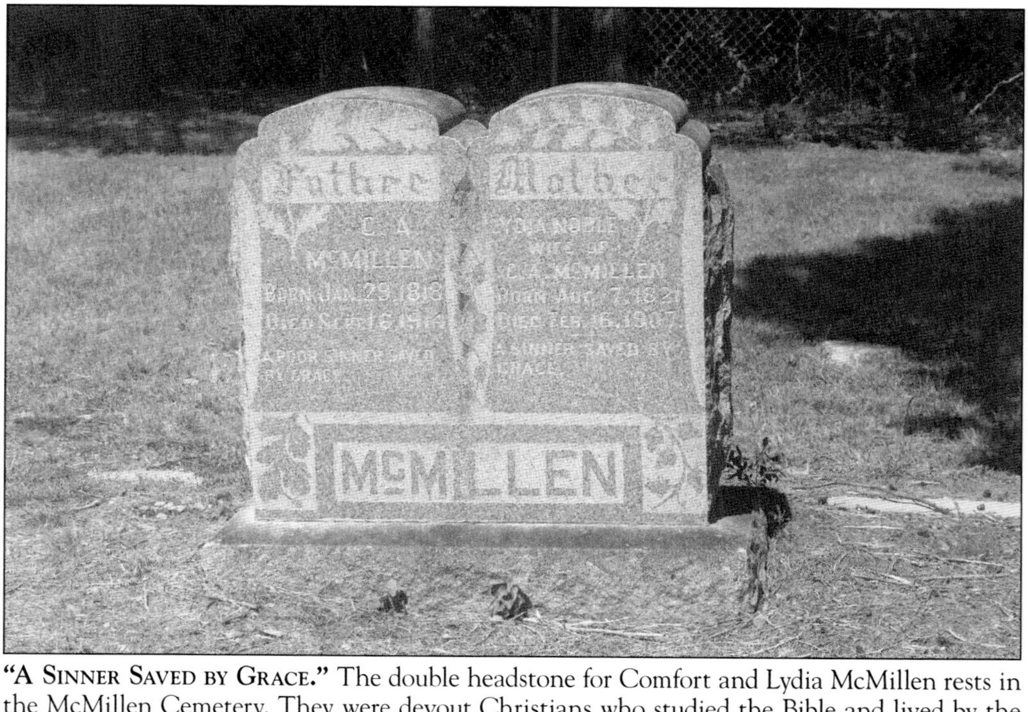

"A Sinner Saved by Grace." The double headstone for Comfort and Lydia McMillen rests in the McMillen Cemetery. They were devout Christians who studied the Bible and lived by the golden rule. A Bible verse is engraved on their headstones. There are many missing and broken stones in the cemetery, which is surrounded by tall cedar trees. (Larry G. Taylor.)

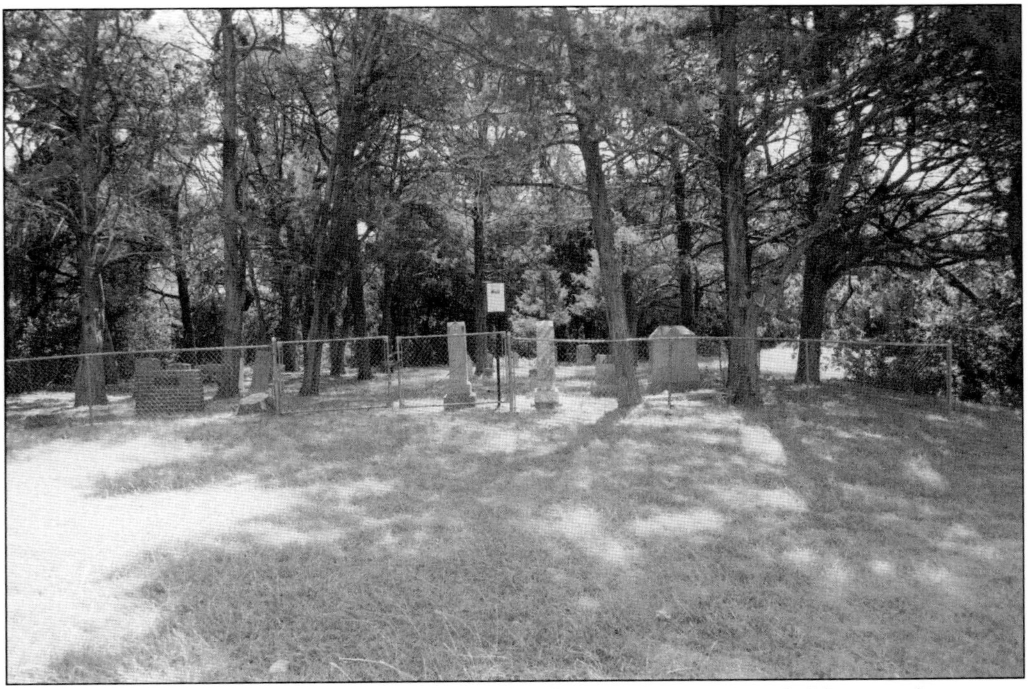

Murphy Family Cemetery. The cemetery is small and contains approximately 30 graves. Sometimes it is also called the Moulden Cemetery, because Susan Murphy married James L. Moulden. Cedar trees planted by the daughters of the Murphy family surround the cemetery. The cemetery is well maintained through the efforts of Dessie Haker. (Larry G. Taylor.)

William Murphy County Marker. This photograph, taken in 2011, displays the marker placed by the grave of William Murphy at the Murphy Family Cemetery, located on Maxwell Creek Road. William and Dorothy are buried in the cemetery on the land they claimed as part of the Peters Colony grant. (Robert L. Jenkins.)

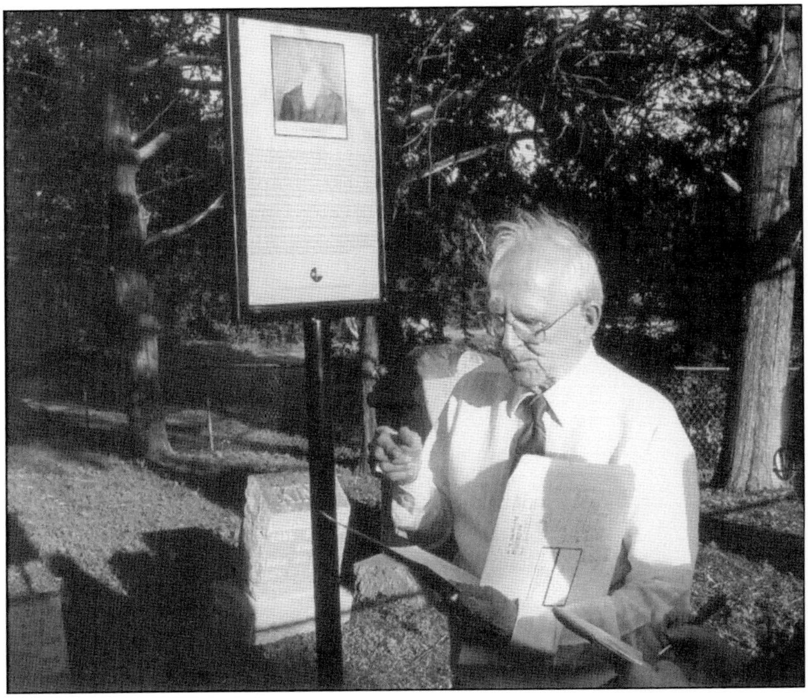

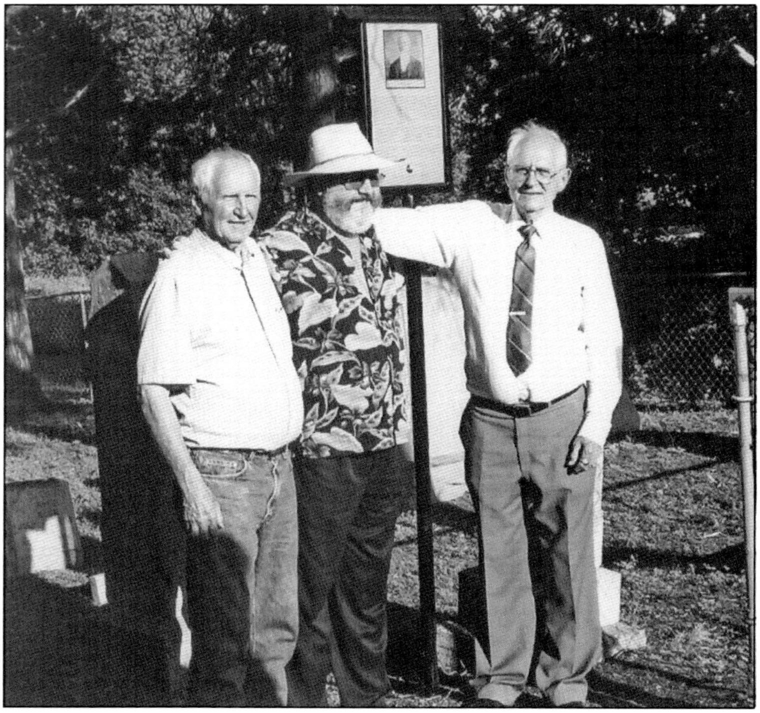

DESCENDANTS OF MURPHY FAMILY. The Collin County Historical Commission unveiled a county marker honoring William Andrew Murphy, the namesake of Murphy, Texas. Descendants attended from all over the state of Texas. Pictured are, from left to right, Roy Murphy, William Andrew Murphy IV, and Ray Murphy. Roy and Ray are the great-grandsons of William and Dorothy Murphy, and William Andrew IV is a great-great-grandson. (Robert L. Jenkins.)

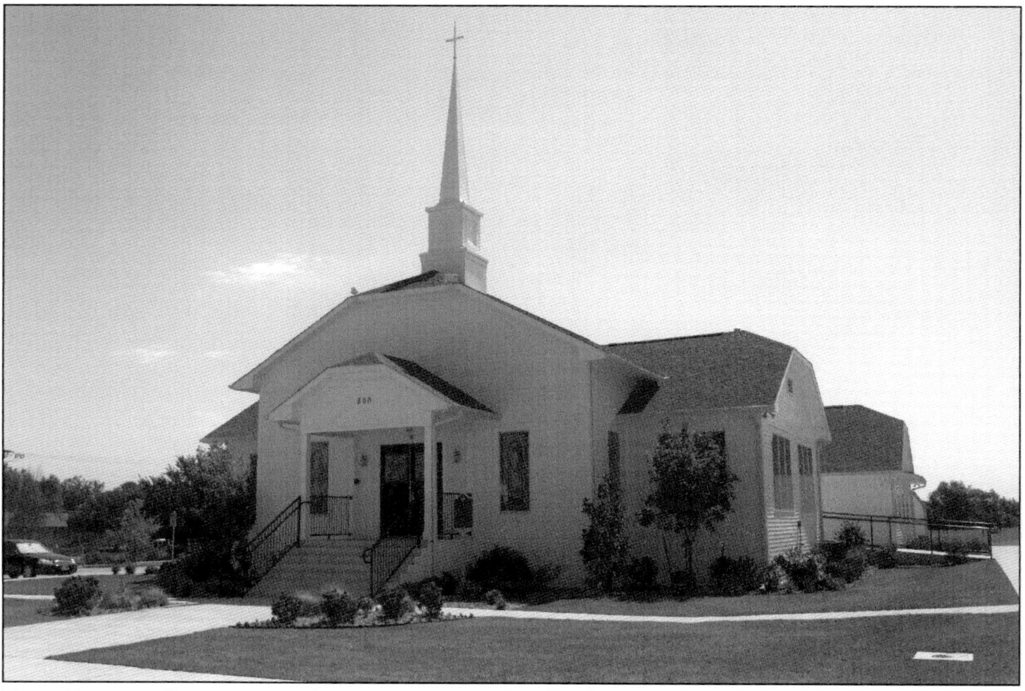

FIRST BAPTIST CHURCH OF MURPHY, 2011. Pictured is the century-old church in its new location at the intersection of North Murphy Road and McMillen Drive. After 108 years, the church moved from the location on FM 544 in the first phase of a new plan of growth and expansion. The church was completely renovated and remodeled, and the first service at the new location was on Christmas Eve 2009. (Larry G. Taylor.)

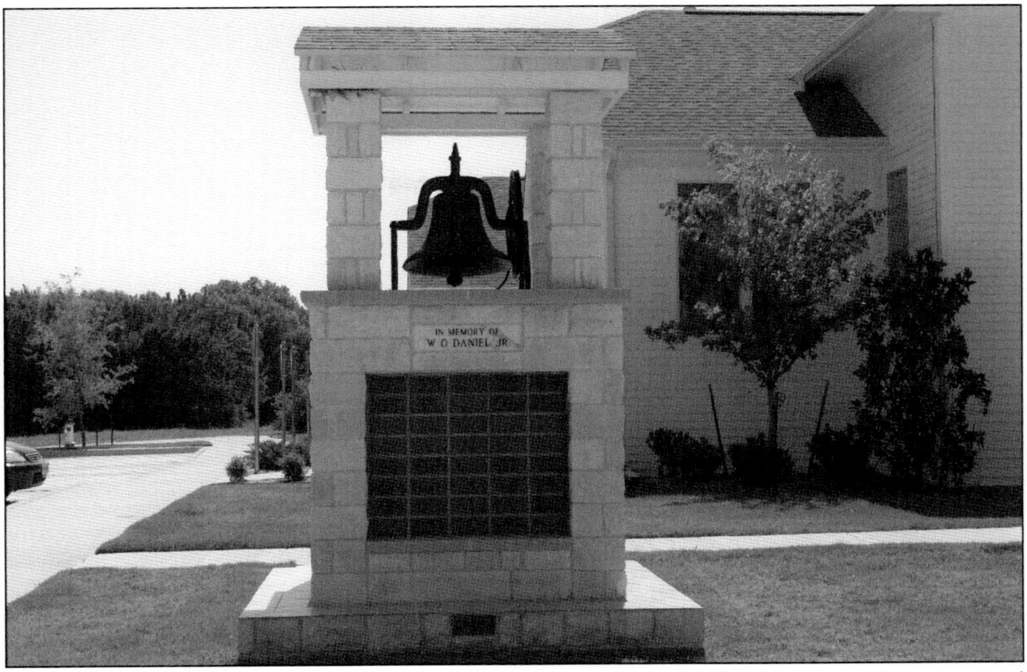

CHURCH BELL STILL RINGING. Shown in the photograph is the black bell that was first mounted in 1978 on a red and white brick structure bearing the name Murphy Baptist Church. The bell was a memorial given by the family and friends of the Daniel family in memory of W.O. Daniel. Today, it is relocated to a place of honor in front of the First Baptist Church of Murphy. (Larry G. Taylor.)

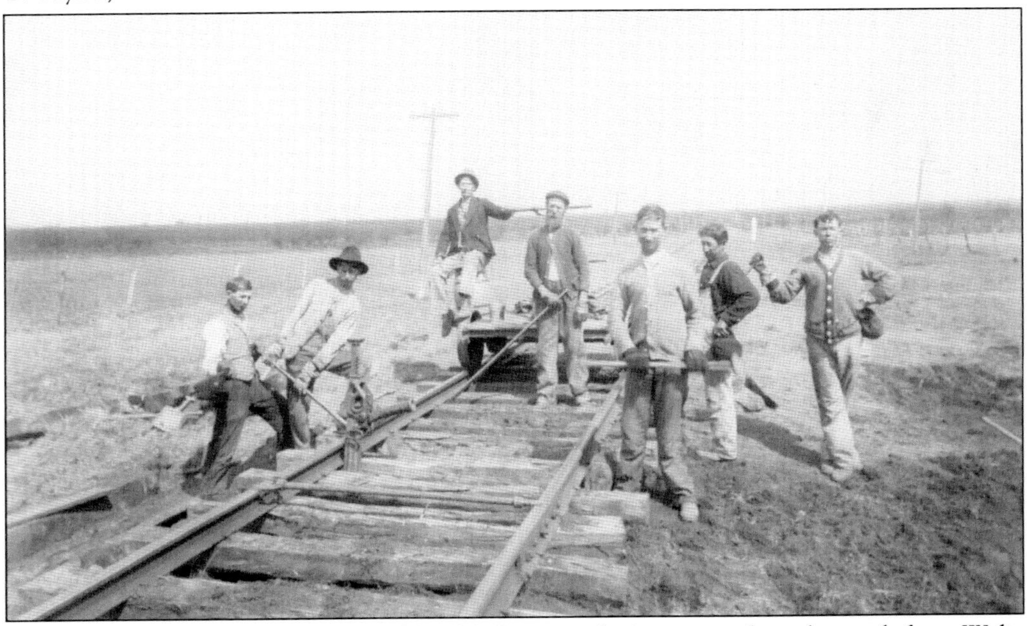

LAYING TRACK. Brothers George and Joe McGuire worked on extending the track from Wylie west to Murphy along FM 544. Posed in the photograph are George, with the beard standing on the track in front of the work cart, and Joe, standing front center and to the right of the track. Other workers in the photograph are unidentified. (Mike Massey.)

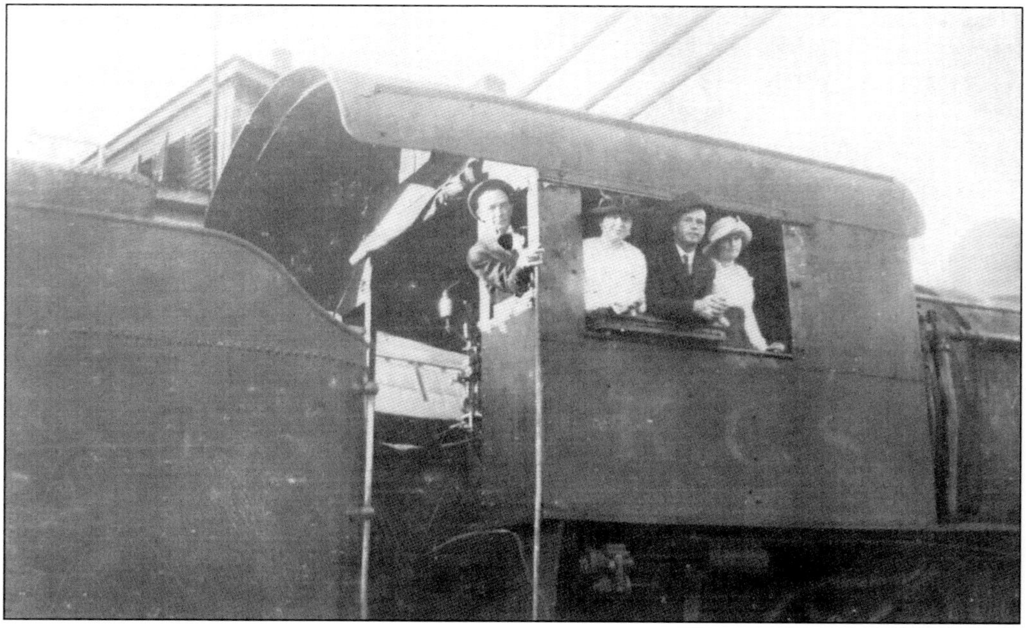

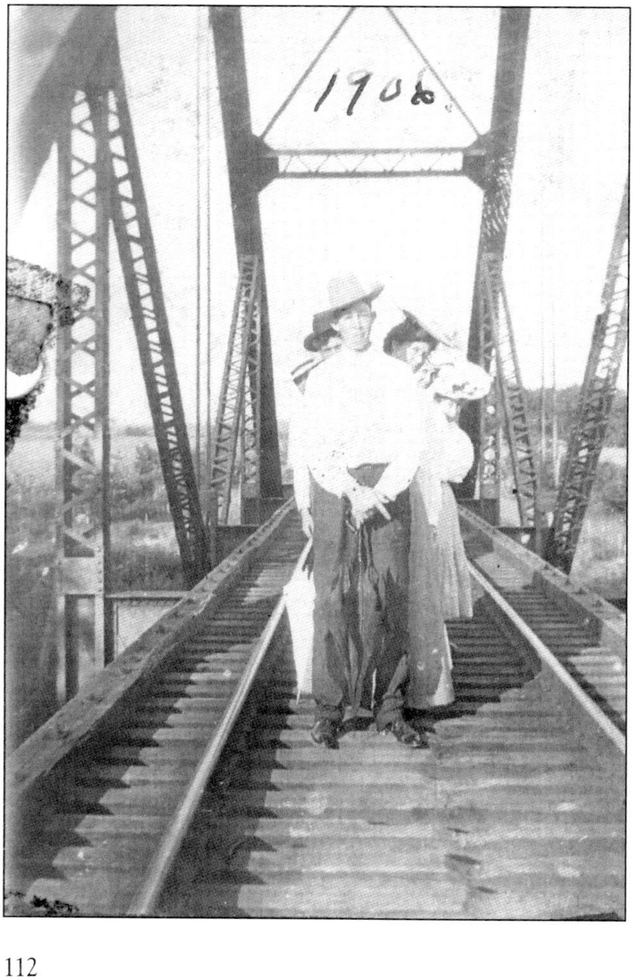

Riding the Train. Frank Brookout, his wife, Lena, and their friends are shown riding the train. In the early 20th century, rides cost as little as 10¢ to 15¢. Citizens did not mind catching the freight train into Plano and then transferring to a passenger train to travel to Dallas for business or a day of shopping. (S. Michael Boyd.)

Taking a Stroll on the Railroad Bridge, 1906. This picture was taken on the railroad bridge overlooking Rowlett Creek. Nelle King Turney and her friends enjoyed a leisurely walk across the bridge. Schoolchildren often walked along the tracks from their farms in Murphy to the Murphy School. (Dessie Haker.)

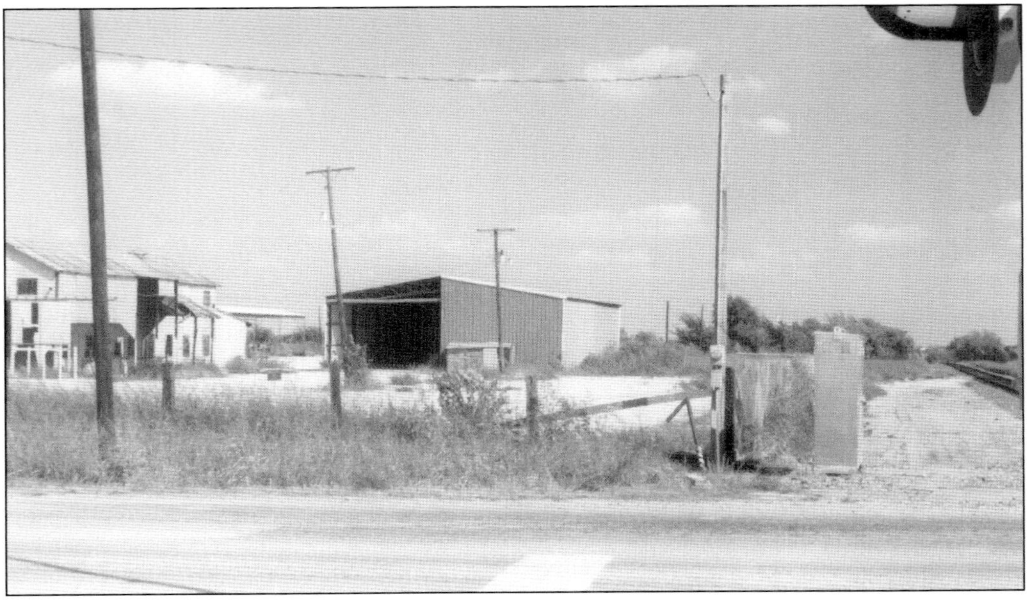

Railroad Tracks, 1989. The building of the railroad enhanced the value of land and helped the local economy. A gin was built on the north side of the tracks along Murphy Road. A depot was placed west of the tracks along Murphy Road when the St. Louis, Arkansas & Texas Railroad came to Murphy in 1888. The first depot had a ticket office and two waiting rooms, one for whites and another for blacks. According to Joe McCreary, kids would hop a train just for the thrill of a short ride while the train was loading cotton, wheat, or onions. They would hide and ride a short distance until the train made another stop to load or unload. These pictures showed the declining role of the railroad and gin by 1989. (Both, Brad Lapsley.)

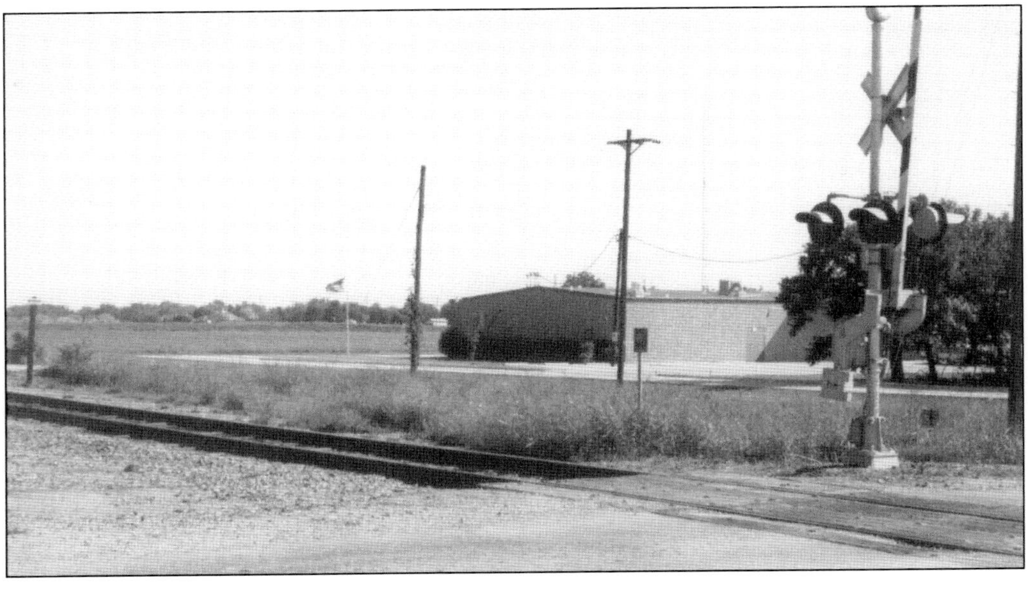

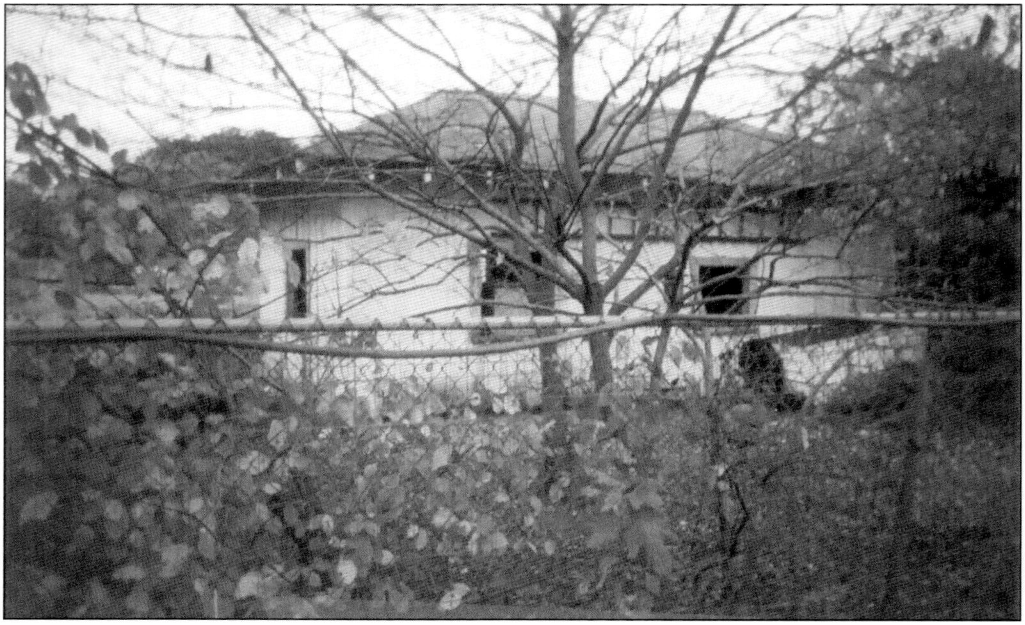

Hear the Lonesome Whistle Blow. Standing in the backyard of a home on Ridgeview Drive is the 1940s train depot with Murphy distinctly painted on the opposite side. Train travel became less popular as cars and buses became the major mode of transportation. A former city council member moved the depot to his home to save it from becoming a fire department practice burn. (Tom Rowe.)

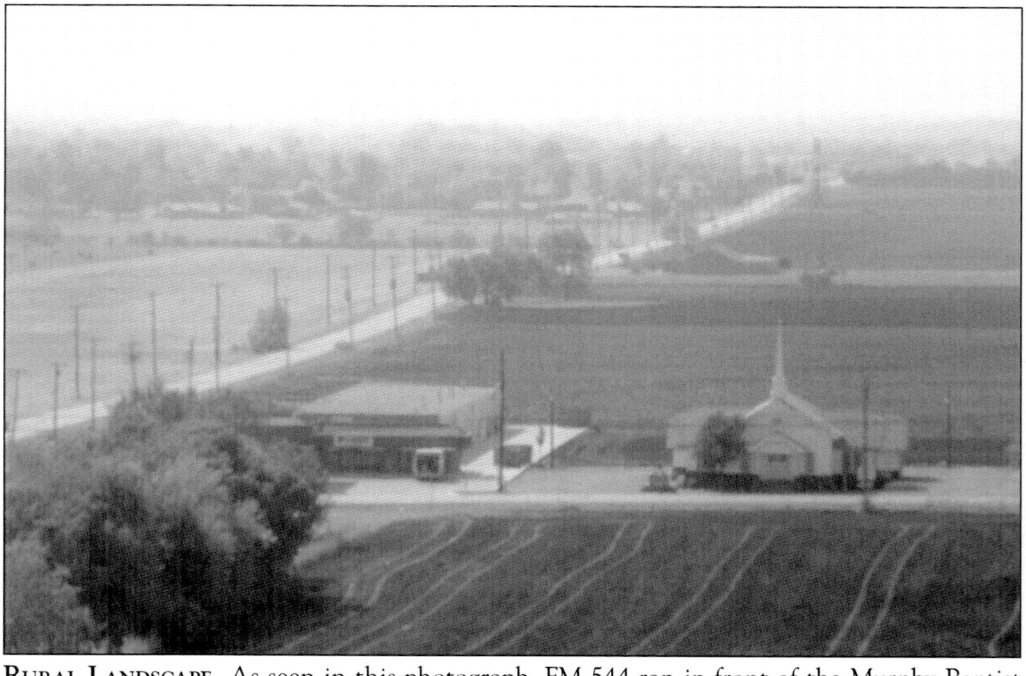

Rural Landscape. As seen in this photograph, FM 544 ran in front of the Murphy Baptist Church and the FINA station. To the south of the church were a cotton field and a farmhouse and barn. The empty field on the left soon housed the first supermarket, Albertsons, and other retail businesses. (Brad Lapsley.)

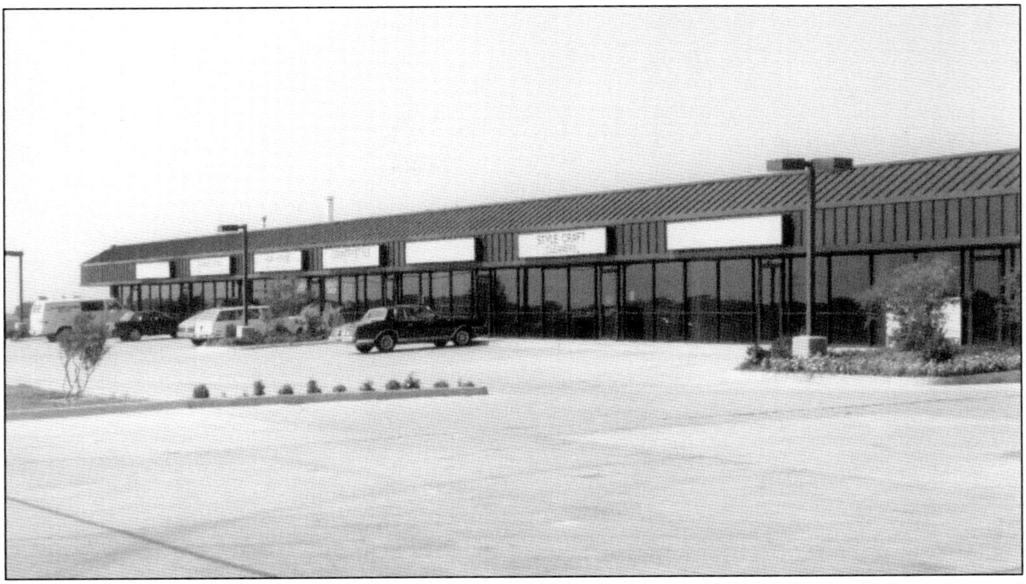

Murphy's First Retail Center. The first strip mall built by Perry Bolin of Bolin Oil was opened in 1986. Called Murphy Corner, it was built at the intersection of Murphy Road and FM 544 south of the FINA station. The building was divided into seven individual spaces. (Brad Lapsley.)

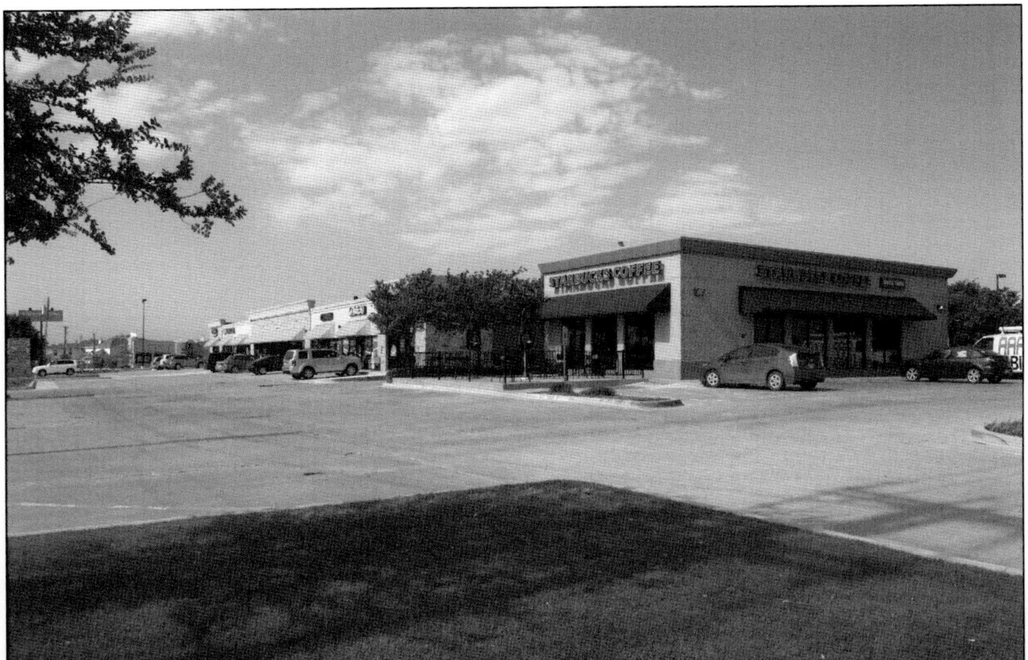

Retail Center Today. The retail center was renovated in 2011, and the outside was replaced with a new facade. A Starbucks has replaced the FINA station. Tenants include a dry cleaner, veterinary clinic, t-shirt shop, and donut shop. (Larry G. Taylor.)

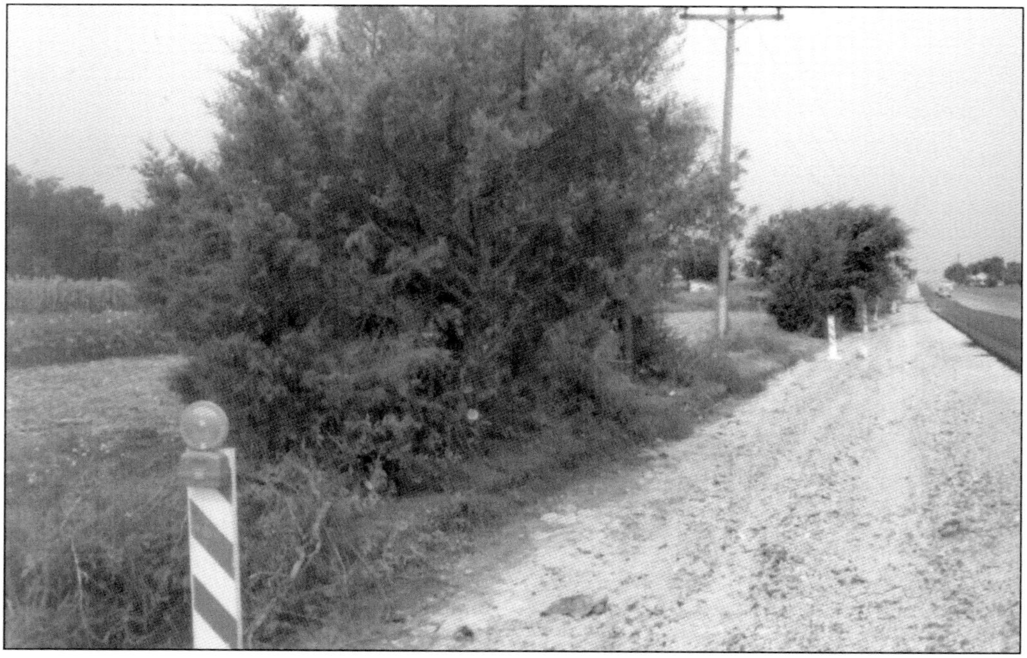

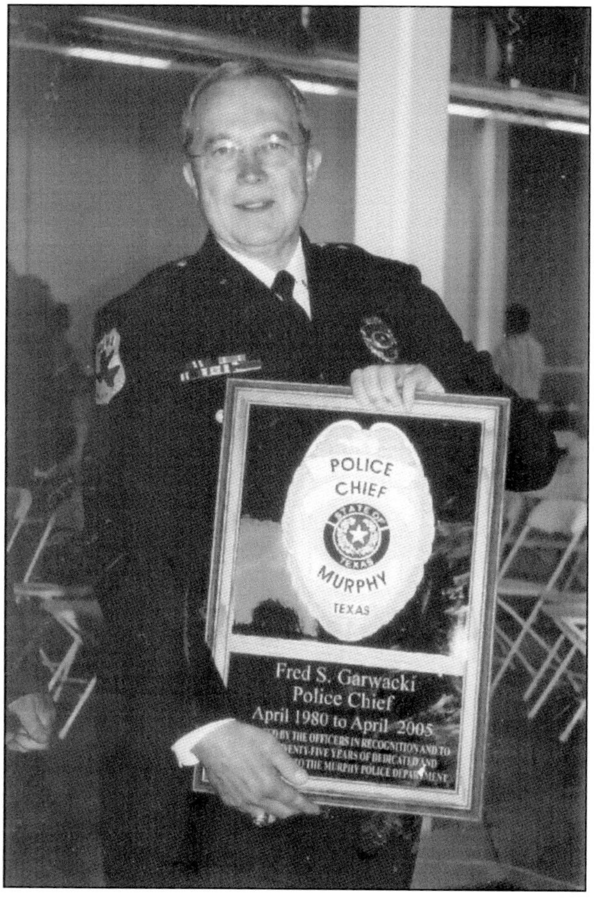

FARM TO MARKET 544. The widening and asphalting of FM 544 took place in the 1980s. The photograph was taken on the Murphy farm looking west. The old Turner house sits on the right side, and beyond is the Murphy Store. Today, the store is gone, and the road has six lanes going through the city. (Dessie Haker.)

FRED S. GARWACKI, FIRST POLICE CHIEF. Chief Garwacki served from 1980 to 2005 and saw many changes in the department. In 1979, Mayor Tom Clevenger appointed Tim Arion to report on the cost of men and equipment necessary to start a police department in Murphy. Garwacki served longer than any officer in Murphy and was instrumental in the growth of the department. Today, there are 31 employees. (Murphy Police Department.)

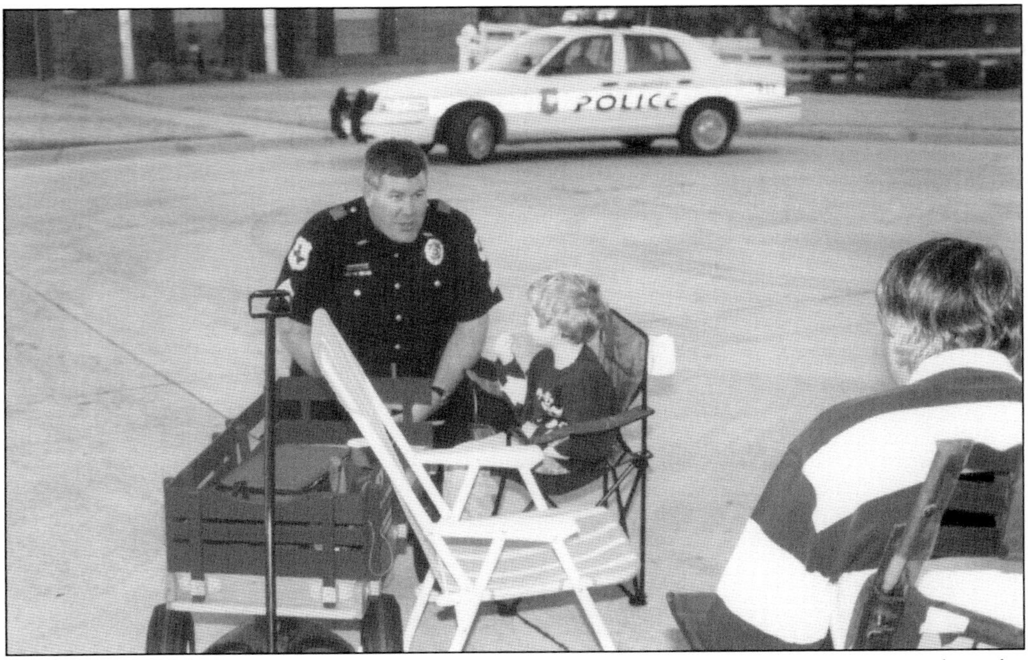

NIGHT OUT. One goal of the police department is to create an environment of teamwork in the department and with citizens of the community. The police department sponsors the Neighborhood Watch, Crime Stoppers, and Citizens Police Academy. In this photograph, an officer is meeting with local citizens in the Night Out Program. (Murphy Police Department.)

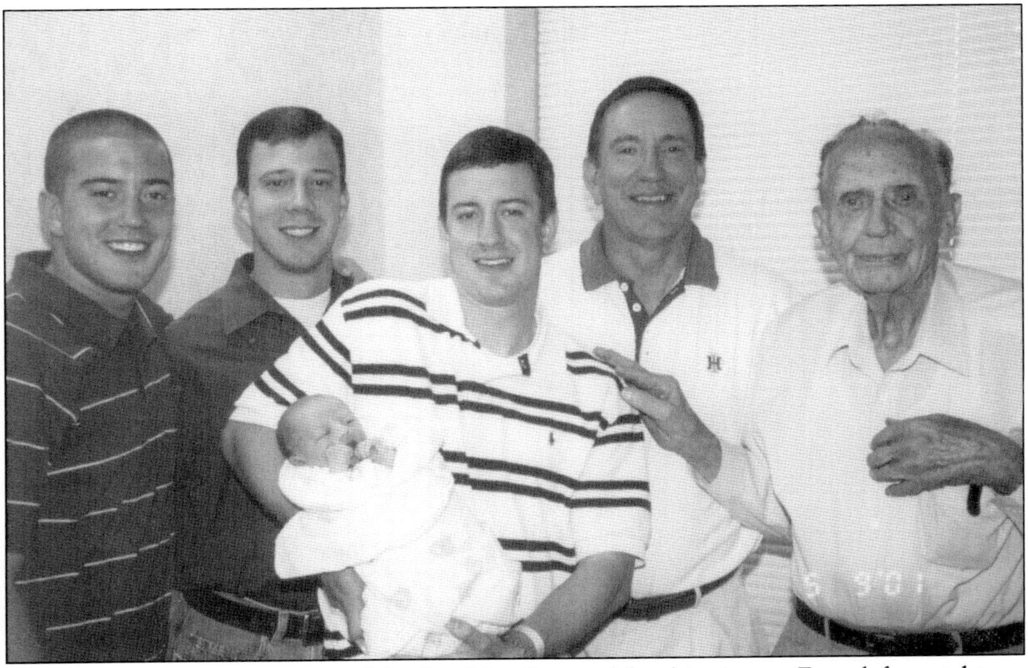

BOYD FAMILY. Four generations of the Boyd family posed for this picture. From left to right are Lucas, Seth, Derek, Dylan (baby), S. Michael, and Edgar Boyd. Ed was the third generation to live in Murphy. S. Michael was the fourth; his son Derek was the fifth. Derek's son Dylan and daughter Hayley are the sixth generation to live in Murphy. (S. Michael Boyd.)

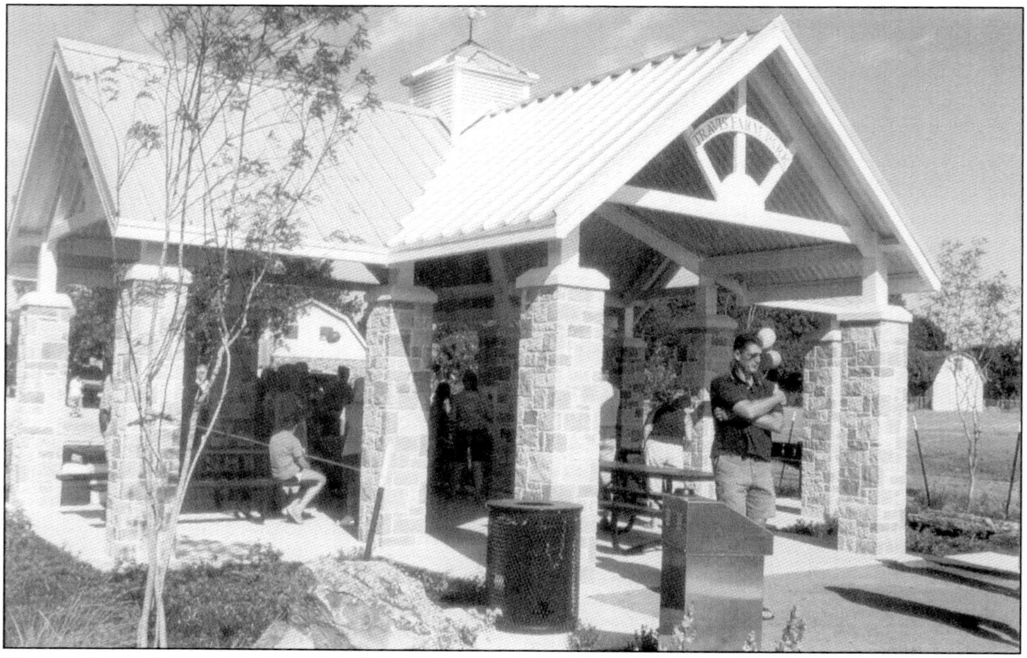

TRAVIS FARM PARK. In August 2010, the City of Murphy dedicated Travis Farm Park in the honor of Charles and Lula Sue Travis. In the 1970s, the farm was divided and sold to developers who built homes in a subdivision named Travis Estates. The remainder of the farm was sold to the Ganis family, who still reside on a portion of the land. (Author.)

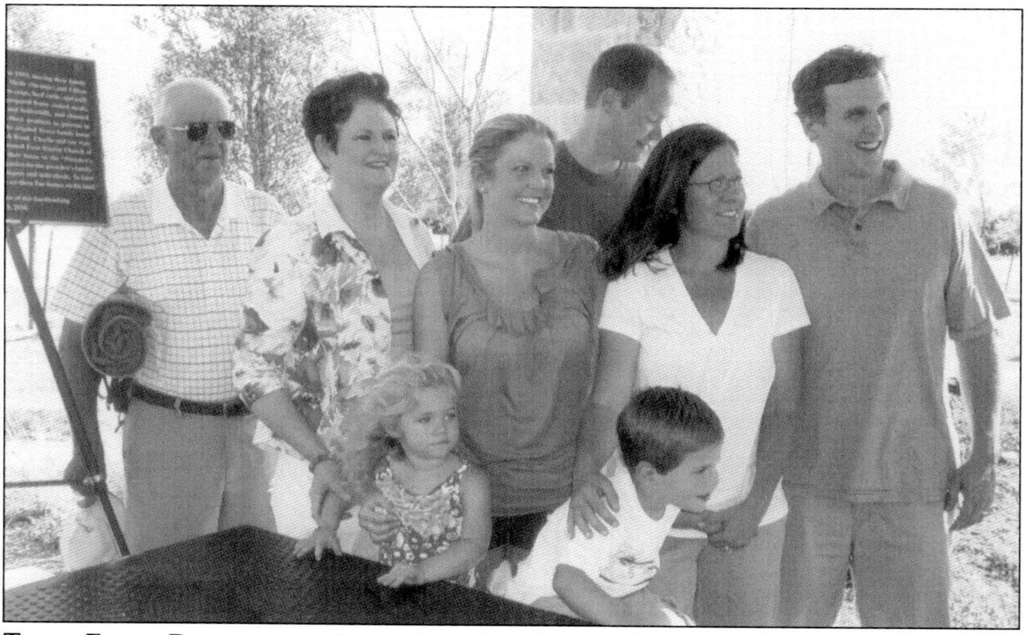

TRAVIS FAMILY DESCENDANTS. Pictured are, from left to right, Lester and Betty Prince, Jill and Kevin Heffeman, and Karen and Glenn Prince. Children in the picture are Kate Heffeman and Gavin Prince. Descendants of the Travis family attended the dedication of the park on the Travis farm. The original Travis home and barn were located northeast of the park. Glenn and his family make Murphy their home. (Betty Strange Prince.)

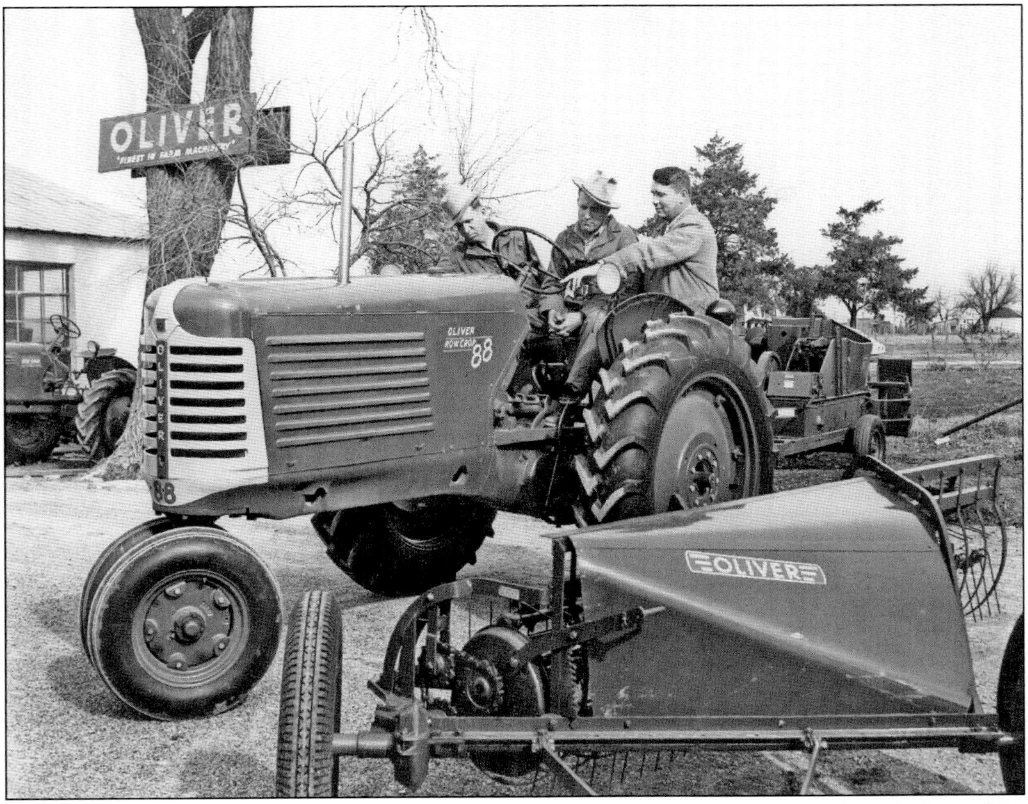

Oliver Tractor. Shown in this photograph, from left to right, are Max Daniel, W.O. Daniel Jr., and W.W. Keeran, Oliver territory manager. Daniel Implement on North Murphy Road began to sell Oliver equipment in 1952 and provided area farmers with new equipment as well as replacement parts for older equipment. (Inez Daniel.)

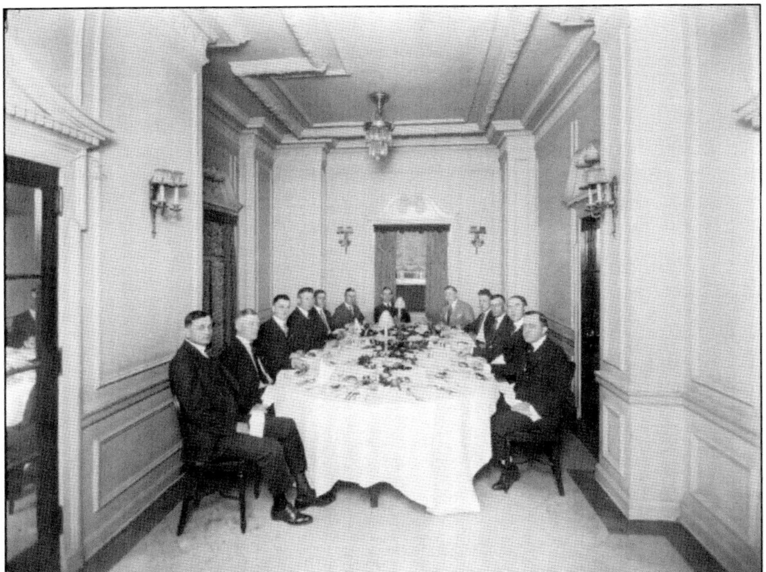

Adolphus Hotel, 1920. This photograph demonstrates the White Truck Company sales meeting at the Adolphus Hotel in Dallas. Lee Turney, third from the left, was one of the top salesmen in Dallas. During the Depression, few citizens of Murphy could have afforded a dinner at this upscale hotel. (Dessie Haker.)

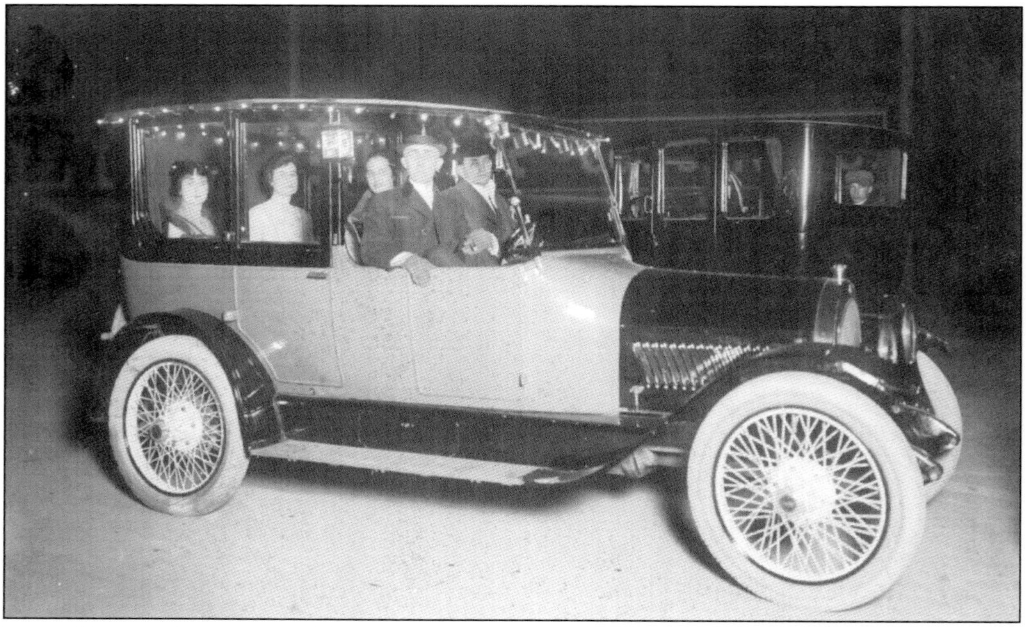

Davis-Turney Automobile Company, c. 1911. S.G. Davis, front left, and Lee Turney, in the driver's seat, were owners of an automobile dealership in Dallas. From left to right in the back seat are Mrs. Wallace, Nelle Turney, and Ollie Davis. Friends said Nelle Turney always drove the latest model car from her husband's company. (Dessie Haker.)

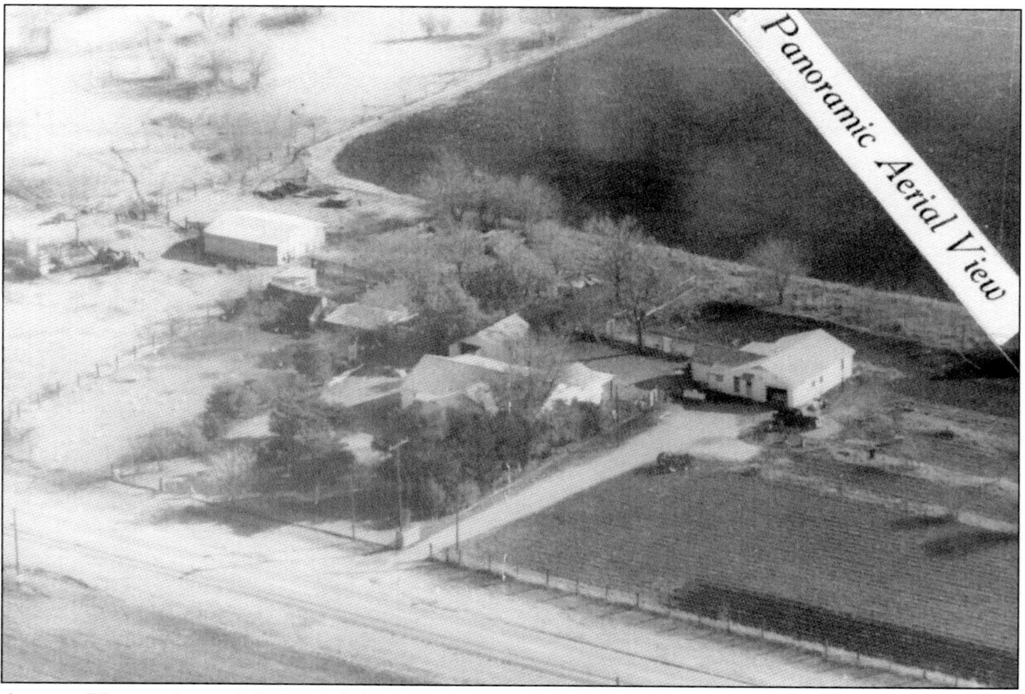

Aerial View, 1970s. The aerial shows the land that was owned by the William Murphy family. Dessie Haker and her husband, Otto Louis Haker, inherited the land from Nelle Turney upon her death. They had the old farmhouse moved and built a modern brick home on the land. (Dessie Haker.)

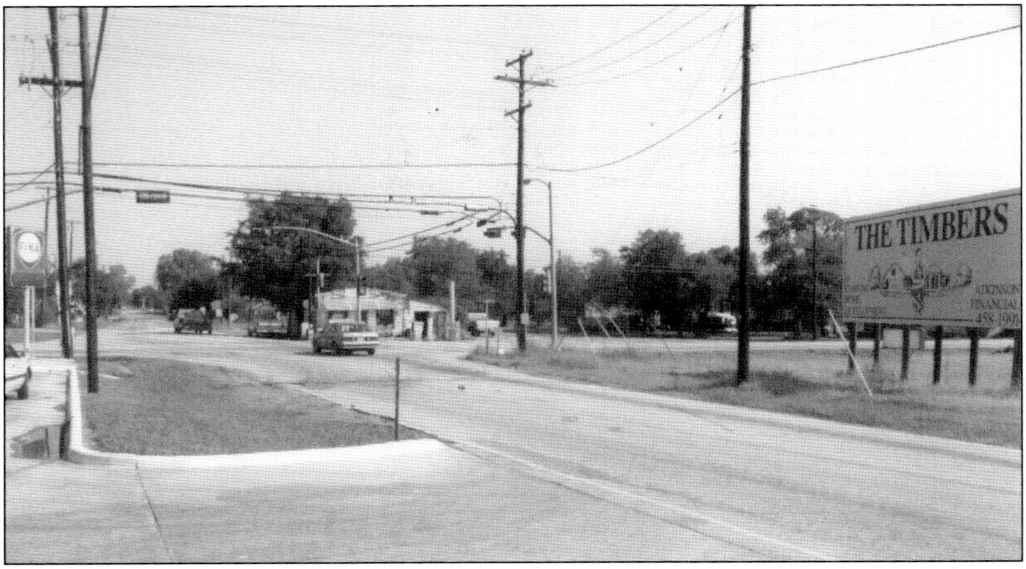

Murphy Crossroads, 1989. The intersection of Murphy Road and FM 544 has seen many changes since its origins. Both roads began as dirt wagon trails. In the photograph, the intersection is shown with a FINA station on the left. On the right side are the Murphy Grocery and an empty field with a sign advertising the Timbers Addition. (Brad Lapsley.)

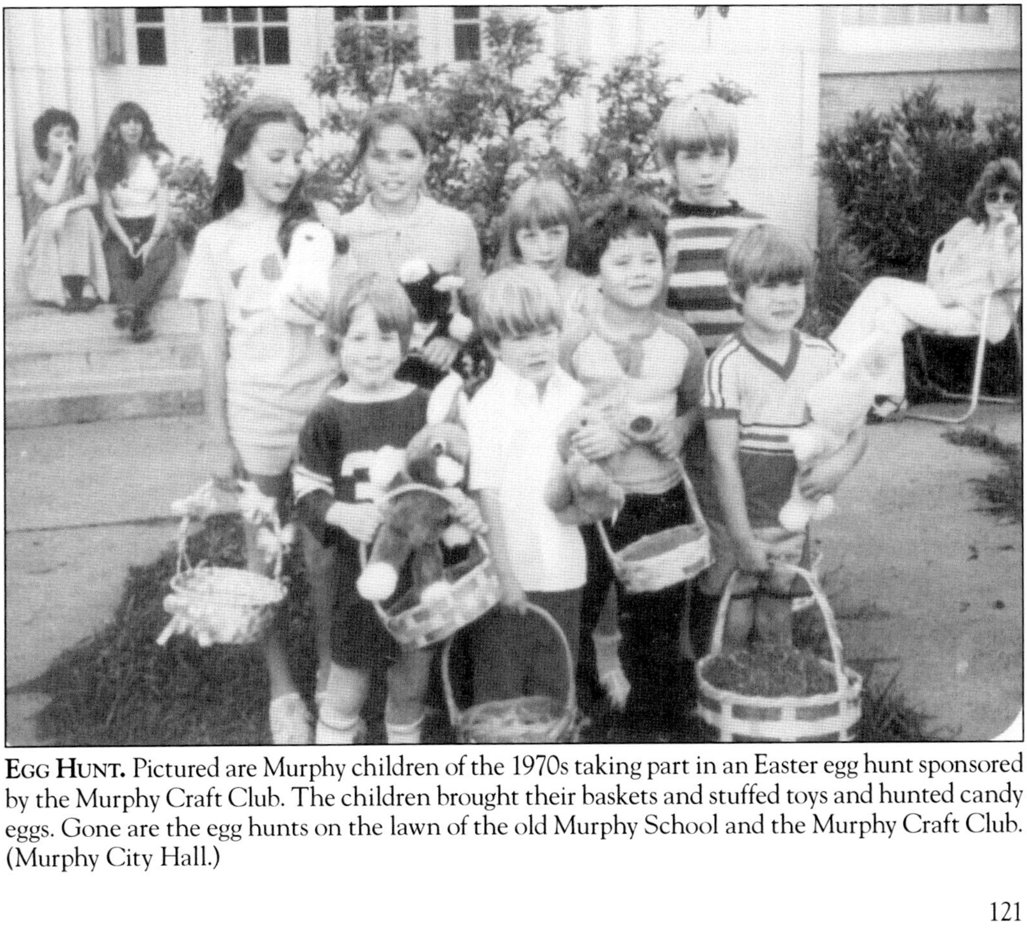

Egg Hunt. Pictured are Murphy children of the 1970s taking part in an Easter egg hunt sponsored by the Murphy Craft Club. The children brought their baskets and stuffed toys and hunted candy eggs. Gone are the egg hunts on the lawn of the old Murphy School and the Murphy Craft Club. (Murphy City Hall.)

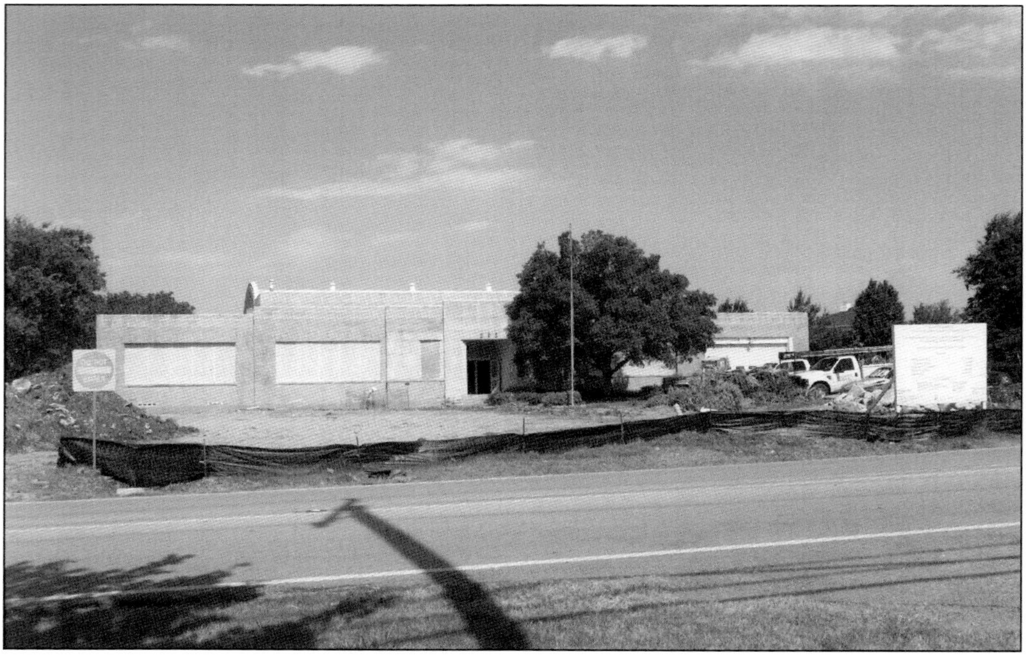

Murphy School Renovation, 2011. This photograph displays the current renovation to the old school. The building has served as a school, fire station, police station, and city hall in its lifetime. After sitting vacant since 2005, voices will again be head in the halls when the renovation is complete in March 2012. (Larry G. Taylor.)

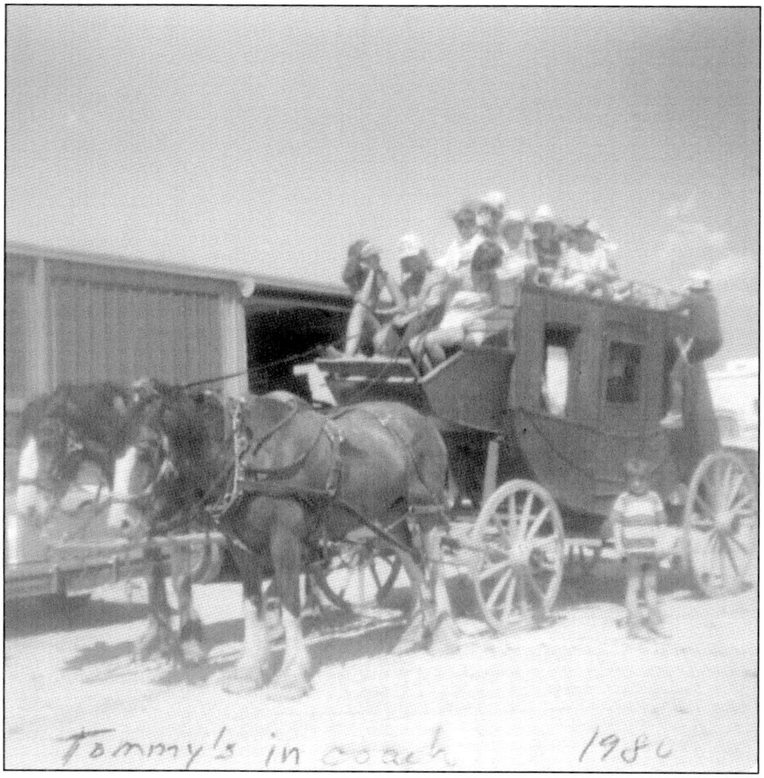

Stagecoach Rides. Gone are the days of chili cook-offs and the Murphy Fair held in the old Murphy School and city hall. Big John's Stagecoach rides are just memories. Instead there is Maize Days, held on the grounds of the Murphy Municipal Complex. It features a kids' zone with bounce houses and a maize market for vendors. (Judy Janasek.)

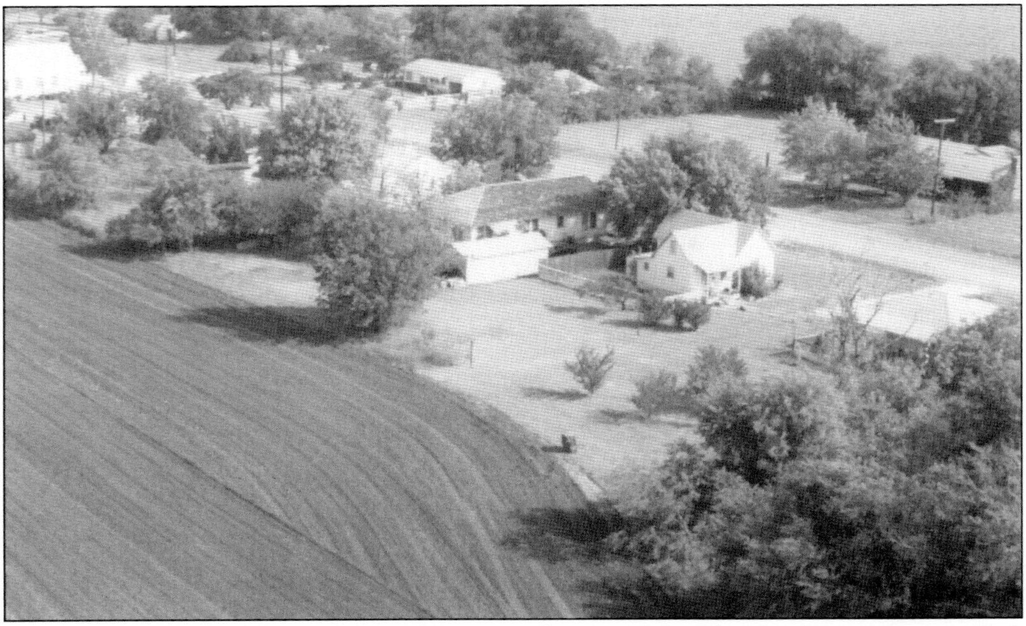

Farmland, 1980s. In the photograph, acres and acres of the Blackland Prairie were tilled, planted, cultivated, fertilized, and harvested. Men and women toiled from early morning until early night to produce the best maize and cotton. The community thrived on hard work and crop production. Today, the farms are gone, replaced by subdivisions with perfectly manicured lawns. (Brad Lapsley.)

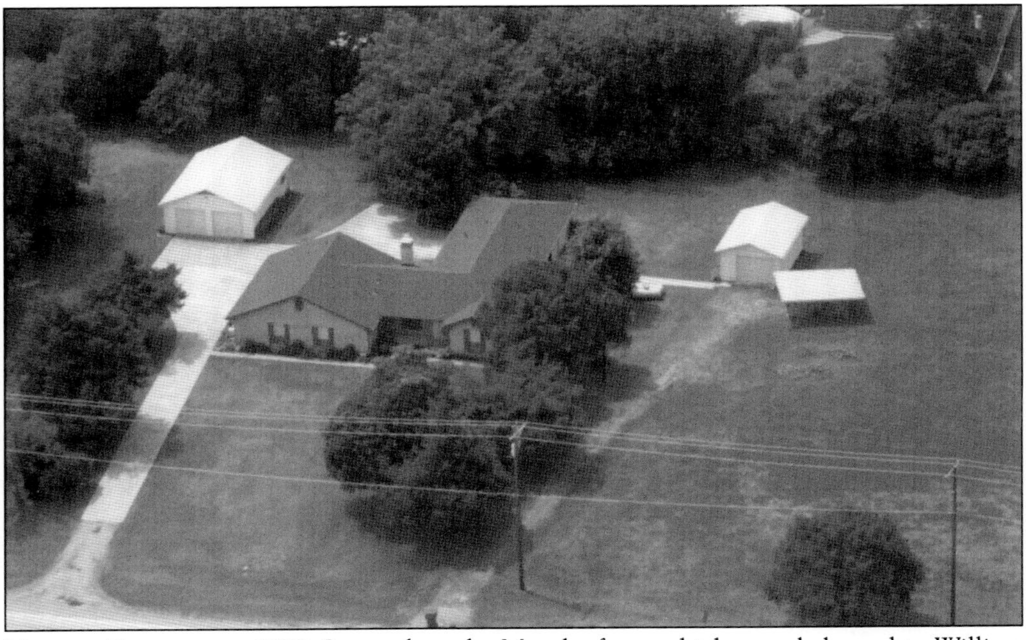

Murphy Farmhouse, 1953. Located on the Murphy farm, which once belonged to William Murphy, was the house built by Dr. William King and Dorothy Murphy King. The house and land was given to their daughter Nelle King Turney. In turn, the land was deeded to Dessie Haker in the 1970s. The farmhouse is gone, but the pecan tree and small branch remain today. (Dessie Haker.)

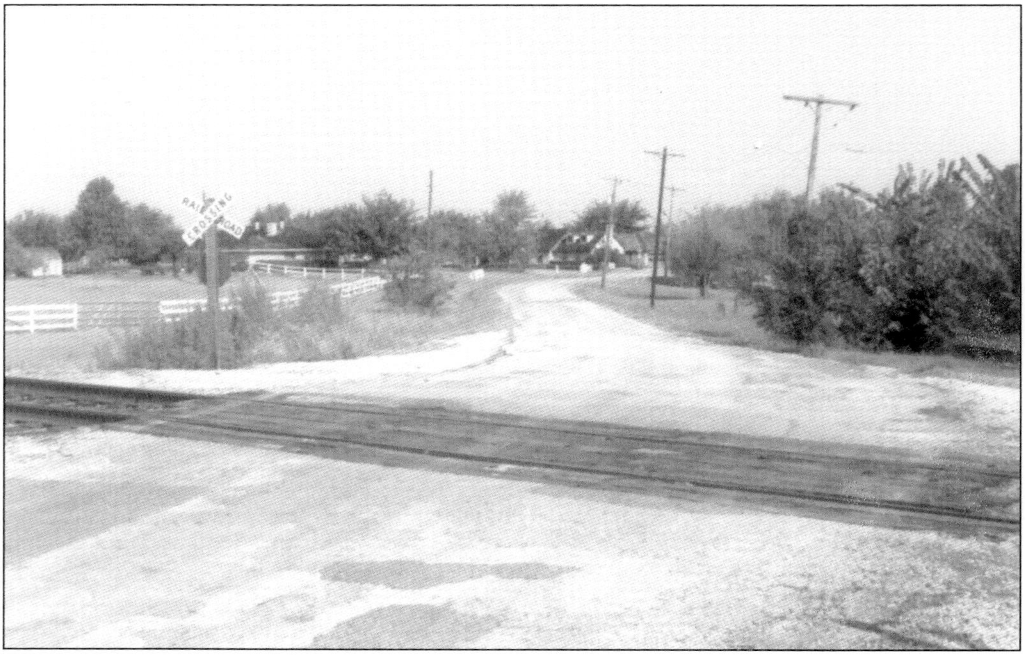

Willow Wood Estates. Skyline Acres and Willow Wood Estates, the two earliest subdivisions, remain today. Pictured is Willow Wood Estates running along North Maxwell Creek as it appeared in the 1980s. This is the land on which Henry Maxwell and William Murphy built their log cabins and settled in the 1850s. (Brad Lapsley.)

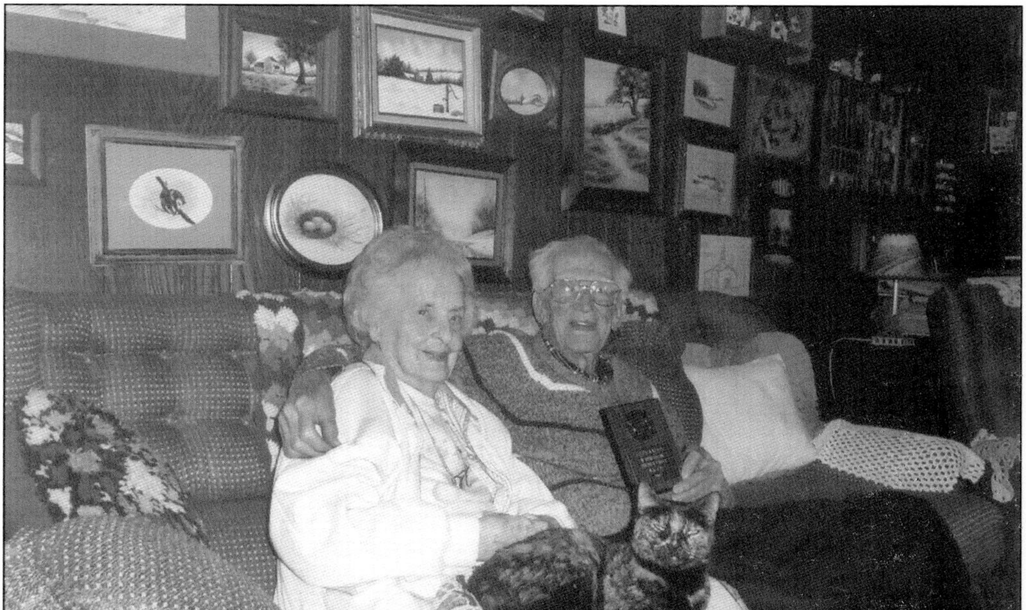

Jules Kappes. In the photograph, former mayor Jules Kappes sits with his wife, Del, and reminisces about Murphy. He proudly displays a plaque given to him by the fire department. He remembers the first renovation on the old school, when citizens pitched in and made the repairs themselves. The volunteer fire department removed walls and made the first firehouse for the city. (Author.)

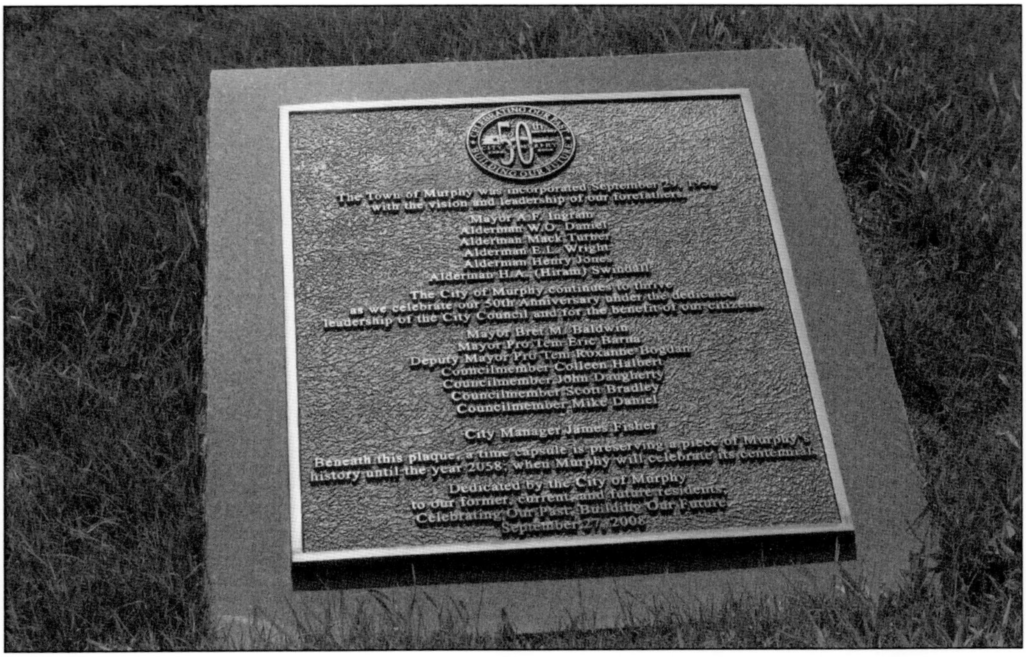

CELEBRATING THE PAST, BUILDING THE FUTURE. The town of Murphy was incorporated on September 29, 1958, and in 2008, Murphy celebrated its 50th birthday. The mayor and city council buried a time capsule with a piece of Murphy's history to be opened in 2058, when Murphy will celebrate its centennial. (Larry G. Taylor.)

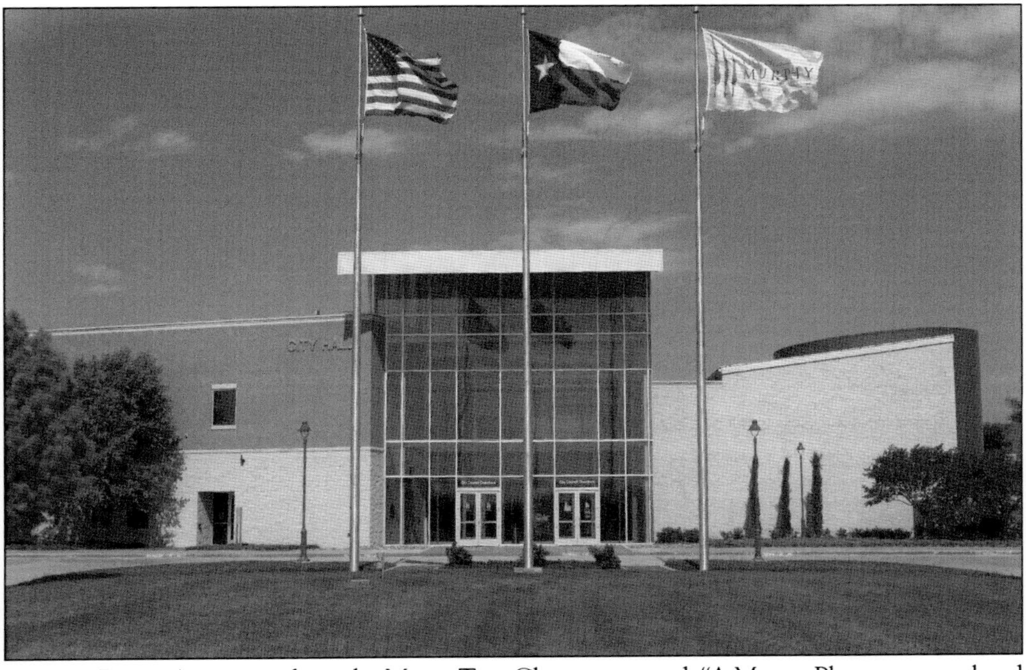

MASTER PLAN. A message from the Mayor Tom Clevenger noted, "A Master Plan was completed in May 1973 to insure our rapid growth would be orderly and protective of both present and future residents." Little did the mayor, council, or residents dream of the growth of the city and the completion of the Murphy Municipal Complex in 2005. (Larry G. Taylor.)

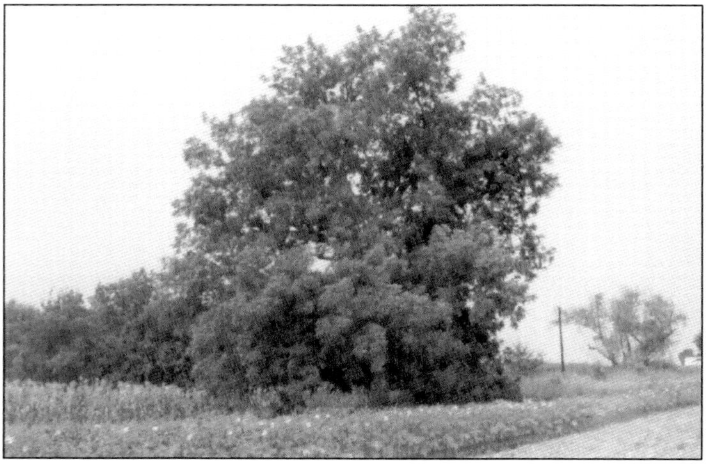

Native Pecan Tree. This tree stood along Murphy Road on the farm of Dr. and Mrs. King. Nelle Turney told the story of her mother talking over the fence with a neighbor when she saw the tiny tree and said, "This is my tree." The tree stood watch over the family garden near the little branch of running water. Okra and corn can be seen planted in the garden. (Dessie Haker.)

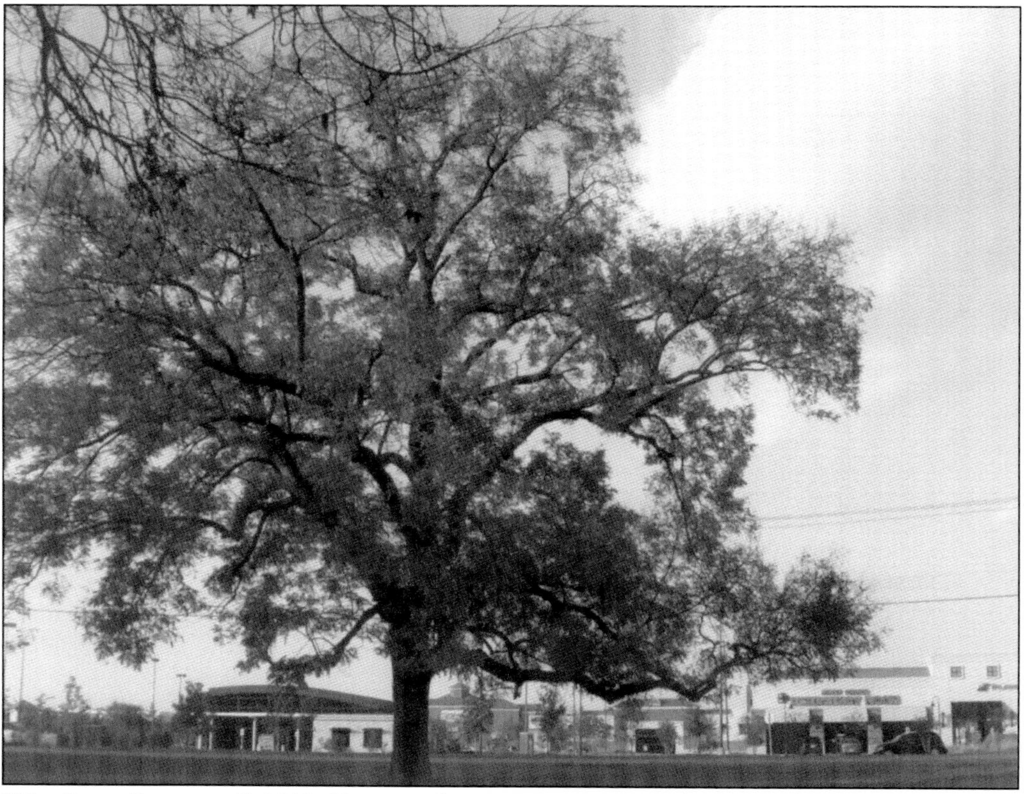

"The Lone Sentinel," 2010. Shown is the tree as it appears today on the land owned by Dessie Haker. Nelle Turney named the pecan tree "the sentinel" because it towered above all the other trees around it. If trees could talk, this tree could relate the history of early days, when there was a grocery store, drugstore, doctor's office, blacksmith shop, barbershop, bank, café, and pioneers. (Margaret Haker Smith.)

Bibliography

http://www.banking.state.tx.us/
Fulkerson, Bev. *Wylie Area Heritage*. Wylie, TX: self-published, 1990.
Gough, Joy. *Decatur-Maxwell-Murphy Cemetery*. Murphy, TX: Cemetery Association of Murphy, 2001.
Gough, Joy and Ned Hoover. *Cemeteries of Collin County, Texas*. Plano, TX: Worldwide, 1995.
Jones, Mary Allene. *Sachse Remembered, 1840–1940*. Wolfe City, TX: Henington Publishing Company, 1990.
Jowers, Marcia. Numerous articles. *Murphy Messenger*.
Laenger, Lolisa. Numerous articles. *Murphy Monitor, Wylie News*.
Maxwell, Henry. *Day Books of Henry Maxwell from 1853–1860*. Transcription provided by Mary Maxwell.
Plano, Texas: The Early Years. Plano, TX: Friends of the Plano Public Library, 1985.
texashistory.unt.edu/
www.tshaonline.org/
Walker, Cindy. Numerous articles. *Murphy Monitor, Wylie News*.
Zavitz, Bev. *Living in Murphy, Texas, Revisited*. Dallas, TX: Jack Kenneth Publishing, 2004.